CREATIVE ECONOMY and CULTURE

SAGE | 50 YEARS

SAGE was founded in 1965 by Sara Miller McCune to support the dissemination of usable knowledge by publishing innovative and high-quality research and teaching content. Today, we publish more than 850 journals, including those of more than 300 learned societies, more than 800 new books per year, and a growing range of library products including archives, data, case studies, reports, and video. SAGE remains majority-owned by our founder, and after Sara's lifetime will become owned by a charitable trust that secures our continued independence.

Los Angeles | London | New Delhi | Singapore | Washington DC

CREATIVE ECONOMY and CULTURE

CHALLENGES, CHANGES AND FUTURES FOR THE CREATIVE INDUSTRIES

John Hartley
Wen Wen
Henry Siling Li

$SAGE

Los Angeles | London | New Delhi
Singapore | Washington DC

SAGE

Los Angeles | London | New Delhi
Singapore | Washington DC

SAGE Publications Ltd
1 Oliver's Yard
55 City Road
London EC1Y 1SP

SAGE Publications Inc.
2455 Teller Road
Thousand Oaks, California 91320

SAGE Publications India Pvt Ltd
B 1/I 1 Mohan Cooperative Industrial Area
Mathura Road
New Delhi 110 044

SAGE Publications Asia-Pacific Pte Ltd
3 Church Street
#10-04 Samsung Hub
Singapore 049483

Editor: Chris Rojek
Assistant editor: Gemma Shields
Production editor: Katherine Haw
Marketing manager: Michael Ainsley
Cover design: Shaun Mercier
Typeset by: C&M Digitals (P) Ltd, Chennai, India
Printed in India at Replika Press Pvt Ltd

© John Hartley, Wen Wen and Henry Siling Li 2015

First published 2015

Apart from any fair dealing for the purposes of research or private study, or criticism or review, as permitted under the Copyright, Designs and Patents Act, 1988, this publication may be reproduced, stored or transmitted in any form, or by any means, only with the prior permission in writing of the publishers, or in the case of reprographic reproduction, in accordance with the terms of licences issued by the Copyright Licensing Agency. Enquiries concerning reproduction outside those terms should be sent to the publishers.

Library of Congress Control Number: 2015937418

British Library Cataloguing in Publication data

A catalogue record for this book is available from the British Library

ISBN 978-0-85702-877-8
ISBN 978-0-85702-878-5 (pbk)

MIX
Paper from responsible sources
FSC® C016779

At SAGE we take sustainability seriously. Most of our products are printed in the UK using FSC papers and boards. When we print overseas we ensure sustainable papers are used as measured by the Egmont grading system. We undertake an annual audit to monitor our sustainability.

Frontispiece: Global Media Culture.

The Shakespeare Duck: Globe Theatre Shop, London.

CONTENTS

List of Figures   ix
About the Authors   xi

PART I   THE CHALLENGE   1

Theory   2

1. Economy + Culture + Technology = Newness   3
2. The Big Picture – Spheres Enveloping Spheres   16
3. The Three Bigs – 'Everyone' 'Everything' 'Everywhere'   25

History   39

4. The Creative Industries 'Moment'   41
5. Back to First Principles   55
6. Creative Industries to Creative Economy   69

PART II   FORCES AND DYNAMICS OF CHANGE: THE THREE BIGS IN ACTION   81

Everyone   82

7. Technology   83

Everything   101

8. Economy (1) Makers   103
9. Economy (2) Scenes   119

Everywhere   127

10. Geography (1) – BRICS   129
11. Geography (2) – MINT, etc.   147

PART III FUTURE-FORMING (WITH THREE BUTS)   **167**

Scepticism   168

12 'Ceci Tuera Cela'   169
13 The Three Buts   180

Optimism   207

14 Future-forming   209

Acknowledgements   231
References   233
Index   245

LIST OF FIGURES

1.1	Culture and technology, exhibit A: 'TV happiness shared by all the family!' 1951 advertisement (*Time* Magazine)	12
1.2	Culture and technology, exhibit B: 'Over 100,000 people live in tiny "cubicle apartments" in the city [Hong Kong] … Residents go about their lives in these confined spaces, sleeping in one corner, eating in another, storing their belongings in a third, and perhaps watching a TV that's found in a fourth'	13
2.1	The Earth System: the geosphere and biosphere combined	17
2.2	Preserved for posterity: V.I. Vernadsky's grave in Moscow – protected by a perspex box	19
2.3	A conjectural diagram showing the growth of human knowledge, correlated with changes in media technologies (x axis) and successive economic epochs (y axis)	21
6.1	Four phases of the creative industries – from industry clusters and services to creative citizens and cities	70
6.2	Urban semiosis: cities as incubators of social network markets	78
7.1	Jiaoshou's mask and his online avatar	90
7.2	Cover pages of *Jiaoshou Weekly*	94
7.3	The tombstone of *Toulushe* (Disclosure Agency)	95
8.1	Growth of Maker Faires	108
12.1	'Ceci tuera cela': illustration for Hugo's *Notre Dame de Paris*	170
12.2	Control: not the opposite of chaos but a position of 'liquidity' or 'antichaos' in a 'poised system'	176
12.3	Order, chaos, poise and policy	178

13.1	Paul Baran's 1964 diagram	182
13.2	Total household stocks of home appliances and electronics in China, 2011	193
14.1	Tavi Gevinson at *Makers: Women Who Make America*, New York	227

ABOUT THE AUTHORS

John HARTLEY
John Hartley, AM (Order of Australia), is John Curtin Distinguished Professor at Curtin University Australia, and Professor of Journalism, Media and Cultural Studies at Cardiff University Wales. Recent books include: *Cultural Science: A Natural History of Stories, Demes, Knowledge and Innovation* (with Jason Potts, Bloomsbury, 2014); *Key Concepts in Creative Industries* (co-authored, Sage, 2013); *A Companion to New Media Dynamics* (co-edited, Wiley-Blackwell, 2013); and *Digital Futures for Cultural and Media Studies* (Wiley-Blackwell, 2012). He is editor of the *International Journal of Cultural Studies* (Sage) and publisher of *Cultural Science Journal* (online). He is a Fellow of the Australian Academy of Humanities and the International Communication Association, Honorary Professor of Zhejiang University of Media and Communications (Hangzhou), and Guest Researcher, Institute for Cultural Industries, Shenzhen University, China.

WEN Wen
Wen received her doctoral degree in creative industries from Queensland University of Technology, Brisbane, Australia in 2012. She is now a Lecturer and Director of the Project Development Department of the Shenzhen Institute for Cultural Industries, University (SZU), China. She was a visiting scholar at Curtin University, Australia in 2014 (February to April). Her main research interests include creative scenes, urban culture and the cultural economy. She has published academic papers in the *International Journal of Cultural Studies*, *International Journal of Cultural and Creative Industries* and *Cultural Science Journal*.

Henry Siling LI
Henry is Senior Lecturer and Director of International at the School of Media, Culture and Creative Arts in the Faculty of Humanities, Curtin University. He has a PhD in creative industries from Queensland University of Technology and MA in simultaneous interpreting from Beijing Foreign Studies University. Henry worked at China Executive Leadership Academy Pudong for ten years and was Executive Director of its Centre for International Courses and Programs before joining Curtin University in 2013. His research covers social media, user productivity and young people in China and has been published in the *Chinese Journal of Communication* and *Cultural Science Journal*.

PART I

THE CHALLENGE

THEORY

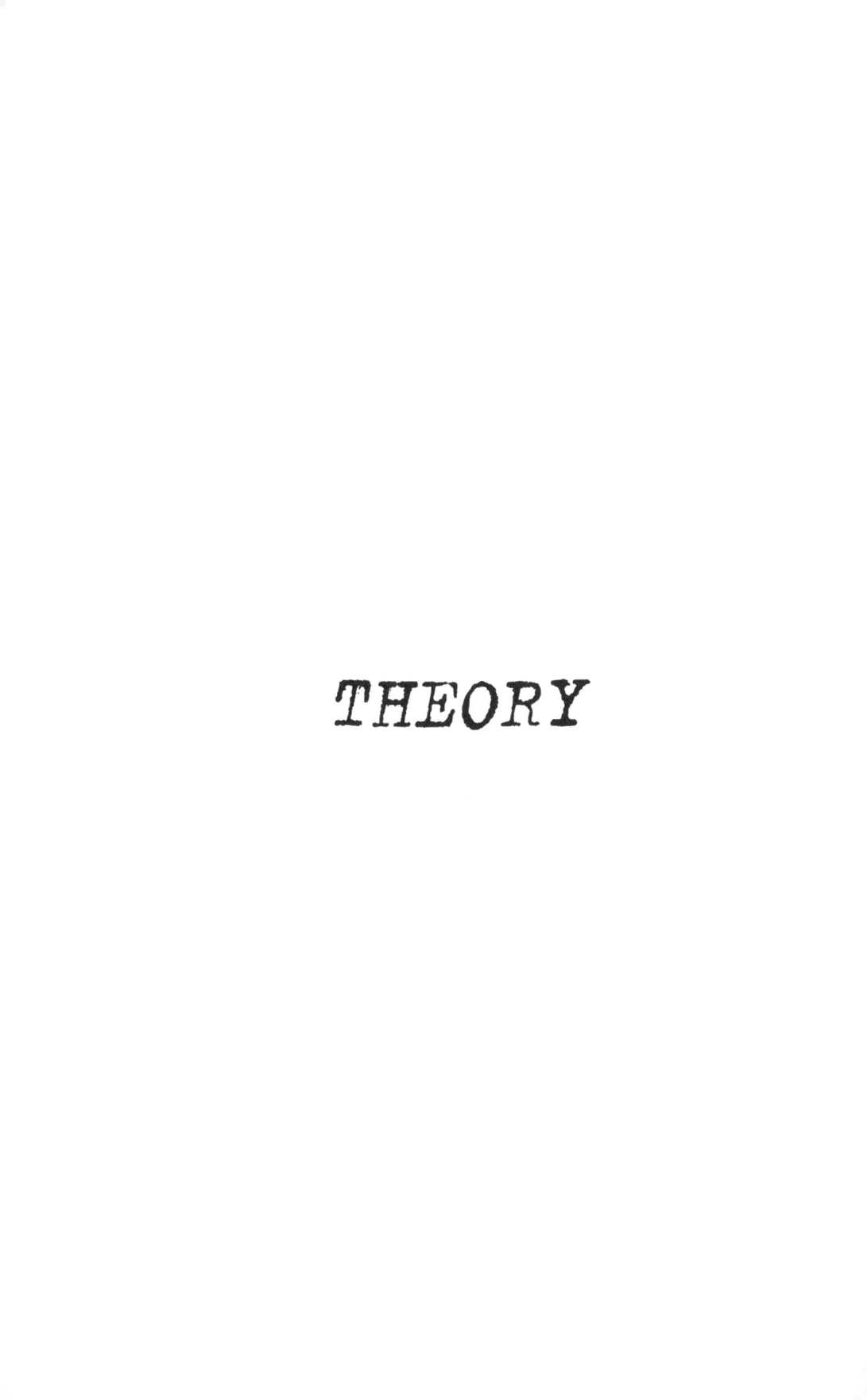

1

ECONOMY + CULTURE + TECHNOLOGY

= NEWNESS

How can a system develop and yet remain true to itself?

(Yuri Lotman, 2009: 1)

Whose creative industries?

The question is: *Whose* creative industries? We need to ask it, because much of the discussion about the creative industries or creative economy (also called the cultural industries), in policy, scholarly and industry circles, presumes quite limited answers to that question. Thus, the standard answers are: 'Creative industries' describes a specialist sector of the economy; only certain types of work or occupations count as creative; not many countries can boast a creative economy. A presumption has taken hold that 'creative industries' refers to the 'copyright' industries, whose business plan is founded on making the creative outputs of talented individuals into 'intellectual property', and then selling that.

We don't think any of these are satisfactory answers. In this book, we want to pose the question anew, by making the answers as broad and inclusive as is possible. Here, the answers – which we call 'the three bigs' – are:

- The creative industries are not confined to an elite of trained artists or firms; they encompass (or could encompass) *everyone*.
- They are not confined to one sector of the economy; they characterise (or could characterise) *everything*.
- They are not a feature of advanced or wealthy countries; they are (or could be) *everywhere*.

The difference between 'are' and 'could' in the formulations above is not meant to be normative, but rather to describe a situation where – we would argue – a more expansive answer is possible, but unnoticed or even unknowable using current approaches. Thus, posing the question 'Whose creative industries?' is to some extent a 'thought experiment', because quite clearly this expansive conceptualisation of the role of creativity in contemporary cultures and economies is not in place as an everyday reality, nor is it part of everyday talk among those who comprise the 'conceptual community' or 'discourse public' of the creative industries, whether they are scholars, policymakers, consultants or industry insiders. Therefore, the overall purpose of this book is to develop a coherent perspective and an argument that will put these answers on the table, so to speak, as an alternative to current conceptual settings. We are not so much arguing that the creative economy and culture *could ever* capture the creative productivity of everyone, everywhere, across everything, but, rather, we want to set that idea as a new bar or yardstick for testing whether the *full potential* of the creative industries is being realised, or *could ever* be realised using existing definitions, ambitions, policies and practices; and if not, what alternative conceptualisations and arrangements can take their place.

We are motivated to do this because we think there is something missing from the picture so far: several 'somethings' in fact. Here they are:

- *Populations*: The most important element missing from current conceptualisations of creative industries is *everyone* – the general population, who, since the emergence of digital technologies, social networks and user-created content, can be seen (not just claimed) to be engaging in mass creative productivity, which we call *microproductivity*, that is a major driver of economic development.

- *Technologies*: This combination of 'everyone' with 'digital networks' is crucial to our purpose, because we do not locate creativity in the individual person, talented or otherwise, but in *systems*. We see culture and the economy as systems too, albeit more complex and multiple (systems of systems) than any technology to date. Because of their scale and variability, 'natural' cultural systems are hard to study. Technological systems, on the other hand, are an empirical form of human connectedness that can be studied (Arthur, 2009). Of these, we think two are more important than others. One is very old: cities. The other is very new: the internet. We see urban and digital technologies, their productivity and capacity to create new ideas and to distribute them across whole populations, as a proxy for those same qualities in human culture. It follows that we think the predominant conceptualisation of creative industries has not integrated 'creative production' sufficiently with 'digital networks' or with what we call 'urban semiosis'.

- *Culture*: We think 'culture' is misunderstood and restricted in most public thought about the creative industries. As we will argue in this book, we see culture as a human invention whose function is to produce *groups* or 'demes' – groups which can survive where individuals do not (Pagel, 2012a; Hartley and Potts, 2014; and see Chapter 3 below). We argue that what binds these groups is *knowledge*; and that the 'output' of culture is not heritage, customs, art, or even artefacts (goods and services), but *innovation*: culture is the mechanism for 'producing newness' in conditions of uncertainty (Potts, n.d.; Hutter et al., 2010). Thus, for us, culture faces the future. It is the driver of economy, and not the other way around. It needs to be reconceptualised and integrated into economic thought and policy; equally, those devoted to culture and the arts as presently configured need to understand its role in economic evolution.

- *The Planet*: Finally, we think something rather larger than the proverbial 'elephant in the room' is missing from most accounts of creative industries, and creativity more generally, whether in its cultural or economic dimension: the planet. It is only since the mid-nineteenth century that 'we' (humans in general) have even known the extent of the planet and what it is made of, where its land and sea masses are located, what its geological, biological and human resources comprise, and how its systems interact. In the long course of human history, *knowledge* of the planet as a whole is less than two centuries old. Among the slowest disciplines to 'globalise' their view of their subject matter are the humanities (culture) and social sciences (economics), which retain a local, sectarian or national perspective, rather than seeking ways to understand their object of study as a planetary phenomenon. It would be weird if geologists, oceanographers, environmental scientists, meteorologists or even miners restricted themselves to this or that corner of the world without seeking to understand how and where it connects with others. But the study of meaning-creation and the study of wealth-production (i.e. cultural studies and economics; which this book will treat as integrated) have both remained aggressively parochial. The idea of a planetary cultural system, or creative economy, is almost *unthinkable* in current circumstances, except by visionaries from other disciplines like Jared Diamond (geography) or E.O. Wilson (biology). Indeed, much 'critical' writing is in a state of denial about the global stretch of culture as a system, seeing 'globalisation' only negatively, as a political issue, for which large corporations or powerful countries are to blame. In this book, in contradistinction to that, we treat culture as a 'semiosphere' (Lotman, 1990), a dynamic system of differences whose local peculiarities (identities and expression, values, artefacts, actions) can only be explained by means of the dynamics and interactions of the systems that generate them.

How to study the creative economy

Attempting a book about the creative industries, or more generally the creative economy, is a risky business from the outset, because 'creative industries' is an unloved concept (Miller, 2004; Ross, 2007; Cooke and Lazzeretti, 2008; McGuigan, 2010; O'Connor, 2010). Nevertheless, it is our belief that its time has only just begun: this is the 'age' or era of the *creative economy*. We see the creative economy not as a sector but as an 'epoch' (see Figure 2.3, page 21 below), following from previous (accelerating) epochs, each one associated with explosive expansions in knowledge-technologies, thus:

- The *Hunter–Gatherer era*, coincident with communication by *speech and stone*; from about 70,000 years ago (Harari, 2014).

- The *Agricultural era*, coincident with *writing*, husbandry and cultivation by hand; from about 10,000 years ago (agriculture) to 5,000 years ago (writing).

- The *Industrial era*, coincident with mechanical communication – *printing*, machines, etc.; unevenly adopted between the sixteenth and nineteenth centuries.

- The *Information era*, coincident with *electronic* communication – the telegraph, cinema, radio and TV broadcasting, computers; late nineteenth to late twentieth centuries.

- The *Creative era*, coincident with *the internet*, and population-wide, planetary communication among interconnected users and makers; now on.

This book, therefore, is about the creative economy as an *emergent* phenomenon in a *longue durée* timeframe. We are interested in its future, which is uncertain, of course, but it may be much more significant than its past, if is well conceptualised, observed and nurtured by those with 'skin in the ne' – economic, intellectual or creative.

In order to imagine and predict how that future may turn out, it is important to understand past and present arrangements: what elements, dynamics and processes are already in train and what actions may help or hinder any future potential to be realised. In the case of the creative economy, this is where the problem lies, because conceptualisation and research to date has been confined to too narrow a band of activities, agents and places – the so-called creative *industries* as a subset of the economy as a whole. As a result, the greater phenomenon that the term seeks to describe often slips from view.

Our study advances the argument that the creative industries need to be reimagined on an entirely bigger scale than heretofore. This is not to fall for 'hype' or 'cultural populism', 'celebrating' some 'neoliberal' ruse to power and profit. Surprisingly little of that sort of talk makes sense in the places we intend to visit. The reason for enlarging the scale of inquiry is to make sure that we have understood where creativity comes from, how it connects people, and what it is used for. That's where culture comes in. As our title indicates, the creative economy and culture are inseparable, the more so as cultural activities based on sociality, identity, communication and meaningfulness have migrated to the web and to digital media, both commercially marketed and self-represented, such that culture, technology and the economy are now a single object of study. This poses a challenge to existing disciplinary distinctions, which have long preserved a distinction between the social sciences, where the economy is studied, and the arts and humanities, where culture is a central, albeit contested, concept.

Part of the problem about the study of the creative industries in the university setting, therefore, is that the 'creative' aspect belongs to one scholarly tradition while the 'industries' part belongs to another. Researchers from these different traditions come upon the topic – and each other – with different skills and training, different methods and aims, housed in different parts of the campus with different measures of success and achievement and, to make matters worse, in-group and out-group allegiances and ideologies that can make each side suspicious of the other. For example scholars in economic or industry portfolios are more likely to work from a pro-market perspective that would minimise the role of the state in creative and cultural affairs, while those in cultural and creative portfolios are likely to support public culture and be critical of market-based commercial culture.

In such a context, where *how* we know seems to have a disproportionate influence on *what* we know, there is a need to work beyond existing disciplinary boundaries, to learn from other disciplines and contribute to them, and to adopt methods of study that take researchers beyond their individual comfort zone (i.e. their specialisation), in order to do justice to emergent objects of study that defy traditional categorisation.

The creative economy is just such a domain. It combines the most intimate levels of personal identity and expression with global-scale markets and systems; and confronts both citizens and researchers with a situation where, in Mehita Iqani's suggestive pun, human 'I contact' (2012: 148) is made through a mediated, symbolic environment in which who 'I' am – and how I establish my identity – is inseparable from the workings of global systems (media, markets) and technologies (networks, 'big data' and communication devices) (Leaver, 2012). Further, technological and social change has been so rapid in this environment that the disciplinary distinctions inherited from the nineteenth century are no longer capable of explaining what is going on (Lee, 2010) – what is cause and what is effect, and how best to study the creative, cultural and economic aspects of contemporary life. In such a context, the challenge for students of the creative economy is not to confine themselves to ever more specialist silos, but to team up with others (see Chapter 14) in order to develop a multidisciplinary approach that can take seriously the *relations* among different phenomena: creativity and economy; selves and systems; culture and technology; existing knowledge and emergent trends or future probabilities.

Culture as the source of innovation

The present authors come to this quest from the perspective of *cultural science* (Hartley and Potts, 2014), which offers a *systems* view of communication, culture and therefore of creativity, rather than an individualist or behavioural view, and an *evolutionary* rather than choice-theoretic view of economics. As will become clear, we do not start, as do most 'industry' or 'policy' definitions of the creative economy (following DCMS, 1998), from 'individual talent'. We don't deny that individuals are talented; in fact we believe that more people are more talented than has been *realised* (especially in the economic sense of that term) and that the creative economy, properly – i.e. ambitiously – conceptualised and enabled, will allow such talents to flower and prosper at general rather than elite-only or commercial-only scope and scale.

But individualism is not our starting point, because we see the flowering of talent as an *output* of *complex systems* (not a cause of individual action). The system that generates creativity is *culture* – not technology or the economy directly, and not individuals by themselves. However, it is in the economic and high-tech sectors that the term 'creativity' has attracted most policy and critical attention over recent years. This is because creativity has become associated with innovation in the business environment. Thus, *creative innovation* is a much sought after quality that is said to drive contemporary post-industrial economic performance as a whole. At the same time, creativity is also the stock in trade of the humanities and the creative arts, which (at least according to one way of thinking) are strange bedfellows for economics and technology. This is, however, the reason for taking an interest in culture, communication, creativity, the arts and humanities, with all their critical and often antibusiness ideological baggage, when trying to understand an apparently simple economic phenomenon like the creative economy.

Culture is the source of what Michael Hutter and his colleagues (2010) call *newness*.[1] Culture is based on communication within and among groups or demes (Hartley and Potts, 2014). It is the *source* of newness because culture works at the level of *groups* rather than individuals; and culture is also the context in which innovation is *used*. Usage impels innovations that adapt new technologies, from steam power to internet connectivity, through myriad acts of tinkering and experimentation, some of which go on to be generally adopted. In turn, newness, as distinct from novelty, is another word for innovation.

The difference between novelty and newness is this: novelty is, as it were, a 'conjecture' or 'experiment', which will not survive unless it is taken up and used across a system or network, be that technical or social. 'Newness' occurs not at the point of invention or discovery but upon acceptance by others, in the socio-instrumental implementation of new ideas (see Potts, 2011). Newness is thus the *use* of novelty – it is cultural rather than technological or economic in nature. In evolutionary terms, novelty is 'variation', which is individual and effectively random, while newness is 'adaptation', which is selected and replicated among a population.

Cultural sources of innovation, albeit at anonymous, artisanal or user-created microproductive scale, may thereby explain macro-level developments up to and including the dynamic growth associated with the Industrial Revolution (Mokyr, 2009), even though 'innovation' is usually seen strictly as a business process. Indeed, it is seen by many in business, technology, economics and government to be the one essential requirement for growth and prosperity in turbulent times. Here's a typical example of how innovation is discussed in business forums:

> Innovate or die has been the catch phrase of the 21st Century. The modern organisation operates in an ether of discontinuous change and is faced with numerous influences that continually challenge its integrity and survival. These include the impact of rapid globalization, discontinuous change, increasing levels of competition, technological change, unstable economic conditions, transition from an industrial to knowledge-based society, diversified workforce and increasing complexity of the external environment.[2]

This mode of expression may be couched in catchphrase and cliché, but that's because it describes a now-commonplace reality: companies that don't innovate are prey to 'creative destruction' (Schumpeter, 1942) by nimble newcomers. Even big firms cannot rely only on industrial scale, organisation and cost-cutting to survive.

Culture drives industry and technology

From start-ups to tech giants, firms need entrepreneurial imagination, adaptability and energy to thrive in an uncertain environment. They also need to pay attention now, more than ever before, to collaboration and relationships (with each other, with users, and with the zeitgeist); and to design, narrative, meaningfulness and fashion-forwardness, not just in 'creative' products like movies but also in telecoms – for example, smart phones – built structures, even foodstuffs. In other words, the humblest commodity, from coffee to quinoa, is saturated with signification, and it is this that determines its economic value. Innovation is thus the process of successfully assigning new meanings (thence, new users and values) to existing objects or processes.

Granted that innovation is now a well-established contemporary business value, what has this to do with creativity, culture and communication? Let one of the tech giants, Intel, answer that question. In 2013, Intel commissioned a survey of 12,000 people over 18 years old, in Brazil, China, France, India, Indonesia, Italy, Japan and the USA. The results reveal that:

> Millennials [18-24 year-olds] globally show a stark contrast to their reputation as digital natives who can't get enough technology in their lives. A majority of millennials agree that technology makes people less human and that society relies on technology too much.[3]

In other words, the segment of the population most immersed in the world of digital technologies, social media and online participation is also the most critical of that world's personal and social impact – it 'makes people less human'; and society 'relies on technology too much'. That's a worry for a firm like Intel, no matter how innovative it may be at the technical level. If there's such a thing as a 'millennial malaise' and young people are beginning to reject the very technology in which they are assumed to be 'native', then the prospects for economic sustainability are uncertain indeed. Is culture *trumping* technology and economics?

Intel is famous for investing massively in R&D for innovation. Its company research budget is said to be bigger than Australia's national one.[4] It has relied on research investment because at the beginning of each year it could not know which invention would be its bestseller by the end of the year, since it hadn't been invented yet. That was because of Moore's law.[5] This is Intel co-founder Gordon Moore's prediction that the number of transistors on a microchip would double about every two years; a prediction that was bold in 1965 when he made it, but has held true for over half a century. The company has risked its future on Moore's law, so far with success (despite the increasing cost of maintaining an exponential rate of development). In turn, the increased capacity of their chips has improved the performance and range of the myriad devices and applications with an 'Intel inside'. Intel has achieved pre-eminence in the technical field by innovating at speed as well as scale. If, now, people think that technology dehumanises them, then Intel will be the loser.

But perhaps culture does not *trump* technology in this direct way. Perhaps culture is the very place where technology finds meaningfulness and usefulness, and thus the determinant of success. It's not an 'either/or' or a zero sum game. Get the culture right and technology integrates with it, to such an extent that people may not recognise what they are using as technological. This is certainly what Australian anthropologist Genevieve Bell thinks. She directs 'interaction and experience research' for Intel, running a research lab with a $35m annual budget and a staff of 100 (again, a much more significant investment in the intersection of culture and technology than is made by most countries). Bell interprets the Intel survey thus:

> At first glance it seems millennials are rejecting technology, but I suspect the reality is more complicated and interesting ... A different way to read this might be that millennials want technology to do more for them, and we have work to do to make it much more personal and less burdensome.[6]

The lesson is not that culture and technology cannot mix, but that they *must* mix. Companies must understand the users of technology at least as well as the physics. At a presentation at RMIT University in Australia,[7] Genevieve Bell entertained the audience with a pair of slides showing the 'image' of the user that typically circulates in company boardrooms and laboratories, compared with pictures of actual users and the circumstances in which the company's technology actually operates. The two images could not have been more different. We can reproduce her thought experiment here, using similarly contrasting images (Figures 1.1. and 1.2). The image of the consumer in the minds of company executives and computer scientists remains pretty much that of the 1950s nuclear family as portrayed in advertising (Figure 1.1). Ads like this one for TV sets were open to criticism even when first published (Spigel, 1992), because 'TV happiness' is proffered to an entirely abstract or idealised white, suburban, heterosexual couple with two children. It's all smiles as everyone gazes at their technological gadgets, each one equally open to being pleasured by advertised commodities. Social realities such as poverty or differences in class, gender, race and sexual orientation are banished beyond the closed drapes, while happiness is construed as the shared consumption of dramatised images of the same nuclear family on the TV screen – without a hint of mutually conflicting preferences.

Culture, as the admitted source of newness, is construed here as 'family happiness', but the family is not the source of *products*. The chain of causation is clear: culture is the source of emotion, affect, and family roles, but all this can be converted into one act – consumption – because those complicated feelings, relationships, identities and meanings, shared or otherwise, can be achieved through purchasing what clever technologies and even cleverer brand names have done to express them in material form 'because of 25 years of pioneering in the electronics industry', as Motorola claims about itself. This kind of thinking is where the *industrial* model of innovation has its own origins, confining invention, technology and the growth of knowledge to producers, and making culture the domain of consumption, seen in strictly behavioural terms, where the main thing is to 'add plenty of pleasure'. The home is seen as a work-free (unproductive) refuge of conspicuous consumption, even as Mother works as provider, where the wants, needs, desires, and shared meaningfulness of 'all the family' are known in advance to the corporate marketing department (Spigel, 1992), but where 'the consumer' plays no role in establishing those meanings beyond the act of purchase. In the Motorola version of 'family happiness', people have relationships with technologies rather than with each other, and the idea of a productive family making creative use of their time together to produce meaningfulness for themselves is not on offer.

FIGURE 1.1 Culture and technology, exhibit A: 'TV happiness shared by all the family!' 1951 advertisement *(Time* Magazine).
*Picture courtesy of John W. Hartman Center for Sales, Advertising and Marketing History, Duke University Library.*8

But the reality, as Genevieve Bell pointed out, can be very different. Figure 1.2 shows an example from Hong Kong. The same elements are present: domestic interior, family member, consumption and electronic devices for screen and sound. Looked at one way, the two images merely record the mismatch between idealised corporate desire and people's so-called real lives. We've moved from WASP monoculture to global, ethnic, multi-culture, and from 'conspicuous consumption' (consumer goods as 'costly signalling' trophies) to 'always-on' connectivity, where technology is integrated into the personal environment. Looked at another way, Figure 1.2 shows *user ingenuity and inventiveness*, given that people can adapt the most unlikely spaces to accommodate their TVs, phones (two in this picture) and other devices, not to mention books, magazines, newspapers and photos. True, the conditions are so cramped that a Motorola family-of-four couldn't fit in the room, so this is not an idealised image, but at the same time it should not be read as entirely negative either. Instead, it shows home not as a refuge but a working user-space as well as resting place, where the outside world impinges on private life, and social connections are maintained electronically.

FIGURE 1.2 Culture and technology, exhibit B: 'Over 100,000 people live in tiny "cubicle apartments" in the city [Hong Kong] ... Residents go about their lives in these confined spaces, sleeping in one corner, eating in another, storing their belongings in a third, and perhaps watching a TV that's found in a fourth'.
*Photograph courtesy of Society for Community Organisation/Publicis Hong Kong.*9

Perhaps most people's experience lies somewhere between these extremes. Either way, and this is what concerns Bell and Intel, if corporate culture gets too far out of step with user culture, the aspirations of one side of the relationship will fail to connect with those of the other. When that happens, it's the corporation that loses out in the end. So companies must understand culture as well as technology. How a given invention fares in the world depends really on a combination of fantasy and reality, where ordinary consumers as well as corporate executives may have an impossible image in their heads (at once nostalgic and aspirational) but a grubbier reality at their feet. Both image and actuality are part of culture, where economics plays a part, especially for those with constrained space and time for leisurely consumption.

Thus, culture does not trump technology; it *drives* it. Although it is true, as Bell suggests, that the big firms 'have work to do' to make technology more 'personal' for young people, they cannot do it in ignorance of the lives that such 'millennials' lead, or without linking their internal innovations to the creativity, purposes and networks of users. This is why a systems approach to creativity is needed, because it exceeds the organisational boundaries or control of any one agency, even the largest and most astute of firms.

Interestingly, the young 'digital natives' who have been among the most tech-hungry early adopters so far may be giving way to different demographics. The same Intel survey found that most of the very people who endure the conditions like those shown in the pictured Hong Kong apartment (Figure 1.2) held very different views, compared with disenchanted affluent youngsters in rich countries. Thus:

> Women in emerging markets across ages believe innovations will drive better education (66 percent), transportation (58 percent), work (57 percent) and healthcare (56 percent). Women in emerging markets would be willing to embrace technologies others may consider to be too personal to improve their experiences: software that watches their work habits (86 percent), students' study habits (88 percent) and even smart toilets that monitor their health (77 percent).

A full 70 percent of Chinese women over 45 who responded to the survey thought that people 'don't use technology enough'.

This is why culture is so important to the economy and technology: it is the source of 'newness' or implemented novelty; the arbiter of uptake, and the determinant of a company's future. It is the domain of meaningfulness, identity and relationships, and these in turn determine the usefulness or otherwise of the latest app. At last, where technology meets usefulness, we can see the beginnings of a much-needed rapprochement between technological sciences, economic strategists, and creativity, understood not simply as clever inventors working for firms but as a population-wide capability that can be developed and improved, or neglected and ignored (at corporate peril).

In this shifting boundary between the sciences, social sciences and arts, we see the creative industries as a kind of *marker-dye* for future trends. It reveals how entire systems operate and interact. We do not see the creative industries as just another sector of the economy. To take this approach further, it is necessary to shift to planetary scale and an evolutionary timeframe. Only then will it be possible to describe and discern how the creative future is formed.

Notes

1. See also www.wzb.eu/en/news/analyzing-innovation; and: www.wzb.eu/en/research/society-and-economic-dynamics/cultural-sources-of-newness.
2. John Kapeleris, writing for the *Australian Innovation Festival* website (n.d.), available at www.ausinnovation.org/articles/innovate-or-die.html. The post also offers a definition of innovation, in terms of new products/services, processes, marketing, organisational arrangements and business models.
3. 'Intel research reveals changing tech advocates and attitudes: millennials are tough on technology, women carry the tech torch and digital affluents share wealth of data', 17 October 2013, available at: http://newsroom.intel.com/community/intel_newsroom/blog/2013/10/17/future-of-technology-may-be-determined-by-millennial-malaise-female-fans-and-affluent-data-altruists.
4. According to CEO Craig Barrett at http://mailman.anu.edu.au/pipermail/link/2002-September/020884.html.
5. The Wikipedia entry on Moore's law is worth reading.
6. Source: http://newsroom.intel.com/community/intel_newsroom/blog/2013/10/17/future-of-technology-may-be-determined-by-millennial-malaise-female-fans-and-affluent-data-altruists.
7. Source: www.designresearch.rmit.edu.au/events/presentation-duck-dolls-divine-robots-designing-our-futures-with-computers-genevieve-bell-friday-28-september-2012.
8. Image source: Item ID: TV0213: http://library.duke.edu/digitalcollections/media/jpg/adaccess/lrg/TV0213.jpg.
9. *Cramped Apartments in Hong Kong Shot From Directly Above*, by Michael Zhang. PetaPixel, 19 Feb. 2013. Available at: http://petapixel.com/2013/02/19/cramped-apartments-in-hong-kong-shot-from-directly-above/; see also www.soco.org.hk/index_e.htm.

2

THE BIG PICTURE – SPHERES ENVELOPING SPHERES

> *The unit of semiosis, the smallest functioning mechanism, is not a separate language, but the whole semiotic space of culture in question.*
>
> (Yuri Lotman, 1990: 125)

In this short chapter we set up a theoretical model for the 'big picture' approach that follows in the next chapter – actually the 'three bigs'. The model is not of our own devising: it has been elaborated over decades, following the insights of two scientists whose location in the former Soviet Union meant that their work and its implications were slow to percolate through to the Anglosphere. They are Vladimir I. Vernadsky and Yuri M. Lotman (also known as Juri Lotman in Estonia, where he co-founded the 'Tartu School' of semiotics). Lotman derived his concept of the '*semiosphere*' (sphere of culture) from Vernadsky's '*biosphere*' (sphere of life). Vernadsky also coined the concept of the *noösphere* (sphere of thought), which, together with the biosphere, he saw as a transformational agent in the evolution of the *geosphere*.

That's a lot of spheres.[1] Bear with us while we explain, because these concepts are now widely accepted in mainstream science, especially in the field of ecology (see Levit (2011) and Figure 2.1). However, the extra step, from the natural geosphere + biosphere to the cultural semiosphere + noösphere, has not been taken with equal confidence up until now, except in specialist fields like biosemiotics (see Kotov and Kull, 2011).

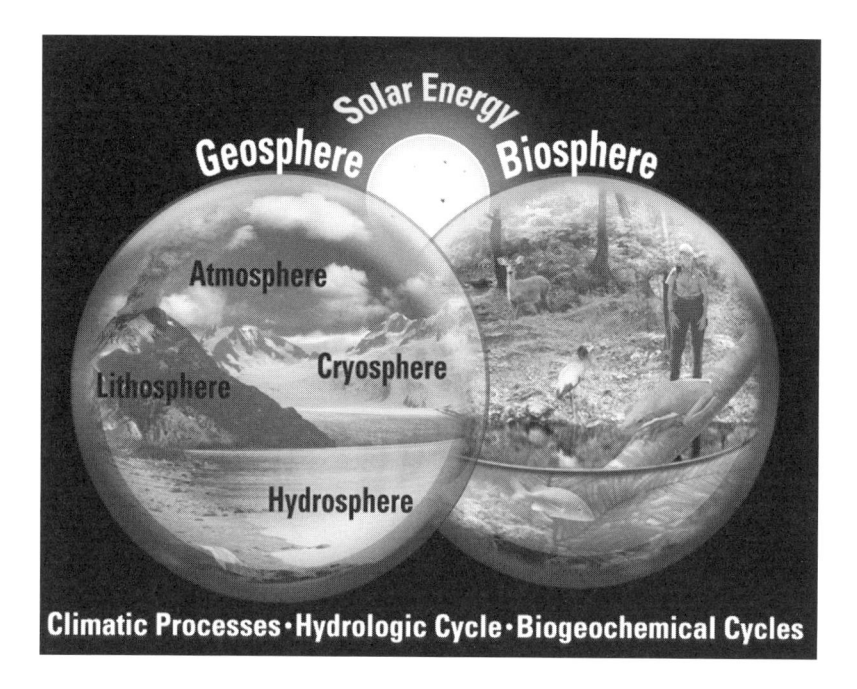

FIGURE 2.1 The Earth System: the geosphere and biosphere combined. *Image courtesy of the US Geological Survey (diagram designed by James A. Tomberlin, USGS)*[2]

The study of culture, and with that the study of creativity and its elaborate exploitation at global scale in the creative economy, could benefit by adopting a systems approach, if only to test current ways of thinking. This is what we do here, contributing to a new hybrid field that Hartley and Potts (2014) have called 'cultural science'.

Concentric spheres: geosphere, biosphere, semiosphere, noösphere

Following Yuri Lotman (1990), whose concept of the semiosphere informs our approach, we see the *cultural system* as planetary in extent – part of the 'earth system' that includes the atmosphere and other components of the geosphere, plus the biosphere, so named by V. I. Vernadsky (1938). The geosphere + biosphere amounts to a coherent unitary system at planetary level (see Figure 2.1), an observable envelope around the crust of the earth, despite myriad internal differences, boundaries and dynamic processes, including localised clashes (competition) and collapse (extinction).

In the case of the biosphere, all life is interconnected, via genetics or environment, including relations of predation as well as symbiosis and habitat-modification, and life is distinct from non-life. Thus, 'life' is a unitary envelope around the earth, extending a few kilometres above and below its surface, at most. The existence of any one species or specimen cannot be explained without reference to the system.

Although in its infancy, cultural science proceeds on the notion that the same applies to culture and knowledge. This is Lotman's revolutionary proposition: that culture is a unitary system, comprising all meaning systems and their interrelations and agents, and it covers the planet as the semiosphere. Evolutionary processes are at work, and increasing complexity characterises the various spheres (where 'life' is just another word for elaborately self-organising complex systems). Naturalistic matter–energy processes (Herrmann-Pillath, 2010), or what Vernadsky calls biogeochemistry, drive change throughout, linking geological phenomena to meaning and knowledge, which he called the noösphere (Vernadsky, 1943) as well as to life.[3]

A differentiated 'system' within the biosphere, the human species is planetary in extent, while displaying myriad differences, boundaries and processes, especially between *groups* that range between tribe and ethnicity in scale. This has been the case for many thousands of years. *Knowledge of* human planetary unity, however, is barely more than a century or two old, and is still not complete. It was only in the nineteenth century that the physical features of the planet (the geosphere) were mapped to a first approximation (although under-sea features remain under-explored). Its living component, the biosphere, is still not fully mapped, and the components of human knowledge (noösphere) and meaningfulness (semiosphere), have barely begun to be investigated as part of the causal sequence of matter–energy evolving with this and possibly other planets. It is perceived in its parts, not systematically; and often appears as static structure rather than dynamic flux.

Such imperfections of perception and knowledge are an artefact of the infancy of cultural inquiry. They do not describe the system itself. It's the unsteady hand of an immature science that needs improvement, not least to modify previous attempts to control natural systems whose self-creating complexity has evolved without benefit of human intervention for the last three billion years and more. Knowledge and culture – noösphere and semiosphere – are not exempt from these processes. They are relatively recent manifestations, thereby likely to prove even more complex than what has gone before. They need careful characterisation, models, predictions, evidence and testing, just as the geosphere and biosphere have received from physics, chemistry and the biosciences.

FIGURE 2.2 Preserved for posterity: V.I. Vernadsky's grave in Moscow – protected by a perspex box.
Picture courtesy of Julie and Keld (July 2012)[4]

Cultural science names the attempt to develop a systems-level and evolutionary account of culture, knowledge and meaningfulness in the Vernadsky–Lotman tradition. Vernadsky (Figure 2.2) wrote in 1938:

> In this period [last 500 years] the entire surface of the planet was embraced by a single culture: the discovery of printing, knowledge of all earlier inaccessible areas of the globe, the mastery of new forms of energy—steam, electricity, radioactivity, the mastery of all the chemical elements and their utilization for the needs of Man, the creation of the telegraph and the radio, the penetration into the Earth ... by boring, and the ascension of men in aerial machines ... Profound social changes, giving support to the broad masses, advanced their interests into the first rank.

Vernadsky saw life and knowledge as transformative of physical (chemical) matter, and thus as a new form of energy. Terrestrial energy and chemistry transforms geological materials (e.g. into igneous and metamorphic rocks). In the same way, life transforms complex chemical molecules into the dazzling variety of species in the biosphere; and these in turn – or at least their corpses – transform geology (via sedimentary rocks). Knowledge, for its part, transforms the geosphere and biosphere directly, for instance by isolating elements that are not encountered in that form in nature (such as aluminium or plutonium), or by deforestation, intensive farming and fishing, sea-defences, urbanisation, pollution and the like.

Geologically, these are recent and rapid changes, but they began a long time ago in human terms: agriculture about 10,000–12,000 years ago and industrial-scale processes about 300–500 years ago. Our observation is that what Vernadsky describes is not something new that is suddenly 'embracing' the planet in its globalising grip. Culture and knowledge spanned the world once *Homo sapiens* had spread to every continent (bar Antarctica; the last place colonised by pre-moderns being New Zealand/Aotearoa in about 800CE). So emerged a single-species planetary system of interconnected but distinct cultures and knowledge that have, however, experienced exponential growth over the past 300–500 years. What we're looking at is a logarithmic scale or power law curve in the growth of knowledge, from the earliest migrations of *Homo* species (hominins) to the latest internet sensation. And this is why it is important both to *link* culture (creativity) to this planetary perspective, since it characterises the latest phase, and to *separate* culture (creativity) from other forms of knowledge (such as mechanics or information), because the rate of change is now so rapid that economic transformations succeed each other at ever shorter frequencies.

In the quotation above, Vernadsky mentions printing and the globalisation of knowledge, followed by the invention of electronic communication (telegraph and radio), alongside new sources of energy and new understanding of materials, as the mechanism for rendering 'the entire surface of the planet' as a 'single culture'. We suggest that this insight can be formalised along the whole curve of human development since 12,000 years ago, such that a correlation can be observed between what might be called technologies of knowledge on the one hand (speech, writing, print, electronic/broadcast, and digital/internet), and economic epochs on the other (hunter-gatherer, agricultural, industrial, information and creative) (see Figure 2.3).

Yuri Lotman borrowed from Vernadsky's idea of the biosphere (see also Samson and Pitt, 1998 and Lapo, 2001), to produce his own concept of the semiosphere: a systems perspective on meaningfulness and culture, seeking to explain language as a globally coherent phenomenon that generated the possibility of difference within it. His key insight is the concept of the 'semiosphere' or 'universe of the mind', within which cultural and textual difference develop through active intra- and inter-system dialogue (including conflict). As he put it, the semiosphere is the 'semiotic space necessary

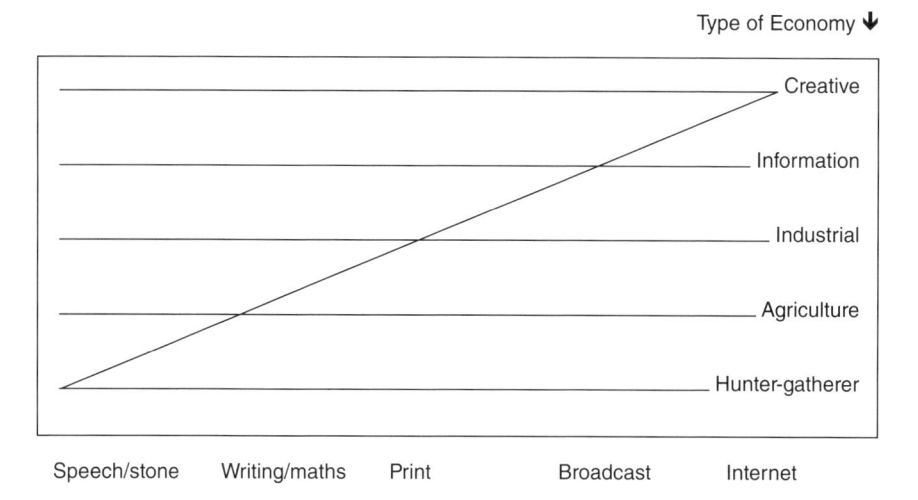

```
                                              Type of Economy ↓
┌─────────────────────────────────────────────────────────────┐
│                                            ╱ Creative       │
│                                          ╱                  │
│                                        ╱   Information      │
│                                     ╱                       │
│                                  ╱         Industrial       │
│                              ╱                              │
│                         ╱                  Agriculture      │
│                    ╱                                        │
│              ╱                             Hunter-gatherer  │
└─────────────────────────────────────────────────────────────┘
 Speech/stone   Writing/maths   Print        Broadcast    Internet
 >70,000 years  3000BCE         1500CE       1900CE       1970CE
```

Time / Technology of knowledge reproduction →

FIGURE 2.3 A conjectural diagram showing the growth of human knowledge, correlated with changes in media technologies (x axis) and successive economic epochs (y axis). The curve is exponential (hence, time is compressed logarithmically along the x axis), showing how the growth of knowledge accelerates as economic systems have evolved (this is a power law curve). The 'creative economy' requires but then supersedes the 'information economy'. *Diagram adapted from Hartley and Potts (2014: 215)*

for the existence and functioning of different languages' (Lotman, 1990: 123–5). His version of semiotics is not founded on the abstract signifier or individual sign, but on 'separate semiotic systems' (like tectonic plates), which can only come into their distinctive and asymmetric being within the envelope of a larger unity, the semiosphere. This is the 'semiotic space or intellectual world in which humanity and human society are enfolded and which is in constant interaction with the individual intellectual world of human beings' (Lotman, 1990: 3). The semiosphere is essentially scale free, encompassing intimate personal interaction, for instance between a mother and her newborn infant, which Lotman called the 'language of smiles' (1990: 144); up to the turn-taking mutual influence of different national literary cultures, say those of France and Russia following 1789; or Italy before and during the Renaissance (1990: 146). Like the atmosphere, the semiosphere is planetary in extent, but every living human breathes it and derives their individual potentiality from it.

The semiosphere is modelled on Vernadsky's concept of the biosphere and the noösphere (which emerges out of the biosphere, modified and made more complex by human thought, invention and intervention). These concepts – biosphere, semiosphere and noösphere – allow systems thinking to shift away from reductive science and methodological individualism, to countenance 'downward causation', from system to species to specimen. But they remain scientific concepts: the concept of the biosphere is itself derived from geology:

> Mankind, as living matter, is inseparably connected with the material-energetic processes of a specific geological envelope of the Earth—its biosphere. Mankind cannot be physically independent of the biosphere for a single minute. (Vernadsky, 1943: 17)

This 'geological envelope' includes the atmosphere – another phenomenon that, like the semiosphere, can be understood as a single object, one that covers the whole planet but nevertheless is breathed in and out by individual organisms (Hartley, 2008: 66–7). The biosphere comprises not only the earth's living organisms and species, but also their interactions, the conditions for the continuation of life and the links and relationships among all 'living matter'. The evolving biosphere provides the conditions of possibility for the life of any species, e.g. *H. sapiens*' dependence on oxygen produced by other life forms, bilateral symmetry, calcium structures for skeletons, the exploitation of 'fossil fuels' and living matter for energy, etc.

Humanity is but an evolved component of chemical and geological matter–energy. However, such systems are always in flux, and 'anthropogenic' novelties can produce system-level changes. Vernadsky (1943: 20) asks, 'Here a new riddle has arisen before us. *Thought is not a form of energy.* How then can it change material processes?' Humankind has isolated metals, produced entirely new materials, and impacted the planet, shoreline, oceans, atmosphere, and latterly even space, with previously unknown structures, materials and activities. What some are now calling the Anthropocene epoch (Crutzen and Stoermer, 2000; Crutzen and Schwägerl, 2011) is changing the geological as well as biological and climatological makeup of the planet.

This idea suggests that *'thought'* (Vernadsky), *culture* (Lotman), *social organisation* (Sawyer, 2005; Runciman, 2009) based on *communication* (Luhmann, 1991, 2012) and *urbanism* (Jacobs, 1985), which between them over a few thousand years have produced the growth of knowledge required for industrialisation and globalisation, should now be considered as a *geological epoch* – integrated with biogeochemical processes and therefore with the transformation and transference of matter–energy. Such large-scale, system-level changes are imperceptible and unconscious at the individual level; they cannot be predicted by reference to individual consciousness, action, intention or rational self-interest alone, which may be why the response to anthropogenic climate change has become so politicised.

Vernadsky's idea of an 'envelope' encircling the earth, and Lotman's application of that idea to culture, language and the creative arts (literature, cinema), offers an explanation of human sense-making, culture, thought and knowledge – as well as the 'product' of those activities, including cities and waste (Maxwell and Miller, 2012) – as forces that are part of the web of causation in material processes. Lotman's concept of the semiosphere starts from the system, and interactions among systems, to explain communication. This is important because, as with the shift from Linnaean taxonomic *botany* (describing difference) to Darwinian evolutionary *bioscience* (describing causation), it offers a way to conceptualise culture as an adaptive, interactive (communicative) system. We are moving from cultural studies to cultural science.

Lotman's semiosphere paves the way for an evolutionary approach to culture, but one that's based on the evolution of systems of knowledge (Boulding, 1977) and technology (Arthur, 2009), rather than genes. It draws attention from the single unit, be that the sign, utterance, speaker, *langue* or language, and directs it towards interactions among whole populations and intersecting systems. Unique utterances are possible only within global systems of rules, structures and processes, and to get started these rules require the mutual interaction of 'at least two' languages, according to Lotman. Thus the elementary act of communication is *translation* (not *transmission*).

Lotman used the analogy of intelligence to introduce the idea of language as a 'mutual psychological process': 'Human Intelligence ... cannot switch itself on by itself. For an intelligence to function there must be another intelligence ... Intelligence is always an interlocutor' (1990: 2). So, 'human consciousness is heterogeneous. A minimal thinking apparatus must include at least two differently constructed systems to exchange information they each have worked out' (1990: 36). Language, culture, and thought are constituted in the *clash of systems*.

Lotman's work was literary in orientation, although he was interested in other textual systems including cinema, but his purpose was scientific, in the sense that he wanted to identify what Thorstein Veblen had called 'cumulative causal sequence' in phenomena, within the 'semiotic space' of culture. Thus, his own analysis is empirical and historical in character, but at the same time it is devoted to theory-building, conceptual modelling and the elucidation of causal process in sense-making systems. A systems approach – one that is also interested in historical dynamics and the causal mechanisms of change – is thus a candidate for the status of an evolutionary approach to culture. And culture, in the form of the semiosphere and the associated knowledge-system or noösphere, is a becoming 'mighty geological force' (Vernadsky, 1943: 19).

How does this force intersect with knowledge and material processes to create newness in uncertain circumstances? This book offers one particular answer to that question.

Notes

1. But wait; there's more! Amy Mandelker (1995) reminds us that Lotman's concept of the semiosphere owes something to Mikhail Bakhtin's earlier notion of the 'logosphere'.
2. The US Geological Survey's own caption to this image is: 'The geosphere and the biosphere are the two components of the Earth System; the geosphere is the collective name for the lithosphere, the hydrosphere, the cryosphere, and the atmosphere. All parts of the Earth System interact and are interrelated through climatic processes and through the hydrologic cycle and biogeochemical cycles. The Sun is the dominant source of all external energy to the Earth System' (http://pubs.usgs.gov/pp/p1386a/plate-earthsystem.html).
3. Numerous accounts of the biosphere and noösphere refer to the Jesuit priest Pierre Teilhard de Chardin, whose theology borrows these terms. His work was more familiar in the West during the Cold War era. However, Vernadsky originated and conceptualised the terms (Lapo, 2001). Teilhard's teleological–theological appropriation of the concept of evolution as well as these terms should not detract from Vernadsky's scientific account. However, there is debate about the extent to which Teilhard and Vernadsky shared a belief in 'directed' evolution (Levit, 2000), a conjecture that has been refuted in subsequent evolutionary bioscience.
4. Picture source: http://image2.findagrave.com/photos/2013/148/20402_136985439217.jpg (www.findagrave.com/cgi-bin/fg.cgi?page=pv&GRid=20402&PIpi=81243867).

3

THE THREE BIGS – 'EVERYONE' 'EVERYTHING' 'EVERYWHERE'

Social systems have Heisenberg principles all over the place, for we cannot predict the future without changing it.

(Kenneth Boulding, 1981: 44)

Conceptual community-formation

We want to take account of the *distribution* of the creative industries idea and its implementation as much as its origin. We think its underlying potential emerges as much in the process of diffusion and adaptation to new circumstances as it does in resolving some of the arguments and hostilities that beset the concept.

The geographer Russell Prince (2010: 121) has observed that:

> The rapid diffusion of creative industries policy is the result of so many policymakers, activists, council and government officers, cultural entrepreneurs, researchers, and academics from so many places being able to incorporate the concept into their political, cultural, economic, and social projects.

Such a view emphasises not so much the concept but the *conceptual community* who gather round – or walk away from – an iterative conversation that may become more elaborate, more effective, and more fit-for-purpose over time (or, it might fizzle out).

Thus, what's important is the *group*, because it is the group that generates knowledge. Hartley and Potts (2014) use the term *deme* (a subpopulation or 'demos') to identify the cultural vehicle or group that can include both situated (located in a place) and virtual or dispersed (connected via publication, communication and dialogue) communities of interest or affinity. A deme in classical Greece was a division of the population of Attica, upon which Athenian citizenship was calculated and organised. The term is still familiar in political rhetoric in the words 'demos', 'democracy', 'demography', etc. Contemporary bioscience also uses the term deme, to denote subpopulations of a given species in which interbreeding occurs (often in isolation from other subpopulations of the same species); such populations can develop distinctive features. These two uses of the term deme combine to describe self-organising populations, which share knowledge, decision-making (citizenship) and genes (intermarriage) among themselves but are distinct from (and often adversarial to) other such demes (i.e. speakers of other languages – known to the Greeks as 'barbarians'). Demes are the basic unit of culture (Pagel, 2012a). Culture makes groups; groups make knowledge. We argue from this that it is in the preservation, adaptation and replication of group-made knowledge, communication, and selves (in both identity and offspring) that *creativity* is to be found. In short, we take creativity to be a property and 'output' of cultural groups, not the other kind of property, belonging to individual persons.

This logic applies just as strongly to those who seek to analyse and explain culture, creativity and their industrial-economic characteristics as it does to those whose activities they study. 'We' – the community of scholars, policy-makers, commentators, students and readers – are involved in deme-formation, in order to know. In this instance, the deme is formed among the interconnected agents mentioned above, who are drawn from *other* demes, both functional (government, cultural institutions, policy and advocacy agencies, academia) and geographic (from different countries, cities and regions). In this era of global communications, these are also 'virtual' demes – communities of affiliation linked by Facebook or fanship, formed and sustained online or in media. When such diverse groups-of-groups come together *as* a larger group, e.g. what Michael Warner (2002) has called a 'discourse public', it is not easy to isolate what characterises the 'we'-identity of that group, and here is where tensions, arguments, unexpected meetings of mind and innovative possibilities are generated, as *difference* rubs up against *purpose*.

This may be why Russell Prince can argue that the building up of a global knowledge and policy community is the most important achievement of the creative industries concept. He cites the easy transferability of the idea across global borders, and the community and infrastructure that have built up around the concept, to support its development:

> The creative industries provide a common reference point for what is a wide variety of projects, all with their own particular political programs and ways of knowing. Through the creative industries concept, otherwise diverging projects that may never have encountered one another are able to speak to each other across the space that separates them. (Prince, 2010: 136)

Thus, the implication of Prince's argument is that the most important conceptual achievement is not to cleanse the definition of creative industries, but to keep the deme together:

> However long the creative industries survive as a concept and the policy community holds together, what all this points to is that the ethic must not be to think it is possible to find some "final solution" that will set the creative industries free and provide rewarding livelihoods for all those that participate in them, but is to recognize that it is the ongoing dialogue and connections across space that give the idea vitality. (Prince, 2010: 136)

Prince's valuable contribution to the debate about the creative industries/creative economy is that the debate itself, and the differences among different parties to it, can be seen as creative group-formation: the 'policy community' is an example of what it seeks to describe, making the idea of the creative industries more real the more it is discussed, no matter what the position of each combatant or contributor.

The take-out message is: keep talking! The rewards may be considerable. Prince concludes that: 'Any new and unexpected connections facilitated by this global form could herald innovative policy solutions and political projects; and the more connections, I would argue, the more likely this is to occur'. The goal is for innovation in ideas and the generation of usefully new knowledge. It is more likely to be reached by dialogic practice than by definitional exclusivity and sectarian division of the group into insiders and outsiders, we and they, right and wrong.

This book takes up the challenge of promoting dialogue, making connections and boosting the vitality of the idea, by taking three risky steps – the Three Bigs – in the run-up to a new conceptualisation (not a 'final solution') of the creative industries.

Orders of approximation – starting from zeroth

In the world of research, there is a vogue for what is called evidence-based policy and publication. When measured against existing yardsticks (e.g. market trading by firms) or statistics (e.g. consumer demand), the creative industries don't necessarily shine, not least because they encompass a wider range of productive activity than is captured in the market, and they deal in novelties, for which there can be no demand in advance of supply. Pretty soon, busy policymakers and politicians lose interest (creative industries aren't big enough), scholars and researchers get bogged down in statistical and conceptual minutiae (creative industries aren't coherent enough), and the general public continues to ignore the whole show (perhaps assuming, from all this professional squabbling, that the creative industries idea has nothing to do with them).

We think that 'evidence-based' policy – research that looks backwards to what has already happened – is premature. More important at this stage is conceptualisation itself, the 'bold conjecture' phase of scientific discovery, as Karl Popper put it:

> Bold ideas, unjustified anticipations, and speculative thought, are our only means for interpreting nature: our only organon, our only instrument, for grasping her. And we must hazard them to win our prize. Those among us who are unwilling to expose their ideas to the hazard of refutation do not take part in the scientific game. (Popper, 2002: 279–80)

Counter-intuitively, the present circumstances may be in need of more rhetoric and less evidence, more conjecture and fewer stats, more imagination and less description, than is usually allowed in the social sciences. Until we can trace the shape of whatever it is that is forming now and will transform the future in unpredictable ways, we are likely to misinterpret the signals we receive – they may be mathematically and descriptively accurate, but miss out on what happens next, or fail to discern the overall system being sampled in the details. Indeterminacy and uncertainty are not cured by accuracy (in physics they are quantum facts as distinct from mechanical ones); understanding comes from piecing evidence together, from *synthesis*, not from the perception of chaotic bits and pieces jostling for attention.

To explain what we mean, the creative industries concept itself offers a good example of how wrong you can be if you conceptualise a phenomenon simply on the evidence of the past. The creative industries were originally described narrowly, to include *analogue* arts (DCMS, 1998), without much consideration given to the elephant that was already lumbering around the room – digital media and social networks. The latter had already begun to transform creative practice, both professional and amateur, and their economic impact can be gauged by looking at the market capitalisation of companies in the tech, telecoms, media and e-commerce (consumer services) lists, and how these 'social network market' companies (Potts et al., 2008) have grown and outcompeted one another increasingly rapidly – market leadership leapfrogging from Microsoft, Nokia and Ericsson to Apple, Google and Amazon.[1] The fact that most of these companies originate in the USA and most are barely out of their teens may have blinded the essentially European-minded proponents of the creative industries idea to the transformational force of the digital revolution, simply because there was not much point in having a UK or EU policy on a sector headquartered elsewhere (other than a desire to break up these competitive giants, as was proposed in a (non-binding) European Parliament vote in October 2014, aimed directly at Google). So a conceptualisation of a creative economy that was based only on the existing forms of creative and performing arts, publishing, design and media was doomed to rapid obsolescence – and policy missteps.

However, such partial beginnings may only represent what scientists and engineers call a 'zeroth order of approximation' (or educated guess), to which a number cannot be put. For instance, a crowd in a sporting arena, shopping mall or demonstration may be estimated at 'a few hundred' or 'a few thousand' or 'tens of thousands' … all of which are 'zeroth' orders of magnitude (zero significant figures), but nevertheless they are informative and real descriptions (from which observers can tell if the crowd was small and disappointing, or big and compelling). Later refinements may allow higher order numerical values to emerge – the 'gate' at a stadium, or 'police estimates' at a demonstration. What these numbers 'add up to' can of course still be contentious when reconverted to meaningfulness.

Whether quantified accurately or not, however, orders of approximation are useful tools in characterising phenomena for which no calibration system yet exists. That's where we are with the creative industries: no-one is certain about what they're made of (where to draw the boundary), so we can't yet tell how many there are, what general category each one is a species of, how they interlink spatially and by sector, or what scale or rate of growth they exhibit. Admitting error and ignorance, and lack of evidence, is not the moment to walk away! The initial conceptualisation of the creative industries is not of zero value just because it can't be quantified, or misses significant elements: it's simply at zeroth order of approximation. The response should be: let's improve it.

But patience does not seem to sit easily with policymakers or theorists, much less practitioners. The very term 'creative industries' sends some theorists into a rage. Other scholars, working in strongly demarcated disciplinary knowledge fields, don't like the term much because it arose in policy discourses – it is seen as an incoherent grab-bag buzzword, or an opportunist bit of marketing rhetoric to boost the profile of a particular ministry or locality, rather than a theorised concept (Schlesinger, 2009; Prince, 2010; Flew, 2012).

Many people *in* the creative industries don't like it because they don't see why their particular specialism needs to be aggregated with others. A good example of how the term sits uneasily with existing crafts and trades is journalism. Journalists tend to be offended if you say their writing is 'creative' (it sounds as though you are accusing them of making up stories), but journalism as a whole is very much an integrated part of the global entertainment industries. Journalism training is now routinely located in 'creative industries' faculties in universities, alongside practical training in film–TV–radio production, the performing arts, creative writing, design and visual arts disciplines, and communication including PR, marketing and advertising (Bromley, 2014). As a labour market, journalists overlap with other fields of creative practice, including media production (TV, radio, online, the press), authorship and publishing, marketing and cultural intermediation, policy and advocacy. Nevertheless, few practising journalists want to admit to being 'in' the creative industries. The occupational ideology is at odds with the industrial form, and both are being overtaken by cultural and market changes. No wonder they're cranky.

Some serious issues underlie all that crankiness. Some of these will be addressed in the course of the book (The Three Buts). But before we get into the details and disagreements, we want to determine the 'angle of attack' that we hope will lift this book above the level of disciplinary turf-wars and ideological squabbles, which cannot be resolved on conceptual grounds alone. We realise that trying to achieve lift-off for a new overall perspective, to find new horizons for the creative industries, is even riskier than describing the concept or the industrial trajectory so far, but we argue that such a move is necessary if the idea and the practice are to thrive. This is because, despite the growing familiarity of the term, there remains a lack of clarity about the future potential of whatever is covered by the creative industries. As a result, current discourse and debate *about* them may be weighing them down – with legacy thinking, conceptual rigidity, lack of an agreed object, purpose or direction, and low expectations. The way public and critical discussion has construed them has set a by-now rather predictable agenda of self-serving claims and counter-claims, critique and celebration, which may hinder rather than help their 'take-off'.

It is therefore worth the attempt and the risk to rethink the creative industries from first principles, because whatever opinions people may have about the terminology, the facts 'out there' are telling a different story.

Conceptual origins

Since its inception in the 1990s, the idea of the creative industries has travelled the world. What is that idea? The most widespread version is this well-known formula:

> *Creative industries have their origin in individual creativity, skill and talent. They have the potential to create wealth and jobs through the generation and use of intellectual property. Creative industries can include music, performing arts, film, television, radio, advertising, games and interactive content, writing, publishing, architecture, design, and visual arts.*

This is not only the famous DCMS definition of the creative industries, first promulgated in 1998, but also the latest word on the subject, still taking pride of place at the head of the Australian Federal Government's 'Creative Industries' website more than 15 years later – word for word, but without acknowledgement, as if the formula has become a natural law, rather than a piece of intellectual property in its own right.[2] The naturalised idea is that 'individual creativity, skill and talent' (belonging to what are called 'natural persons' in jurisprudence) is what generates 'intellectual property' (exploitable by 'legal persons' such as firms and governments), and this is what creates 'wealth and jobs' (economic value). That is not so much an explanation of creativity, however; it is a description of how property rights can be established, and how creativity can be shifted conceptually from culture to economy, leaving nothing behind.

It was this private-property definition of creative industries that caught the attention of policymakers, ministers and their advisers around the world. Conceptually it is still dominated by its origins in the UK, which, with Australia, is a leader in research and policy discourses (in which we've participated). The term has also gained traction in the EU, although much less so in the USA.

Strong scholarly and policy research does not always mean strong policy implementation (and vice versa). Australia, for instance, shows a bizarre asymmetry between the strength and richness of creative industries research in universities and policy forums, and an almost complete neglect of it in the political and governmental sphere. In the Federal government, 'creative industries' is subsumed alphabetically under traditional arts and heritage within the Arts portfolio (arts.gov.au):

- Collections
- Creative industries
- Cultural diversity
- Film and television
- Indigenous
- Literature

- Movable cultural heritage
- Music
- Performing arts
- Public consultations
- Regional touring and arts
- Visual arts

The Arts portfolio itself is tucked away in the Attorney General's Department, meaning that the minister responsible for artistic expression and innovation is also the chief enforcer of censorship and copyright. The incumbent minister (as we write) is most famous for deciding that provisions of the Racial Discrimination Act should be repealed on the grounds that 'people have a right to be bigoted'.[3] On the creative industries, his most passionate utterance to date has been on copyright reform (to simplify legislation and improve enforcement).[4] There's very little cross-fertilisation between this portfolio and other relevant government responsibilities, such as industry (innovation; R&D), communications (broadband; media), trade (international collaboration; tourism; treaties), education (research; training). National policy on the creative industries is not the place to look for innovative conceptualisation and new, unruly or disruptive energies.

Coherent attempts at scoping, mapping and conceptual modelling are carried out in university research centres (especially the CCI, but there are good centres of research in many places). Unfortunately, central government in Australia tends to keep its own academic research community at arm's length (it's a low trust/high audit regime), with the counterintuitive result that ideas coming from Europe and the Americas are much more likely to be welcomed in policy circles than ideas from local experts.[5] Hence, most of Australia's good ideas about the creative economy are exported. Australian researchers may in fact do better if they can ventriloquise their ideas via high-prestige foreign destinations – much as Australian actors, writers, journalists and musicians are more highly thought of if they address the home crowd from Hollywood, New York or London.

In Britain, the concept has fared better. It survived the risky transition of government from one side of politics to the other. The Department of Culture, Media and Sport was founded (from a previous department of national heritage) within the ethos of the 'New Labour' government (1997–2010). It was not dismantled after the 2010 change of administration. It still boasts a Cabinet Minister with direct responsibility for the creative industries, along with arts and culture, broadcasting, cultural property, heritage and the historic environment, gambling and racing, libraries, media ownership and mergers, museums and galleries, the National Lottery, sport, telecommunications and online, and tourism.[6] There are also active policymaking and debate in the UK, through agencies such as Demos, NESTA and the British Council, private consultancies such as BOP, across the university sector, e.g. FOCI in Manchester, the Big Innovation Centre (sponsored by Lancaster University), or Loughborough University in London (LUiL); in public advocacy (Hargreaves et al., 2013) and parliamentary debate;[7] as well as via the research funding councils.[8]

In both Australia and the UK, however, 'creative industries' as an arm of governmental responsibility is sliding backwards in ambition, to be more or less coterminous with traditional arts and national heritage, although in the UK it is also connected with the media, communications and the online environment. But here, as in Australia, the oft-quoted idea of 'joined-up government', where policy objectives are carried through across multiple portfolios, is not readily evident. Apart from the Prime Minister or Treasurer/Chancellor, who generally seem to have their minds on other things, no Ministry 'sees' the creative industries as a whole, in economic and innovation terms as well as in aesthetic and heritage terms, or as a wealth-creating as well as a spending portfolio. The way is not cleared to develop the creative industries with tax breaks (Treasury), trade and industry incentives, infrastructure investment (e.g. fast broadband), education, R&D and training schemes, and the support of those who argue strongly for innovation in every other domain. Instead, the lobbyists for incumbent industries rule the roost. Therefore there's little incentive for public-policy formation that tries to draw economic and cultural values together: synthesis and systems thinking are not 'in demand'. The 'suits' and policymakers go one way; the 'creatives' and academics another, often with negative opinions about each other.

A global conversation, not individual property

'*Born in the UK; theorised in Australia; implemented in China*'. That's the shorthand version of a short history (Hartley, 2010; Prince, 2010: 134). But it's not the end of the story. The main issue is not to determine what has already happened, but to imagine and plan for future formation. For full-scale implementation of the creative industries as a means towards economic development of the country as a whole, you have to look towards China, Brazil, Indonesia, Nigeria and other emergent and developing economies, where very large-scale investments, both public (state-funded) and private, have been made to develop creative precincts and cities, creative sectors of the economy, and a creative workforce (Li Wuwei, 2011).

Meanwhile, the internet, digital media and social networks have played a game-changing role in extending economically useful creative practice throughout the population. Now, you can create in your home and reach directly a potential market of billions. Or you can link through social networks with crowd-sourcing solutions or other kinds of group action (e.g. crowd-funding, activism, p2p information and tutorials) that can pack economic and political clout far beyond the capabilities of each private individual. Most people don't immediately turn into internet entrepreneurs, but few are unconnected completely, and the process of diversification and niching that now attends social media, digital technologies and internet connectivity resembles the equally game-changing uptake of technologies by myriad anonymous artisans during the Industrial Revolution in Britain in the nineteenth century (Mokyr, 2009).

Given the rapid dispersal of the creative industries idea, and the rapid growth of digital and social media across an equally rapidly globalising marketplace, it is time to consider whether the 'property' approach is still adequate to explain and organise creativity in complex societies. Our approach is very different, because we do not accept that individual 'natural persons' are the source of creativity. They are, rather, a fiction, or figment of jurisprudence and methodological individualism, not real people you can bump into on the street. When it comes to national policy, they are always transformed into 'legal persons' – i.e. firms – whose property (monopoly rent-seeking rights) has to be protected from 'piracy' by the very 'natural persons' who comprise the citizens and voters legislators nominally represent (but rarely bump into on the street).

We see creativity as a feature of semiotic and noetic systems, in particular cultural systems like language, which individuals certainly use and make their own without being or owning their source. Such cultural systems, in turn, are a feature of groups, not individuals: our culture, language, creativity and communication are all posited on the sociality of our species, not our individuality. Creativity is a common resource, not private property. Individuality is therefore better seen as a *product* of such systems, not their source.

The 'Three Bigs'

How do you think about creativity as a group-made common resource, belonging to whole populations: to everyone (not just owners of intellectual property); everywhere (not just in advanced countries); across all of their activities (not just in one sector of the formal economy)? This question yields three very clear answers: the 'Three Bigs'.

1. First, we want to start our discussion of the creative industries by thinking about the *planet* (using a 'biogeochemical' rather than 'globalisation' perspective). We want to think about the creative industries as a planetary phenomenon. On the model of the geosphere→ atmosphere→ biosphere→ semiosphere→ noösphere, we see the creative industries as the → *future-sphere*. Its main characteristic is openness, 'becoming' (always in a state of making itself), not-yet-ness; potentiality in uncertainty; indeterminacy; youthful irresponsibility; childishness; playfulness … experimentation with the capabilities (including the rules) of existing systems. Understood at system level ('sphere'), this experimentation with probabilities and with the process of becoming is (with varying success) what the creative industries *do*.

2. Second, we are not interested in confining the idea of the creative industries to the art and design or the creative and performing arts sectors of the economy; nor with the popular-culture versions of these – consumerism and entertainment. Equally, at the other extreme, we are not trying to advance a general, psychology-based 'everyone is creative' argument. Instead, we want to identify what *creativity is* in economic terms. Our answer is that it is the *production of newness in complex adaptive systems*. New knowledge and innovation allow *systems to renew and change*, for themselves, endogenously. The creative industries are the ones that *form the future*, in whatever section of the economy.

3. Third, we do not make '*individual talent*' (DCMS, 1998, etc.) the very foundation of the creative industries. Our approach does not start from individuals and build up, but from relational systems in which every individual is understood as an agent (not just the 'talented' individuals), and any one individual is only recognisable as such in distinction from all the others. Indeed, we do not employ methodological individualism, where individual desire (wants, needs) is the motivation, individual behaviour is the object of study, and individual rational choice is quantifiable.

Because the creative industries are system-based, we see individuals and their behaviours and actions as the *output* or 'precipitate' of the process, not an input. Instead, we're interested in *groups*, at three levels of scale and complexity:

- *Macro*: population-wide abstractions (audiences, citizens, consumers, the public);
- *Meso*: particular but still potentially vast organised and institutionalised groups such as 'social networks' (Twitter, FB, YouTube);

- *Micro*: various forms of self-organising group entity, such as firms or other enterprises, community associations, cultural institutions and ephemeral groups in digital culture: flash-mobs, crowd-sourcing networks, companies of players/performers ... etc.

We define a group – a deme – as *purposeful non-kin*, a concept with affinities to citizenship and publics, as well as to consumers and audiences. We see the creative industries as being driven, organised and implemented by *group purpose* (a 'plot'), agreed among more than one agent, although sometimes conceived and carried out in secret ('commercial-in-confidence'). In the creative industries, a group may gather around a relatively weak notion of purposefulness – to play a game, join an audience, or build a public, in order to express co-subjectivity with others of like mind or culture. What we seek to identify in this is not strength of purpose but the way that such groups become the sources of newness or innovation *as groups*, rather than simply on the basis of individual behaviour or decisions.

Communication – not individual creativity

How can you understand the creative industries this way? The fundamental answer is that we see creativity in terms of *communication*, not talent, genius, professional expertise or artistic training, much less intellectual property. It takes two to communicate; the minimal system of communication includes two different units (addresser and addressee), which are already 'semiospheres' or meaning-systems. In principle, such systems are characterised by difference not sameness. The basic fact of communication is 'clash' between different systems: incommensurability, untranslatability, asymmetry and possibly conflict. Meaningfulness emerges along the boundaries of difference (untranslatability; incommensurability) between systems.

The basic *act* of communication is translation across borders (personal-micro, organisational-meso, cultural-macro), which are thereby maintained as well as crossed or altered. Hence, moving or renegotiating borders is highly productive of new information, which may take the form of irritation (Hutter), creative destruction (Schumpeter) or innovation (Potts; Leadbeater and Wong). In all cases, newness emerges from the clash and interaction of difference.

Our model of creativity, then, is organised around communication in this mode. It operates at all three levels of Dopfer and colleagues' (2004) 'MMM' or 'Micro-Meso-Macro' conceptualisation of how economies work:

1. *Macro*: Taking a planetary systems approach (but not globalisation) (Lotman, Vernadsky, semiosphere) – '**everywhere**' being interconnected and mutually determinant.

2. *Meso*: Taking an '**everything**' approach … economic transformation based on newness and innovation, evidenced by digital media, social networks, DIY/Maker culture, and as-yet-unfulfilled potential across all of the economy (and this includes not just 'sectors' of the commercial economy but social enterprises based in community and regional action).

3. *Micro*: Taking an '**everyone**' approach, where everyone forms into *groups*, especially during a stage that everyone has to go through: *youth* (including childhood).

An immediate implication of this structure is that it messes with what has until now been incorporated into the micro (individual) and meso (institution) levels of organisation, because now we can identify *microproductivity* arising from distributed individuals (e.g. social networks – including users and the agents formerly known as consumers) as an economically significant source of value, not only cultural but also economic. However, 'productivity' is a term that is normally restricted to organisations and industries – a 'meso' term – whereas individuals are not normally calculated in disaggregated form in economics. The smallest unit of economic organisation is the firm. Individuals may be abstracted as consumers or workforce, even households, but not as *producers*. In our model, as in the real world, the boundary between consumer and producer is in crisis and in flux, with innovations coming from users and interactive participation, DIY culture and the 'maker' movement as much as from traditional enterprises. The 'holotype' example is YouTube (Burgess and Green, 2009), compared with previous 'mass media' platforms. Broadcasters were professional and exclusive content-creators, but users create (or copy) all YouTube content. As a result of this redefinition of the boundary between producer and consumer, extraordinary amounts of new information ('big data') are released into the system as a whole. We aim to capture some of the dynamic fluidity of boundary repositioning in 'the three bigs', a scale at which it is possible to observe how relations between previously distinct systems are changing.

At the same time, the discussion above should have indicated what we think about the 'macro' level. It's not an abstract aggregate of smaller realities; it is a causal agent, in the form of complex systems and their interactions. You can't understand the individual without knowing about the macro-system, any more than you can understand how humans work without knowing about the atmosphere (and how it got to have so much life-sustaining oxygen in it).

Thus, we think the '3 Bigs', taken together, will assist in producing a synthesis that situates creativity, culture, the economy, technology and policy too not in the realm of property to be exploited, but in the domain of newness, from which adaptation to changing and indeterminate circumstances can be hazarded by demes or groups, albeit groups that 'cooperate' competitively, adversarially, and in secrecy from one another.

Notes

1. Source: PwC Top 100, 2008–13. Available at: www.pwc.com/gx/en/audit-services/capital-market/publications/top100-market-capitalisation.jhtml.
2. See http://arts.gov.au/creative.
3. Senator George Brandis, Attorney General and Minister for the Arts (www.attorneygeneral.gov.au/Pages/Portfolio.aspx): 'People have the right to be bigots you know', Brandis said in answer to a question by the Indigenous Labor senator Nova Peris. 'In this country people have rights to say things that other people find offensive or bigoted' (24 March 2014: www.theguardian.com/world/2014/mar/24/george-brandis-people-have-the-right-to-be-bigots).
4. Senator George Brandis, 'Address at the opening of the Australian Digital Alliance Fair Use for the Future – A Practical Look at Copyright Reform Forum', Canberra, 14 February 2014: www.attorneygeneral.gov.au/Speeches/Pages/2014/14February2014-openingoftheAustralianDigitalAllianceForum.aspx.
5. Thus Senator Brandis' speech on copyright reform for the creative industries (see previous note) opens with reference to an 1841 speech by Lord Macaulay in the UK House of Commons, and refers to an industry report by global firm PwC. Nowhere does he mention local work on creative industries or copyright (led by Brian Fitzgerald) done over the past decade (with government funding) at the CCI.
6. See www.gov.uk/government/ministers/secretary-of-state-for-culture-olympics-media-and-sport. The Secretary of State is supported by an Under Secretary of State (minister) for Culture, Communications and Creative Industries (www.gov.uk/government/ministers/parliamentary-under-secretary-of-state-culture-communications-and-creative-industries).
7. For example, House of Commons (www.publications.parliament.uk/pa/cm201314/cmhansrd/cm130619/debtext/130619-0002.htm#13061976000001); House of Lords (www.parliament.uk/business/publications/research/briefing-papers/LLN-2011-032/debate-on-3-november-the-creative-industries).
8. For example, www.ahrc.ac.uk/Funded-Research/Research-Creative-Economy/Creative-Economy-Showcase-2014/Pages/Watch-highlights-from-the-day.aspx.

HISTORY

4

THE CREATIVE INDUSTRIES 'MOMENT'

It is totally addictive.

(Kate Moss)[1]

Context

This chapter is about a 'moment' in the sense in which that term is used in cultural studies, following the work of Stuart Hall and his colleagues in the 1970s: 'in one moment we can observe the shape of a whole ... process' (Hall et al., 1978: 82, 162, 217, 293). In *Policing the Crisis*, Hall and his colleagues analysed how one event, in this case a law-enforcement crackdown on 'mugging', can mark a crisis or turning point in longer-term historical processes, which they call a *'conjunctural'* moment: 'the *moment of mugging*' (1978: 323).

Although the development of creative industries discourse does not bear comparison with a Hallite 'crisis of hegemony' (Hartley, 2012: 43–4), it should be noted that its 'moment' came when the UK government issued the influential *Creative Industries Mapping Document* (DCMS, 1998), which precipitated international responses among governments, and in educational as well as business development circles. Among those international responses was our own, in Brisbane Australia. This chapter and the next one start from that local instance to explore the creative industries 'moment' as a 'conjuncture'. This was not a 'law and order' crackdown, but it was certainly seen as a highly political intervention by observers at the time, and has suffered somewhat as a concept ever since. In order to refresh the 'moment', we start from where we were at the time (on the other side of the planet), in order to explore some of its repercussions without over-politicising it in advance.

All three of the present authors worked together at Queensland University of Technology (QUT) in Australia during the 2000s. All of us have moved on to new appointments in Australia, Wales and China, and we've kept in collaborative contact ever since. But for us, the story starts in Brisbane. QUT was among the pioneers of international research and education in the creative industries. The world's first Creative Industries Faculty was launched there in 2001, under Hartley's leadership as foundation dean. It was clear from the start that teaching, and especially research, needed a new 'proposition' in a non-traditional, technology-oriented university that was located in a non-metropolitan city in a mid-sized, out of the way country. To make a worthwhile contribution to knowledge from there would need more than a gradualist approach to internal change; it needed what Yuri Lotman (2009) calls an 'explosion': exponential change. It also required attention to profiling and reputation, to produce something that could be seen from afar, which means research (no matter how good the teaching may be, or how well the local community, economy and culture are served by it).

Here again, though, business as usual would not suffice. We needed not only to modernise the creative curriculum and research agenda, but also to connect these with technology, law, business and community engagement. Established disciplinary boundaries and methods had to be rethought, not just in presenting a package of courses but fundamentally, to grasp changed realities outside of the university. Local (city-based) education needed to connect with international competitive trends, and international students too. Critical and creative practice needed to connect with entrepreneurship and commercialisation. Research in the arts needed to connect with developments in other fields. We needed an intellectual, institutional and international makeover.

The creative industries 'brand' initially drew together three previously distinct teaching areas:

- *Media and communication*, which was strong in journalism, creative writing, radio–TV–film production, and media studies;
- *Creative and performing arts*, which were strong in music, dance, drama (acting, technical production and drama education), and visual arts;
- New areas based on *digital design*, especially fashion and 'communication design' (human–computer interaction). Eventually – after a decade – these disciplines were conjoined with an existing design school, which had until then been located in the Engineering Faculty, teaching architecture, landscape design, urban design and planning, industrial design, and product design.

Almost all of these disciplines are 'practice-based', filling the needs of the local (i.e. Queensland) economy, including teacher training. They were not research-oriented, except for pockets where 'studies' components accompanied 'practice' programmes.

However popular such offerings were with students (who liked the 'creative' bit) and their carers and financial supporters (who liked the 'industries' bit), the Creative Industries initiative was not going to make any waves beyond the local context unless it could also achieve a pre-eminent research position. Reputation rested on striking out in new directions, whether at the 'pure' level of conceptualisation, methodology and invention, or at the 'applied' level of content-creation (invention), or policy, business and community uptake of new ideas. Gaining a good reputation also meant convincing others, on the world stage, that this new direction was worth taking, by becoming competitive in an open field of knowledge innovation. In order to compete from the margins for agenda-setting pre-eminence, we needed to win the most prestigious research funding awards, publish in the most visible and high-ranking outlets, and so on.

It was clear that we needed to do more than simply beef up the 'studies' component of our existing 'practice-based' research. For one thing, practice-based research is perhaps the hardest area of all for which to win Research Council funding. For another, it did not deal in the insights required to face a creative future beyond artisanal production innovations. Creative practice was sufficiently established to see the future in terms of what it could already do well. It was not interested (in a formal, disciplinary way, although individuals wanted their work to succeed) in what happened to creativity once it left the studio. We needed an even more widely interdisciplinary approach, based on an 'end-to-end' model of the creative process: including *origination* (creative and performing arts, media, design), *legal* frameworks (intellectual property, copyright, commons), *business* processes (including entrepreneurship, start-ups and innovation as well as business process management, distribution and marketing), a whole new approach to the *uses* of creativity among publics, audiences, consumers, communities and citizens; and thence new approaches to *education* (both formal and informal), for a creative workforce and independent enterprises. So we built a distributed team of research experts, not only in 'creative' disciplines but also in the Information Technology, Law, Business, and Education Faculties, and across multiple institutions in Australia, wherever the best talent was to be found, to ask what role creativity plays in innovation in contemporary cultural and economic life.

All of this was taking place during a period of rapid technological change, with the emergence of the internet, digital media and social networks, globalisation of markets, and exciting new opportunities for users in creative innovation. Thus, the time was ripe for 'creative destruction' of traditional disciplines in the knowledge domain and in business practices alike, just at the moment – the 'tipping-point' – when culture, media, design and knowledge came to be seen as drivers of economic growth and transformation, and users began to displace consumers in popular media productivity.

In 2005 – the same year that YouTube was launched, marking the moment when the internet could carry audio-video as well as text – we won funding from the Australian Research Council for an ARC Federation Fellowship for Hartley, and an ARC Centre of Excellence for Creative Industries and Innovation. It was based on this interdisciplinary mix, and from the start sought to *integrate* (not just to sample, chaotically) 'practice' and 'studies' as well as 'pure' and 'applied' research, across multiple knowledge paradigms and methodological traditions, for the attention of international knowledge agents – researchers, readers, students, policymakers, entrepreneurs, activists, advocates, artists, designers, writers, performers and producers ... and their children – whose own traditions and expectations may be very different from each other's and our own.

We made a start with a programme of research designed to:

- Account for the *creative economy* (what's special about it, economically, if anything?);
- Investigate various *creative sectors*, ranging from popular TV and film to fashion (what impediments are there on the pathway from creativity to market?);
- Ascertain what is needed to educate a *creative workforce* and wealth creators (in both formal and informal education);
- Experiment with prototypes of *content creation* and distribution, especially among non-specialist populations and socially disadvantaged groups; and
- Promote the inclusion of *creative innovation* into national innovation systems, where policy settings in many countries at the time were heavily skewed towards bioscience, ICTs and nanotechnology (why do countries need a creative economy?).

Thus our research began to focus on problems at the intersection of culture, technology and economy. On the cultural side was creative talent both 'expert' (artists) and population-wide (consumer co-creation); in the technology space were digital media and social networks; and on the economic side were innovation and growth in a knowledge-based economy.

Policy

An existing science, or social science, did not develop a theory of creative industries that might then be tested using formal hypotheses, experiments, fieldwork, data-analysis and the like. Instead, government departments sought to benefit from the 'new' or 'weightless' information or knowledge-based economy (Leadbeater, 1999), from existing competitive advantage in certain industry sectors, especially in the UK which boasted a large creative economy in the capital, and from seeking to redefine culture as an earning sector (growth) rather than spending one (heritage, welfare).

All of this came together during the first New Labour government in the UK, when in 1998 culture minister Chris Smith sought to boost his portfolio's clout by yoking culture and creativity to wealth-creation, jobs and GDP, in order to get more support from the Treasury for culture. The idea worked. You don't have to agree that it was a stroke of genius to admit that it was timely, productive and had far-reaching consequences, many unforeseen. Although the Treasury remained as flinty-hearted as ever, the 'creative industries' genie was unleashed from the knowledge-domain bottle, and Smith's department of Culture, Media and Sport (DCMS) gained first-mover advantage in defining the creative industries.

The important policy move here was to get culture away from the back door of the economy where it traditionally sat, tin cup in hand, crankily biting the hand that fed it, right around to the front entrance of innovation strategy, where suddenly it was revealed as a high-growth sector, outperforming other services (including prestigious but sluggish manufacturing). It was dynamic and emergent, with multiplier effects on other sectors, a high rate of entrepreneurial initiative, and lots of start-ups, micro-businesses and sole-traders, some of them – ageing rock stars – worth more than many large-scale companies.

Flaws

One question did not even make it on to the agenda of a department whose main jobs were to boost business and keep the arts lobby docile, and that was this: Is it possible to have a 'creative economy' based on the creativity of the *whole population*, not just on existing artistic elites, professional designers and an 'expert pipeline' model of copyright-protected creativity? That question has still not been addressed in policy circles; that's why it forms the basic proposition of this book.

Meanwhile, there were other flaws in this turn-of-the-millennium policy initiative. First was the insistence that the creative industries, based as they are on individual talent, could only prosper in a world where *intellectual property* was strongly enforced. This left out of account the burgeoning world of consumer-created content and user-led innovation; and it forgot that creativity involves a lot of copying from past masters and contemporary competitors.

Second, it anchored the idea of the creative industries in the *analogue* era, where individual artists produced individual works either for public institutions or in a traditional marketplace dominated by single-platform firms or industries (broadcasters, record-labels, film studios, publishers, newspapers, fashion designers, etc.). It missed out not only on the affordances of *digital* technologies, but more importantly on the *internet ethos* of 'knowledge shared is knowledge gained' and on the non-market or 'gift economy' aspect of social networking, crowd-sourcing and communities of affect.

Third, City of London hubris. After all, didn't the Brits have a world-beater in the shape of the City's financial services industry? And wasn't London a great creative capital in showbiz, publishing, media, broadcasting and cultural tourism as well? So what could be more appropriate than to model an ambition for the creative industries on the success of financial services, Britain's biggest export: all market, no regulation (this was pre-Global Financial Crisis when 'light-touch' or hands-off regulation by the Financial Services Authority still seemed like a good idea); high levels of 'creativity' in product design (where the value-add is in the sophisticated inventiveness of products); high liquidity; high debt ('leverage'); high compensation – all adding up to high-growth services. It all looked great as long as growth continued and credit was abundant. Surely the creative sector – like Pygmalion – could undergo a makeover, and 'be like that'?

The creative sector certainly produced some winner-take-all celebrities, like J. K. Rowling and Damian Hirst, and both creative and high-tech winners made it to the under-40s Rich Lists. But that did not translate into a creative economy more generally, nor did the creatives out-compete the bankers on the Hertfordshire-mansion-buying circuit. The richest person in Britain was still the Duke of Westminster (property), later overtaken by Lakshmi Mittal (steel) and Roman Abramovich (oil). And in any case, the City of London was in for a shock, in September 2008, when the head office of Lehman Bros in the US phoned to say, 'London, you're on your own.'[2]

A fourth weakness was its *nationalistic* bias. Everyone from the then UK Chancellor (finance minister) Gordon Brown downwards believed that here was an example of 'competitive advantage' for the UK *as opposed to* other countries. All the talk was of how to *lead* the world, not *join* it. No-one paused to wonder how countries might collaborate rather than compete in a globally networked system whose real motive force was located offshore.

Chris Smith's successor at the DCMS, Tessa Jowell, made speeches about how the UK could leave low-cost manufacturing to the Chinese and concentrate on high value-add creative goods and services. She forgot to mention that the Chinese themselves might have other ideas about that, and were listening carefully to foreign advisers (CCI experts among them) who were telling them that they needed to shift from a low-cost 'made in China' economy to high-value 'created in China' (Keane and Hartley, 2006; Keane, 2007) by growing their own creative sector, encouraging domestic consumption, and aspiring to turn around the 'creative trade deficit' where they imported more ideas from the West than they exported Chinese culture, media, branding and knowledge.

Technology

While the creative industries initiative of the DCMS in the late 1990s was inspired, it was also self-serving and 'irrationally exuberant', as central bankers say. The bubble obligingly burst in March 2000 with the dot-com crash, bringing the NASDAQ back from 5000 points to 1300. Fifteen years later, it was still not back to 5000.

Although a good many ICT ventures lost their money, the digital media and the internet did not go away, any more than railroads or automobiles had collapsed after previous stock-market crashes in the 1850s and 1930s. Nor did the creative industries suffer as much as other sectors with exposure to ICTs. However, it was a chastening experience to see how precarious creative enterprise could be, among both (venture) capitalists and (artistic) workers, once culture had been redefined in market terms rather than in those of heritage or subsidy. It was an early lesson in risk, uncertainty, indeterminacy and the clash of systems.

By this time, however, it had become clear that high-tech ICTs – fat pipes – were going to be crucial to the creative sector, not the death of it. European-style 'analogue' creative industries and cultural institutions did not amount to much without US-style digital technologies and market-based new-media platforms.

Here the European tradition of public culture and cultural institutions met the American tradition of individualism and the entrepreneurial ethos. Where 'Britart' artists might aspire to place their work in a museum (preferably the Tate Modern, Cool Britannia's latest tourist attraction), Californian computer geeks aspired to turn their string of code into a global corporation. Was it possible to integrate these aspirations – intermingling artistry and entrepreneurship, individual talent and global scale, public culture and consumer demand, creativity and computing power, individual artistry and digital global networks?

In short, might digital technologies enable us to take creativity to population-wide participation and global scale? Did 'global media' have to imply 'monopoly control' by the usual suspects – Hollywood and international media moguls like Rupert Murdoch? Or could anyone get a look-in?

If so, might smaller or emergent economies (say, Australia or China) benefit from technological advances and join in too? Although 'big media' remained prominent as they migrated to the net, it was obvious from the start that online creativity could now also include a bottom-up, peer-to-peer element, since that's how the whole thing was invented in the first place. There was no reason in principle why such inventiveness had to be located in California.

Geography

Even so, California was a formidable competitor. Silicon Valley provided the model of a geographical *creative cluster*, where concentrating garage start-ups together seemed to make it easier for some of them to burgeon into global corporations in just a few years.

Richard Florida, an entrepreneurial sociologist of occupations, argued that the 'creative class' of knowledge professionals and ideas entrepreneurs was numerically small (only 150m people worldwide), but it was disproportionately responsible for economic growth and creative innovation (which were increasingly the same thing). Its members included a lot more occupations than the traditional idea of creatives. There were the computer and mathematical geeks; architecture and engineering; life, physical and social-science occupations; education, training and library occupations; the arts, design, entertainment, sports and media.

These 'no collar' professionals, who also liked to live in an 'experience economy', were mobile and went where they liked, so you'd better make your city creative-friendly if you wanted to attract them. Florida's message struck a nerve with city planners worldwide, resulting in the surreal scene of mayors and bureaucrats puzzling over their 'creative class indexes' to see if they had enough students and gay people to make a viable creative city.

But could anywhere be a creative city? Even Florida didn't think so. Eventually he settled on 40-odd 'mega-regions' as the crucibles of global creativity: 'The places that thrive today are those with the highest velocity of ideas, the highest density of talented and creative people, the highest rate of "urban metabolism"' (Florida, 2009). Most of them remain in the USA, according to Florida, but worldwide you can also find them in Europe (Greater London; Am-Brus-Twerp) and Asia (Greater Tokyo, China's Shanghai–Beijing Corridor, and India's Bangalore–Mumbai area).

Growth

At this point, with the *convergence* of telecommunications, computer and media technologies, it was possible to imagine content-creation as a globally distributed user-created system (Jenkins, 2006). *Everyone* (with access to the web) could produce and publish their own media content, or share favourite stuff with their peers. Creative content converged with telecommunications. Instead of trying to make money out of unique items (this film; that painting), you could make it by promoting *creative traffic* among peers who made (or shared) the creative content for themselves. In other words, once the World Wide Web could handle video (by 2005), it was possible to imagine how something like Bit-torrent or YouTube might replace broadcasting as the 'platform' for creative media – not 'one-to-many' mass entertainment but 'many-to-many' messages (more like telecoms than media).

'Platform' is the wrong metaphor here, implying something stable upon which to build the castle where – as they said at the time – 'content is king'. The speed of change on the technical side continued to obey Moore's Law – growth was faster than exponential, doubling the extent of creative infrastructure, speed, connectivity, users, uses and content every couple of years. And of course much of the resultant content was shared, pirated, unpaid or amateur, making it very hard to erect a viable business plan over any new platform.

This produced further uncertainty and dynamism in creative enterprise. This year's hot new platform or 'killer app' – literally in the case of the wildly popular *Dumb Ways to Die* (said to be Kate Moss' favourite app)[3] – was next year's landfill. In turn, wastefulness gave rise to a not altogether welcome new 'creative industry' – that of processing e-waste, in which the Chinese town of Guiyu in Guandong was a world-leader (see Chapter 13).[4] Continuing growth was driven by technological innovation, by the extension of digital participation across an ever-wider population, and by the burgeoning uses to which all this capability could be put, both within businesses and in informal social networks.

One very interesting aspect of this growth was how it outpaced public policy settings. Although (as ever) crucial technological breakthroughs were part-funded by the defence industry, most of the energy came from non-government agencies, some set up for profit and many not. When public policy did catch up – in the shape of the 1998 DCMS initiative – it focused exclusively on *economic* growth, as a sort of updated industry policy. It was not focused on the wider and more important question of *the growth of knowledge* (Loasby, 1999; and see Metcalfe and Ramlogan, 2005); and not at all on the growth in capabilities of the population at large (human resources or human capital). Thus, relatively little public investment was made in the *propagation* of digital take-up across populations, in education for digital literacy, or in support for creative development and organisation (other than business services for creative firms).

In the nineteenth and early twentieth century, modernising countries had invested vast public resources in achieving universal print-literacy through compulsory primary schooling, but no such effort was contemplated in relation to digital media. As far as the growth of knowledge via computers, telecommunications and media networks went, 'the people' were 'on their own'.

Social networks

In short, the *growth of knowledge* was a problem not for the government but for the market – and that was government policy. If people wanted a creative economy benefiting from global digital technologies, and if individuals wanted to hook-up with like-minded others worldwide, then they must 'do it themselves'.

The dotcom crash and the digital revolution emboldened some to say that the problem had been caused not by too much creativity but too little. Attention had been focused too narrowly on connectivity and the use of IT for internal business operations. What might the population at large like to do with this network? Enter DIY culture, Web 2.0 and the new global players, Google, Facebook, YouTube, Wikipedia and Flickr.

Here the true nature of the creative economy crystallised in a way that had not been clear till now. The creative industries were not the 'copyright' industry; they were not the 'arts' industry; they were not creative 'professions' (designers, media producers etc.); they were not the 'media industries'. The creative industries were characterised by something rather different: they were – and are – *social network markets* (Potts et al., 2008).

Social network markets have two main peculiarities. The first is that people's choices are determined by the choices of others in the network. The second is that choices are status-based. Why are these characteristics peculiar?

- *Choice is 'crowd-sourced'*: Markets are supposed to be based on self-interested choice, which is assumed to be individualist and rationalist, not determined by the choices of others. In social network markets *choice is externalist or system-based*, produced by relationships not reason – reason is the *outcome* of collective choices in a system of relations, not an *input*.
- *Status-based choice*: Choice is meant to satisfy wants or needs. But in social network markets it expresses *status relations*. Thus, the creative industries don't look very much like a neoclassical market. The choices of high-status celebrities will often be preferred, and those of low-status people avoided, creating a market in celebrity endorsement. Celebrity itself is not a product of but an input into such a market. You won't be asked to endorse a product unless your name is bankable already.

'Entrepreneurial consumers' too can gain status by making admired choices (Hartley and Montgomery, 2009); not just in high fashion but also in street fashion, like Harajuku in Japan, which gave rise, among other things, to the 'traumatic cuteness' of blogger, model and singer Kyary Pamyu Pamyu, whose debut single gained 62 million hits on YouTube.[5] And because status is both relative and transient, the continuing process of making choices in social networks has an impact on status and thus on values (and further choices), both cultural and economic.

This is what Jason Potts calls 'choice under novelty' as opposed to choice under uncertainty or choice under risk, both of which have been studied in behavioural economics (Potts, 2010). When faced with new knowledge, new connections, or new ideas, people cannot reduce uncertainty by getting more information, precisely because what they're facing is new. Thus, suggests Potts, 'rational economic agents' – that's everyone – observe and learn from how others are making choices, and thus how to respond to the new. This is how they get into social network markets in the first place. Once there, observing and connecting with others, not least by random copying (Bentley, 2009), new possibilities open up, including other opportunities for 'consumer productivity' and co-creation.

Further, much of what constitutes social networks, and therefore the creative industries, is not market-based at all, at least not in the usual sense. This is because social networks exist prior to and outside of markets (among families, friends, neighbours, enemies, etc.); and because they belong to the '*economy of attention*' as much as to the monetary economy (Lanham, 2006).

People place value on the *attention* they give and receive. This is an economy of *signals* as much as one of monetary values, which is why it needs a 'convergence' of cultural studies (semiotics, anthropology, media analysis) with economics to make sense of what's going on (Herrmann-Pillath, 2010, 2013). People may invest time, creativity and material resources in creating the right signals to attract more attention. They also value *paying* attention to favoured others. Fans, for instance, invest in the attention they offer to their idols. Attention may be 'payed' in many ways, not all of them monetised. Choice may just as easily end in a marriage or friendship as a sale.

Consumers = producers

The very concept of a consumer is irrelevant in social networks. Self-organising networks of people, who are in it for the value of the relationship with others, are not really consuming anything. Quite the reverse. What's important is not what they buy, but what they make and how they signal, whether that's simply 'making sense' of stuff they like, or making contact with each other, or making their own creative content, from photos or text to competitive gaming strategies or open-source code. The erstwhile 'consumer' is now the focus and engine of the *productivity* of the system.

Social networks are not made up out of passive consumers, waiting to be persuaded whether to buy the blue one or the white one, or to push this button rather than that. They are strictly peer-to-peer, self-created and sustained, multi-nodal and mutually interconnected *networks*, not the endpoint of a linear product pipeline. A *ballistic* strategy, where you 'target' this or that consumer profile and then 'bombard' them with well-aimed messages, that too is wrong-footed, hence the change in marketing ideologies, towards 'viral', 'Groundswell' and 'Herd' conceptualisations of marketing communication (Earls, 2007; Li and Bernoff, 2008).

In a social network market you can't *make choices for* the consumer. The whole point is that users are doing the social networking for themselves. In essence this is a socio-cultural rather than an economic activity. What people are doing is about *their* status, and those they admire (or otherwise), including their own personal identity-forming activities and people in their own private circle.

Creative destruction

From this perspective – the perspective of the DIY user or 'productive consumer' – the status of organisations is not all that crucial. People interact with *content* and with *others*, not with *firms*. Maybe that's why people don't think of sharing as piracy – they don't see themselves as being in a proprietary environment. It is easy to see that established distinctions between producer and consumer, public and private, property and piracy, expert and amateur, agent and institution, are undergoing a thorough process of Schumpeterian 'creative destruction'. This is 'remix culture' with a vengeance (Lessig, 2008).

In this context it is unwise even to hang on to 'the firm' as the obvious unit of agency or enterprise, since firms are by no means the only (certainly not the first) source of innovation in the online environment. Other forms of association, organisation and institution have been established, from self-selecting networks of mutual interest to giant enterprises based on attention (Perez Hilton), the gift economy (Gutenberg Project), corporate branding (MIT's free courseware), or friendship (not just Facebook).

Many of these start out as amateur hobbies (genealogy), which subsequently prove robust enough to sustain both commercial and community forms of organisation. In these kinds of networks, firms co-exist symbiotically with community networks. Very often the 'generative edge' of a new affordance is not motivated by profit, but unforeseen popularity may create a market, which firms can stabilise. In other words, there's an evolutionary process where the necessary variation and experimentation precedes selection (firms), adoption (markets), and retention or extinction (competition). Thus the system as a whole is larger than the market aspect of it, and includes more kinds of enterprise than the firm, and more kinds of motivation than profit or price incentives.

So here's another peculiar thing. If, as government departments and industry analysts tend to do, you focus exclusively on the *producer* end of an industry, then you're likely to miss the creative industries altogether. They cannot be deciphered by looking at what *firms* do; only by looking at what *people* do, especially when they are interacting within very large-scale open complex systems.

But at the same time it's no good reducing 'people' to the status of an atomised and individualist 'self-contained globule of desire', in Thorstein Veblen's words (Veblen, 1898). Individual identity is itself a social project, *produced in and by* the systems, institutions, networks and relationships in which they participate, all the way up from family and oral language to mass mediated celebrity.

When you consider the 'identity' of global celebrities – let's say Paris Hilton – it is clear that this identity is a constantly produced work in progress, and that Ms Hilton is more like a global brand or firm than an individual. Of course, as a winner in the economy of attention she has amassed myriad more networked connections than 'ordinary' consumers, which means that in Barabási's terms she's a 'hub' rather than a 'node' (Barabási, 2003). She's a spike and you're part of the 'long tail' on a 'power law' curve of attention connections in a 'scale free network'. Or, to put it another way, *everyone* is part of this interconnected network. Thus, despite individual difference between Paris Hilton and those who live 'the simple life', the identity of all is a product of connections in the same dynamic system.[6]

Notes

1. Kate Moss' 'favourite phone app' is *Dumb Ways to Die*, made in Australia by McCann agency to promote rail safety. See: www.dailytelegraph.com.au/entertainment/sydney-confidential/kate-moss-reveals-favourite-phone-app-is-aussie-train-safety-campaign-dumb-ways-to-die/.
2. See http://everythingneednotfit.blogspot.com/2008/10/betrayal-of-london-unheard-in-new-york.html.
3. See the epigraph to this chapter; see the app game at https://play.google.com/store/apps/details?id=air.au.com.metro.DumbWaysToDie&hl=en; and the video – with nearly 90 million views – at https://www.youtube.com/watch?v=IJNR2EpS0jw.

4. See 'Electronic waste' and 'Electronic_waste_in_Guiyu' (Wikipedia); and www.china-pix.com/multimedia/guiyu/.
5. See www.japaneselifestyle.com.au/tokyo/harajuku_fashion.htm; for Kyary Pamyu Pamyu see www.theguardian.com/culture/australia-culture-blog/2014/mar/21/kyary-pamyu-pamyu-tinges-j-pop-horror-show.
6. Paris Hilton's reality TV series *The Simple Life* (2003–7) won her the 'Innovator Award' at the 2009 Fox Reality Awards.

5

BACK TO FIRST PRINCIPLES

The short career of the creative industries global form ... illustrates how transnational communities of experts are emerging that are able to influence policymaking across large parts of the globe.

(Russell Prince, 2010: 135)

Radical rethink

To proceed on a business-as-usual business plan – where the script says that if firms target consumers then industry prospers – prematurely closes down the transformational potential of the times. Instead of this, and precisely because we seem to have entered a topsy-turvy world where it is no longer clear what anything means, we need to take a good hard look at how open complex systems work, and what the role of creativity – not to mention industry – may be in that context.

As mentioned in the previous chapter, that is exactly what the CCI (Centre of Excellence for Creative Industries and Innovation), funded by the ARC (Australian Research Council), set out to do. As its researchers grappled with these issues over the years, it became increasingly clear that a radical rethink about first principles was needed. As part of the work of the CCI, Hartley won a Federation Fellowship, also funded by the ARC, to investigate 'the uses of multimedia'.

That research followed what happens to previously popular media, especially broadcast television, in the digital and interactive era, and sought to think through what *could* happen with population-wide digital literacy, if the internet proves to be as significant an invention as printing was in the early modern period (Hartley, 2009). Printing with moveable type was initially used (from the 1450s) for ecclesiastical and state purposes. Inadvertently, however, by the seventeenth century it had enabled the society-wide adoption of *realism* through three great textual systems, all of which required printed books and periodicals. These were: *science, journalism* and the *novel*.

Given that history of unforeseen consequences and an out-of-all-proportion growth of knowledge resulting from the adoption of a new communications technology (Castells, 2001), what might be the consequences of interactive computer-based communications and the concomitant spread of *digital* literacy? It still is too soon to tell, but it is obvious that we ought not to be thinking about the instrumental purposes of the opening players.

Lucy Montgomery (2010) was one of the postdoctoral fellows working on the Federation Fellowship team. Others included Jean Burgess, on 'vernacular creativity' (Burgess, 2006; Burgess and Green, 2009), and John Banks on the relationship between games companies and players, observing the 'community relations' aspect of games companies. Here the whole question of user-created content, and the distinctions between producer and consumer, expert and amateur, become life-or-death issues ... for the games company. If their player community didn't like a game, and the games developers wouldn't listen, the company could founder (Banks and Potts, 2010; Banks, 2013).

Meanwhile, PhD students from China, Germany, Turkey, Canada, Venezuela and Australia worked with the Federation Fellowship team to develop in-depth studies of how creativity, new media content and economic enterprise were transforming each other in the era of user-led innovation. Among them were co-authors Wen Wen, who studied the meso-level establishment of creative clusters and districts in Hangzhou, China, and Henry Siling Li, who studied micro-level creative productivity via the phenomenon of popular amateur video spoofs in China. Wen and Li are co-authors of this book.

Our Centre's project benefited from contact with specialists in other fields, especially Centre Fellows Jason Potts (evolutionary economics), Michael Keane (China's creative economy and policy), and Brian Fitzgerald (copyright and intellectual property law). During the course of our work, which also featured decisive contributions by the sinologist–economist Carsten Herrmann-Pillath (2010, 2013), it became increasingly clear that the definition of the creative industries could not be accepted at the going rate. There had to be a revaluation.[1]

History

We started this discussion off in the previous chapter by historicising the very idea of the creative industries. The creative economy did not emerge from a definition, but from a situation, and therefore the idea (as a 'mentifact') is not scientific but historical. Thus, in *Creative Industries* (Hartley, 2005; and in Hartley, 2009: Ch. 2) Hartley posited that the creative industries could already be seen as a dynamic, evolving concept even during the decade or so of its current usage. But before we get to that, a longer history needs to be acknowledged, going back to the European Enlightenment, and thence to Classical (Graeco-Roman) antecedents. The public function of creative and cultural practices is constantly reinvented for each new era, so that the stage on which the creative industries debuted was already crowded with *dramatis personae*:

- From the *Enlightenment* notion of liberal arts and civic humanism (the public virtue of the gentleman), comes the idea of the creative arts as noble, civilising, uplifting, aristocratic, '*noblesse oblige*'.
- From the nineteenth-century rise of the *nation state* came the idea of national culture and public arts, when European aristocrats turned their pictures over to national galleries and their palaces into museums.
- From *industrial culture*, especially in America, came the idea of popular arts – fiction, cinema, media – based in the marketplace not the public institution, giving rise to the citizen-consumer as an amalgam of democratic values (freedom, public) *and* capitalist ones (comfort, private)[2] – Walt Whitman *and* Wal-Mart.
- From *modernism and the artistic avant-garde* came the idea that creativity equals 'the new' and that anything produced at mass scale is a mere reproduction; thereby recasting aristocratic elitism into intellectual elitism, where the newest idea rules.
- From the *Frankfurt School* and anti-capitalist leftist academics came the idea of the *culture industries*, where media and state power were coterminous and the state was controlled by capital; creative 'industries' were but a capitalist mouthpiece.
- *Regional policy* around the world often (but not always) depoliticised the idea of the *cultural industries* (an exception was the Greater London Council in the 1980s) and sought to attract them to set up in this or that country or city, resulting eventually in the idea of 'cultural capitals' and 'media capitals'.

- From the *information industry* came the idea of creativity as part of the 'weightless', new or knowledge economy, adding high-value creative content to information infrastructure and connectivity, making creative 'inputs' part of value-added services or intangibles.

All of these traditions were in place – and some of them in contention with each other – when Chris Smith had his good idea that the creative industries were an emergent economic sector. Now the question became: what kind of economic sector was it?

Evolution

Not surprisingly in such a fast-moving and turbulent context, the very idea of what constitutes the creative economy is equally dynamic. Barely a decade on, the concept has shown four distinct phases over its short life. Each phase designates a different field of creative practice, each wider than and encompassing the one before.

Thus you might model the creative industries idea as a virus, spreading through a population via various hosts until everyone is infected with it. The phases are (see Chapter 6):

CI-1   Creative clusters (industry) – closed expert system

CI-2   Creative services (economy) – hybrid system

CI-3   Creative citizens (culture) – open innovation network

CI-4   Creative cities (complexity) – interaction (clash and mixture) of systems

Such a vastly expanded definition of creative agency is only 'thinkable' with complexity/network theory and the notion of open complex systems. It is most easily evident in computer-based social networks, but is not confined to the digital domain. Creative citizens are 'navigators' rather than 'consumers'; they may also act in concert as 'aggregators' to produce 'crowd-sourced' solutions to creative problems.

Following this line of thought it is easy to see that there's more to creativity than what is taught in art schools – or in business schools. Creativity is generalised as a population-wide attribute, it requires social networks, and its 'product' is the growth of knowledge, sometimes within a market environment, sometimes not.

This is a radically democratic move, although it is far from universally adopted and its implications have barely begun to be worked through. But it is possible to identify the new value propositions associated with an evolved and expanded notion of population-wide creative industriousness in this formula:

Agents (both professional and amateur)

+ *Network* (both social and digital)

+ *Enterprise* (both market-based and other forms of purposeful association)

= *Creative value* (in a complex open system)

= *Growth of Knowledge*.

More models

This 'social network markets' model of creative industries was first elaborated in an article by Jason Potts and others (2008); it has gone on to become widely influential. A different model, seeking to account for the creative economy along a different line of thought, was published by Potts and Cunningham (2008). Instead of showing the phases by means of which creativity ripples out from industry, via economy, to culture and back again, this approach sought to show that differing economic theories and approaches brought a different model of the creative industries into view. These four models are:

1. *Welfare* (market failure model of culture), requiring a *negative* policy of welfare subsidy;
2. *Competition* (nothing special here), requiring a *neutral or standard* industry policy;
3. *Growth* (creative industries as a dynamic sector – DCMS-style), requiring a *positive* investment and growth policy;
4. *Innovation* (creative industries as general dynamic of change), requiring an *evolutionary* policy of innovation.

All of this modelling[3] is characterised by one major concern – the role of creativity in change, both cultural and economic, and its location as a property of agency in open complex systems or networks. It is probably clear by now that we favour the fourth model, while recognising the force and legacy of the other three.

The creative industries were looking less like a small but sexy sector in affluent economies (Currid, 2007), and more like a general *social technology* for enabling change. It may even be argued that the 'creative industries' are the empirical form taken by innovation in advanced knowledge-based economies. This would place *creative innovation* on a par with other enabling social technologies like the law, science and markets. The creative industries may be regarded as the social technology of distributed innovation in the era of knowledge-based complex systems (Hartley, 2009: Ch. 2).

Whichever way you look at it, we were heading for an *evolutionary* approach to culture in general. Modelling not just the economy but also culture as evolutionary, and seeing creativity as part of the general process of innovation and adaptation to change, has led us towards a new kind of intellectual enterprise that goes under the heading of 'cultural science'.

Throwing BRIC(K)S at the MINT

But just before we get to that, we must bring geography back into the picture. If the creative industries can be seen in terms of 'social network markets', then any industry has to go through a 'creative industries' phase at some point, because the creative industries 'involve the creation and maintenance of social networks and the generation of value through production and consumption of network-valorised choices in these networks.'[4]

Thus there is a development aspect to creative industries thinking, because if adaptation to change, access to technologically enabled digital networks, and the production and consumption of network-valorised choices among a creative population, do constitute the creative industries, then developing and emergent economies need them more than anyone.

Furthermore, without being encumbered by industrial-era investment in smoke-stack industries and rust-belt regions, emergent countries may aspire to become 'leapfrog economies', using the creative industries as a social technology of modernisation, global engagement and urban development (UNCTAD, 2008). This stimulates their SME and NGO sectors and promotes the development of indigenous micro-business.

It also helps to develop the most abundant resource available to developing countries, *creative human capital*, especially with their predominantly young populations. For young people especially, creative expression is itself an attractant to enterprise. In developing countries, a creative economy is also a powerful tool for promoting and valorising diversity, of both population and cultural expression, both traditional and modern. Thus creative industries are the generative edge of innovation among the billion or so young people worldwide who are now moving through their teenage years towards full economic productivity.

That is why it is just as important to consider countries like China as the USA or UK – indeed the model of creative industries inherited from the latter may be disastrous for emergent economies, based as it is on analogue technologies like painting or the record industry.

Thus whatever model of the creative industries is adopted, it needs to take account of the 'creative destruction' that may imminently be wrought on the global economic and cultural scene by the BRICKS countries – Brazil, Russia, India, China, Korea, South Africa ... and one may add, Indonesia (and many others – this being the point). Former Goldman Sachs economist and Bloomberg columnist Jim O'Neill coined the term 'BRIC' (to which others have added Korea and South Africa to give BRICKS); he is also responsible for the 'Next Eleven' or N-11: Bangladesh, Egypt, Indonesia, Iran, Mexico, Nigeria, Pakistan, the Philippines, Turkey, South Korea, and Vietnam. Among these, four have emerged as international investment prospects: the MINT countries – Mexico, Indonesia, Nigeria, Turkey (see Chapter 11, below). Montgomery (2010) is one of the first books to take the idea of the creative industries and work through it in the context of an emergent economy – in this case the strategically crucial one of China.

Copyright conflict

In a context such as this, it is unwise to carry forward a definition of the creative industries that is based on record-label and Hollywood notions of copyright. Militant enforcement of owners' IP rights and anti-networking stratagems like DRM are predictable responses by existing investors, but that doesn't make them good policy for new ones (Potts and Montgomery, 2009).

But at the same time it is obvious that commercial value requires that you have something to sell, and if that something is an idea there has to be a way to monetise it. Hence there is no escaping the fact that copyright and intellectual property are *the* point of tension for contemporary cultural, creative and commercial conflicts for the foreseeable future.

Here is where old and emergent enterprises clash, and if the overall 'growth of knowledge' is the ultimate object of study, then there are a few more pressing questions than who owns that knowledge, how it can be shared and through what media of distribution, by whom it can be accessed (and on what terms).

Yet neither economics nor cultural studies have thought as carefully as they should about the problem of copyright (see Chapter 8). It's not an old-style 'Left v. Right' struggle between libertarian progressives and control-culture reactionaries (though it does look like that sometimes). It is a problem of how to coordinate and organise innovation, dynamism and change in an existing complex system without snuffing out either the system or the change.

Cultural science

And so it is more important than ever to get a clear idea of what's going on. Within the flux of change and differences of approach, opinion and purpose, it is never going to be possible to derive an analytical understanding from mere observation of the immediate to-and-fro of policy, debate, promotion and critique. However, it is equally clear that continuing to approach the creative industries using existing templates – whether by means of business plans, public policy or academic disciplines – will miss much of what has been described above.

This is what has led us to a work in progress that we're calling 'cultural science'. It is an evolutionary approach to both culture and the economy, combining evolutionary economics, cultural studies, and complexity or network studies. It seeks to investigate the growth of knowledge. It sees cultural and biological systems as co-evolutionary, and sees culture as a complex open adaptive system.

An immediate problem is that the fields closest to the study of creativity, including media studies, cultural studies, area studies (i.e. the cultures and languages of particular countries) and various branches of the social sciences, have been among the very fields most resistant to 'taking the evolutionary turn' in relation to their object of study. Furthermore, the traditional 'two cultures' distinction between science and the humanities, and the lack of numeracy among many of the latter, serve to make empirical studies of complex evolving systems hard to attempt.

There are equally gaping holes in the knowledge, skills and aptitudes of those coming to creativity and culture from economics or the sciences. They can do circulation, but they're not so astute about meaning. On both sides there is a tendency to adopt a 'heads down' attitude to concentrate on the micro-scale of local and familiar problems, leaving the macro scale of systemic coordination, hierarchy, growth and interconnection with other systems out of the analytic picture.

Just because the phenomena under observation are both dynamic and multivalent, it is therefore necessary to move from single-discipline research to problem-solving research; from solo hyper-specialisation to team-based collaboration; and from national silos to international research networks. Most important, it is necessary to develop a coherent conceptual and theoretical framework through which to advance from an observational to an analytical approach.

Since embarking on this adventure, those of us pursuing a cultural science approach have become more firmly convinced that this is worth pursuing by finding that – under various banners – plenty of others are pursuing it too. There are well-established programmes of research into cultural and biological co-evolution in anthropology, language, neuroscience, economics and social science.[5] More recently, evolutionary studies of stories, art and technology have been published.[6] The use of complexity studies and game theory to model and analyse social networks (both analogue and digital) is well advanced.[7] Cultural science is but one strand in this general current, and very much in its infancy.

However, it is worth the effort not only to find out how the growth of knowledge works, but also for more immediate gains. Those trained in the humanities have found it hard to make an impression on public policy-formation or engagement with business, especially in relation to innovation. It is hard to persuade policymakers and business strategists to take creativity seriously without systematic and numerate evidential data to back up any claims.

Thus, while many agree that it is vital to add the cultural and human sciences to national R&D investment, to add creativity to science, technology, engineering and medicine (STEM) as an integral part of the innovation system, and to foster creative ideas as well as going for the technical fix, none of this will happen if those who are interested in culture and creativity can't speak the same language as those who are interested in the growth of both the economy and the knowledge base.

In the meantime, opportunities are being wasted, by government, business and cultural experts alike, to make better use of our growing understanding of the interfaces between cultural and economic values, between ideas and markets, between users and technologies, between elite expert systems and consumer populations, and between emergent and mature national systems.

Superseded?

First-mover advantage rarely lasts long, and in the creative industries change has been unprecedentedly rapid. Today's start-up becomes tomorrow's global corporation; this year's technological wonder is next year's landfill (if not bedrock platform). The same relentless logic has affected universities and academic disciplines too, as knowledge grows exponentially (see Figure 2.3 in Chapter 2), and the percentage of those in tertiary education expands to include about half of all school-leavers in many countries.[8] Change, expansion and acceleration are normal; the medium in which we live. So what about the 'creative industries': do they have staying power, or were they an ephemeral or transitional idea, a flash in the pan? Obeying different logics, but with the same effect, political priorities change rapidly too; and public affairs discourses are prey to changing fashions. Compelling idea or not, does the idea of the creative industries continue to catch the attention of politicians and policymakers, commentators and consultants, lobbyists and advocates, activists and citizens?

In the UK, where 'a week is a long time in politics' (attributed to PM Harold Wilson), the 'cultural and creative industries' survived as a policy priority even in the political turbulence of the later Blair/Brown years, when Gordon Brown took over from Tony Blair as Prime Minister in 2007, only to be faced with the GFC (Global Financial Crisis) the following year, then losing the 2010 General Election. The creative industries idea had been strongly associated with Blairite 'third way' politics (Giddens, 1998), but as Chancellor of the Exchequer (finance minister) and then PM Brown supported it too, right up to the 2010 election, when he launched his party's 'cultural and creative industries' policy with a twin appeal to economics and culture:

> *Of course I'm proud that our creative industries now account for ten per cent of Britain's GDP. They earn Britain billions internationally, and bring millions of visitors to Britain each year. But so much more than that, the arts inspire the best of our potential as human beings. We have a hunger at the deepest levels to be part of something bigger than ourselves – to know that whatever we are feeling, whatever we have been through, somebody has been there before and whispers through the ages that we are not alone.*[9]

Brown lost the election, but the incoming Conservative–Liberal Democrat Coalition government maintained the Department of Culture, Media and Sport, gave the Creative Industries ministry to moderniser Ed Vaizey, and by January 2014 were boasting that the creative industries were 'generating just over a staggering £8 million pounds an hour' for the UK economy, or £71.4 billion per year. They reported 'growth of almost 10% in 2012, outperforming all other sectors of UK industry', accounting for '1.68 million jobs in 2012, 5.6 per cent of UK jobs'. The Secretary of State, Maria Miller (later replaced after an expenses scandal), was cock-a-hoop:

> *These incredible statistics are confirmation that the Creative Industries consistently punch well above their weight, outperforming all the other main industry sectors, and are a powerhouse within the UK economy.*[10]

It seems from these statements, not to mention the statistics, that the 'creative industries' idea has remained robust. But at the same time policymakers in both government itself and in funding organisations such as arts councils, research councils, and regional development agencies, were falling out of love with the creative industries, while creative activists were falling out of love with government, as analyst Julian Sefton-Green reported in May 2014:

> *Voluntary organisations ... have also benefited from recognition, research and, to a certain extent, the attention of policy makers. But*

> the relationship has never been a happy one and government policy towards the creative voluntary sector has swung back and forth from under-investment to over-scrutiny. The result is that for many, hostility and suspicion of government has become a default position – funding is received grudgingly, grant administrators are regarded as the enemy, while within the funding bodies, such organisations are often seen as difficult and contractually non-compliant.[11]

In other words, both activists and policymakers had returned to a mutually adversarial default position, in which voluntary organisations and 'bottom-up' or self-organised creative activism were opposed in principle to 'top-down' government and quasi-governmental agencies, reproducing the old stand-off between culture and commerce, private sector and public sector, the arts and the economy. The commitment to a Blairite 'third way' approach to creativity as an economic good had never been accepted (or even understood) among arts activists, while funding agencies, including departments of government, sought 'evidence-based' (i.e. quantitative, numerical, statistically significant) arguments for public subsidy for creative organisations and activities, including training. As a result, the 'creative industries' idea itself was tarnished, dismissed on the one hand as a weasel-term for 'the market', and disliked on the other hand because its advocates were deemed to be devoted to special pleading designed only to maintain public funding.

In such a context, ministers prating about the size, growth and employment statistics of the creative industries sector only confirmed the suspicion that this was a restricted, business-as-usual model of creativity. Meanwhile, public policy professionals became increasingly cautious about the term. Some prefer the term 'creative economy', partly because this is literally a known quantity, relying on measures and methods of economic analysis that are already familiar to the Treasury and other government departments. At the same time, the idea of a creative *economy* allows scope for creativity to be measured across 'everything', not simply the arts, culture and heritage sectors.

In such a context – well-rehearsed adversarial positions going back to a time long before the 'creative industries' idea was broached – some policy activists began to rethink the term. Prominent among them was NESTA, originally the National Endowment for Science, Technology and the Arts, which (under the Conservative–Liberal Democrat Coalition government) became Nesta, 'an innovation charity with a mission to help people and organisations bring great ideas to life'. Nesta's new mission is based on its belief 'that we're living in a time when there's more need than ever for creativity, experimentation, and risk-taking'. The director of Nesta's 'creative and digital economy policy and research' is (at time of writing) Hasan Bakhshi, a former Treasury economist.[12] In 2013 he co-authored *A Manifesto for the Creative Economy* (Hargreaves et al., 2013), which is described as follows:

> This manifesto sets out our 10-point plan to bolster the creative industries, one of the UK's fastest growing sectors. Key findings:
>
> - The UK creative economy provides jobs for 2.5 million people, more than financial services, advanced manufacturing or construction.
>
> - The creative economy is one of the few industrial areas where the UK has a credible claim to be world-leading, but history shows this position of leadership cannot be taken for granted.
>
> - Our 10 recommendations include incentivising experimentation with digital technologies by arts and cultural organisations, developing local creative clusters, adopting our new definitions of the creative industries and economy - which are simple, robust and recognise the central role of digital technologies - and ensuring government funding schemes do not discriminate against creative businesses.

The description uses 'creative economy' as its main title, glosses it as 'creative industries', which are seen in the text as having a 'central position in this creative economy' (Hargreaves et al., 2013: 14), with a nod both to 'digital technologies' and to 'arts and cultural organisations'.

The *Manifesto* defines the 'creative industries and economy' as '*the use of creative talent for commercial purposes*' (2013: 13–14), a formula that is intended to move beyond the earlier DCMS definition's reliance on intellectual property, to allow for the influence of creativity on 'other parts of the economy', and to give scope to 'digital technologies' and other innovations. At the same time, the *Manifesto* is clear about where the creative economy is to be found – in 'commercial purposes'. While that is hardly a radical statement in the context of economics, it does leave unresolved the problem of the radical, adversarial, activist, voluntary sector (often not just non-commercial but also anti-commercial), which sees itself as a creative and critical avant-garde. It also makes it hard to admit those activities among the general population that are pursued for cultural and social purposes (not for commercial purposes), for instance in DIY culture, user-created content, copying and sharing, social networks and mediation, which nevertheless are crucial sources of innovation for a creative economy.

This is to say nothing about the burgeoning 'sector' of social enterprise and activism that has no commercial purpose but is nevertheless organised along firm-like lines, and may integrate environmental, community, creative and even retail values without being 'for profit' (examples range from Sea Shepherd to GetUp!). Such enterprises are often innovative and catch early trends in popular culture or technological affordance, turning them to new uses based on entirely non-commercial values. As Jocelyn Bailey has put it in relation to differing notions of a 'maker' (see Chapter 8, below):

> For the creative industries, the term 'makers' signifies something quite different from what the Treasury might think. Not steel magnates, chemical suppliers or factory owners, but artisans and inventors... Industrial policy needs to be hauled into the 21st century. We need to update our language, our thinking and our departmental structures, to shake off the false dichotomy between 'the creative industries' and other parts of the economy.[13]

Thus, holding on to a notion of the creative industries as having a 'central position' in a creative economy that is defined in terms of commercial purposes is a welcome step beyond an industrial (big firms, high-tech), 'consumerist' definition of creative industries, but it still relies on a definition of creativity in its 'commodity form' as something that *can* be used for commercial purposes. It doesn't take the crucial next step towards a *relational* or *systems* approach, where it's the tension between opposing purposes – commercial and non-commercial, market-based and activist, entertainment and artistic, private and public, corporate or community oriented – that drives and 'incentivises' creativity.

How can analysts recognise in their mutual differences and antagonistic purposes the need for a *conceptual community* (as discussed in Chapter 3, and see Prince, 2010) to work through these multivalent relations, which are the source of both economic and cultural dimensions of creativity? It's not possible to restrict the idea of creativity to 'commercial purposes' if you want to understand a creative economy; but equally it's not possible to quarantine creativity *from* the economy if you want to understand culture. As many have pointed out, the creative economy has not been incompatible with capitalism from the time when capitalism was invented: artists from Shakespeare onwards were entrepreneurs, shareholders of joint-stock companies, and suppliers of novelties to anonymous audiences for profit; conversely, some claim that Silicon Valley is the Renaissance Italy of our times, and that Steve Jobs was today's Leonardo Da Vinci.[14] This is why, in this book, we have adopted the clumsy formula of 'creative economy and culture'. Artistry, entrepreneurship, culture, wealth – it's one system. It needs an integrated conversation not an adversarial system of explanation.

Notes

1. See http://cultural-science.org
2. In *Popular Reality* (1996) Hartley dubbed 'freedom' and 'comfort' as the 'twin energies of modernity' since the French and American Revolutions: the desire, among ordinary (non-aristocratic) citizens, for freedom, driving the political struggle for emancipation (French Revolution), and for comfort, driving the economic struggle for material wellbeing (Industrial Revolution).
3. Potts (2008) found 17 models of 'creative industries'!
4. Potts, 2008: Definition #12. See also Potts, 2009.
5. For instance the Centre for the Coevolution of Biology and Culture at Durham University (www.dur.ac.uk/ccbc); and see Richerson and Boyd (2005); Mesoudi (2007); Hurford (2007); MacNeilage (2008); Bickerton (2009); Runciman (2009).
6. See Arthur (2009); Boyd (2009); Dutton (2009); Lotman (2009).
7. Most obviously in the work of the Santa Fe Institute; see also Sawyer (2005); Beinhocker (2006); Ormerod (2007); Bentley and Ormerod (2010).
8. OECD (2012), *Education at a Glance 2012*: Highlights, p. 13, OECD Publishing. Available at: http://dx.doi.org/10.1787/eag_highlights-2012-en?NIR.
9. Brown's speech, made in Sunderland in May 2010, can be found at www.totalpolitics.com/print/speeches/35333/gordon-brown-prime-minister-and-labour-party-leader-speaking-at-the-national-glass-centre-in-sunderland-to-launch-labours-culture-and-creative-industries-manifesto.thtml.
10. Figures and quotations at https://www.gov.uk/government/news/creative-industries-worth-8million-an-hour-to-uk-economy.
11. Julian Sefton-Green, 'The Creative Industries and the Big Society', posted at the Creative Economy 2015 blog at http://creativeeconomy2015.com/2014/05/19/the-creative-industries-and-the-big-society/.
12. Quotations taken from various pages on Nesta's website at www.nesta.org.uk/about-us; www.nesta.org.uk/about-us/what-we-want-achieve; www.nesta.org.uk/users/hasan-bakhshi.
13. Jocelyn Bailey, 'The Other March of the Makers' posted on the Creative Economy 2015 blog at http://creativeeconomy2015.com/2014/04/25/the-other-march-of-the-makers/.
14. Comments attributed to Tom Byers of Stanford University: 'Silicon Valley's entrepreneurs are the artists of today's tech renaissance'; and 'the Mayor of Florence came out with a statement, saying Steve Jobs was the Da Vinci of our times': http://thedishdaily.com/2013/03/05/stanford-professor-tom-byers-on-humanity-as-the-core-of-entrepreneurial-success/ (March 2013).

6

CREATIVE INDUSTRIES TO CREATIVE ECONOMY

It is conventional to represent the arts and Creative Industries broadly as suppliers of cultural goods and services. Yet this may be systematically underestimating their contribution to 'the economy'. Why? – Because the Creative Industries also produce another class of outputs, namely innovation.

(Jason Potts, n.d.)

Four phases/models of creative industries

Most policy discussion to date has focused on the 'industries' part of creative industries. But the sector has evolved and broadened since it was first identified in the 1990s. Already, four different phases or models can be identified (Hartley, 2009: Ch. 2). Each one has supplemented – not supplanted – the one before, which is how they can be both sequential phases and co-present models. The upshot is that it is now much easier to see how creativity relies on citizen-consumers as much as on enterprise-artists, and how much cities rely on their citizens as well as their economy to achieve creativity. Thus, for a truly creative city, what is needed is not just one model of the creative industries, but four *creative systems*: each of them separately describable, often overlapping, and clashing in creative tension as they grow and change in relation to each other. The four models of the creative industries are summarised in Figure 6.1.

CI-1: Creative Clusters

Industry definition

- Closed expert pipeline of innovation (internal to the firm)
- Clusters of different industry sectors that together produce creative works or outputs: advertising, architecture, publishing, software, performing arts, media production, art, design, fashion, etc.
- Provider-led or supply-based definition: institutional (meso level) creativity; elaborate production by specialist organisations
- Indicators: 'Creative outputs', i.e. consumer goods priced on creative values (i.e. adding value to information or material), including music, writing, design, performance

CI-2: Creative Services

Business services definition

- Closed innovation system
- 'Creative services' – creative inputs by creative occupations and companies (professional designers, producers, performers, writers)
- Value-added to 'non-creative' sectors (e.g. health, government) by creative services: institutional (meso level) creativity
- Indicators: employment of specialist creative people (professional designers, producers, performers and writers)

CI-3: Creative Citizens

Cultural (user) definition

- Open innovation network (innovation from beyond firms and professionals)
- Number of 'creative citizens' – population, workforce, consumers, users, and entrepreneurs, artists
- Personal (micro level) creativity/microproductivity; market-based and non-market
- Focus on user productivity (social networking, making, crowdsourcing, etc.)
- Social media/user-created content
- Indicators: emergent production from social networks; scaled-up via microproductive institutions (e.g. YouTube, Google)

CI-4 Creative Cities

Complexity (and clash) definition

- Clash and friction between systems: industry/economy and culture (e.g. conflicting interests in the sharing of intellectual property)
- Sites for social meeting and mixture as well as friction: connecting culture and economy, diversity, tolerance, civility
- Creative cities are therefore those that cohabitate all four types – industry, economy, culture and 'urban semiosis'
- Population-wide (macro level) creativity, combined with institutional (meso-level) enterprise, and personal (micro-level) productivity
- Coordination of economic value (GDP; jobs) and cultural value (meaningfulness, identity, relationships, boundaries)

FIGURE 6.1 Four phases of the creative industries – from industry clusters and services to creative citizens and cities *(adapted from Hartley et al., 2012)*

CI-1

The first phase, CI-1, is the *industry* definition (DCMS, 1998), which we call 'creative clusters'. It is made of clusters of different 'industries' (a misnomer, applied metaphorically) – advertising, architecture, publishing, software, performing arts, media production, art, design, fashion, etc. – that together produce creative works or *outputs*. This is a 'provider-led' or supply-based definition.

The sector is reckoned to be anywhere between 3 and 8 percent of advanced economies, and claimed to be high-growth, with an economic multiplier effect. It was first identified in advanced economies (UK, USA, Australia), and is of growing importance to emergent economies (e.g. China, Indonesia, Brazil), given its claimed high-growth, economic multiplier effect.

Looked at this way, the creative industries are nothing other than *firms*, especially those whose livelihood depends on creating intellectual property and protecting it with copyright, enforced against both commercial copying and consumer 'piracy'. It is modelled on the industrial-era closed expert pipeline, which you can see in operation in 'big pharma' or automobile companies:

$$\text{invent} \rightarrow \text{patent/copyright} \rightarrow \text{manufacture} \rightarrow \text{distribute} \rightarrow \text{sell}$$

The industrial model retains all of these functions within the one firm, from R&D labs or design studios, via legal and manufacturing processes, to distribution agents such as car dealerships. A direct line is forged, from intellectual property to purchase – but *not* a direct *communicative or cultural* line from 'creator' to 'user', since neither side knows who the other is, and creators cede their rights to the firm.

CI-2

The second phase, CI-2, is the *services* definition, which we call 'creative services'. It is characterised by the provision of creative *inputs* by creative occupations and companies, most obviously where professional designers, producers, performers and writers add value to firms or agencies engaged in other activities, from mining or manufacturing to health, government and other public services (Howkins, 2001). By one estimate, creative services expand the creative industries by at least a third (Higgs et al., 2008). Again, the input is high value-added, indeed, it is thought to add value to the economy as a whole, boosting the profitability of otherwise static sectors (e.g. manufacturing).

It is this kind of creativity that transforms old-style services like transport into creative services like 'experience'-based tourism. Because this version of the creative industries is economy-wide and involves *occupations and agencies* other than firms, it may be regarded as a hybrid system, in which social networks play a role, but it remains focused on market-driven activity; it is only 'demand-led' in a b2b environment. Nevertheless here is where innovation policy can gain traction, encouraging firms of all kinds to collaborate with creative entrepreneurs and to innovate using creative inputs.

CI-3

The third phase, CI-3, is the *cultural* definition, which we call 'creative citizens'. Here is where creativity spills out of the economy, being an attribute of the population at large – the workforce, consumers, users and entrepreneurs, who become hard to distinguish from artists in how they go about pursuing an idea and creative reputation and a market for it. This is a user-led or demand-side definition. The expansion of the creative industries to cover everyone (at least in principle) allows the possibility that the energies of everyone in the system can be harnessed, adding the value of entire social networks and the individual agency of whole populations to the *growth of knowledge*. It is the domain of experimentation and adaptation, where *individual* agency may have *network-wide* effects: thus it is the dynamic 'edge' of systemic *emergence*.

CI-4

The fourth phase, CI-4, is the *complexity* definition, which we call 'creative cities'. Obviously, cities predate the emergence of a creative economy, although that very fact reminds us that much of what is now associated with the term may have been around for a long time, previously unnoticed in economic or cultural theory. However, what is new is that urban living is now (since around 2008), for the first time, the majority human experience. Further, cities have been identified as a more intensive crucible for creativity than regions or nations (e.g. Currid, 2007). This is because they are in fact an evolved autopoietic solution to problems of complexity and coordination in elaborately interconnected systems. As a result, cities not only display many different *systems* (for instance, different industries, ethnicities, levels of wealth, function, and mixtures of work, leisure, childrearing and tourism), but these systems overlap, clash, mix, and change their relative boundaries and prominence in a continuing dynamic process of inter-system interaction that produces meaningfulness, newness, and experimental solutions to emergent problems. In other words, cities themselves are creative agents, in the way that semiospheres are.

Urban semiosis

The first two models – CI-1 and CI-2 – are based on the economy as we know it. CI-3 is based on 'technologically equipped' culture (Papacharissi, 2010). In Clay Shirky's (2008) phrase: 'Here comes everybody!' In this model, everyone's creative potential can be harnessed for innovation, which can come from anywhere in the system. In fact CI-3 is radically different from CI-1 and CI-2, because: it focuses on culture not economy, consumer or user not producer, and whole populations (social networks) not firms; it is the beneficiary of the digital revolution, posing a direct and fundamental challenge to 'industry' business models; and potentially it is a more productive model of creativity than the ones that are tied to expert-systems alone, because it encompasses many more, potentially all, of the agents in the system as active creators, rather than passive consumers, and so it opens up the space of experimentation and prototyping (new ideas) as well as that of microproductivity (economic activity at sole-trader level). Further, when citizens act in concert, or as associations (formal, like advocacy groups, or informal, like street artists), their group activities contribute to the creative productivity of the city. And when they congregate for festivals, competitions, activism or special events, this too has the potential to generate new meanings and thus to enrich urban semiosis. The 'character' of a city emerges from these sources – which explains why Berlin is more creative than Bremen, or Melbourne more than Brisbane (Hartley et al., 2012).

CI-3 is therefore another example of how the clash of systems is proving to be the driver of change in creative productivity. Rather than being seen as the output of an industry, creative innovation becomes a property of complex systems, socially-networked relations, and the interaction of cultural and economic activities. Furthermore, social networks themselves are sources of innovation; they are not simply distribution media. The force of innovation coming from CI-3 is putting pressure on CI-1, as can be seen in the realm of intellectual property rights (IPR), which have become heavily skewed towards industrial providers, as legislators quail before corporate lobbyists. The 'rights' of those who want to copy and share creative content are not recognised. A ruthless enforcement regime made criminals out of consumers, notably in the recorded music industry, which then served as a model for others, even in industries where copyright had never played a role like haute couture fashion, where some design firms are attempting to assert IPR restrictions over patterns that once would have seen imitation as a sincere form of flattery. The negative effect of this policy on both innovation and the industry itself has begun to be recognised in recent moves to reform IPR law (e.g. Hargreaves, 2011), although the lobbyists have ensured that resultant legislative action is watered down at best.[1]

Thus the four models are not based on trying to define ever more tightly how 'creativity' is 'an industry' but, on the contrary, on showing how it needs to be accounted for at an ever-increasing distance from industry. It is not until we reach stages CI-3 and CI-4, where creativity reaches cultural dimensions located in cities, rather than being confined to production processes located in firms, that the productive connections between culture and economy, individual talent and societal scale, can come into focus.

Furthermore, it is only at that point that we can take proper account of technological systems – the growth of ICTs, digital media and the internet – because these are now not simply in-company efficiency-technologies (as IT once was when IBM – International Business Machines – ruled the roost), but whole-of-society cultural forms with embedded 'social technologies' (as the internet now is). In other words, if we confine the notion of creative industries to the traditional (i.e. analogue) creative arts and their industrial or occupational form, we cannot account for the importance – both economic and cultural – of user-created content and the burgeoning scale of computer-enabled social networks. Since these are clearly important drivers of the creative industries, we need all four models before we can explain creative innovation and the integration of cultural and economic meanings and values. What distinguishes CI-1/2 from CI-3/4 is that the former are cushioned by legislative protections and well-established business apparatus, while the latter are generally informal, often evanescent (e.g. crazes), and tied to someone else's proprietary platforms and IPR. If you're a company, the talk is all about freedom (to trade); if you're not, the talk is all about control (you must obey copyright regulations on pain of criminal prosecution). As a result, un-enterprising firms can get away with rent-seeking behaviour, and enterprising citizens can go to jail. There is no policy setting or government department for freeing up, protecting, and supporting or improving *citizens*. They remain objects rather than subjects of policy.

Governments do not reward civic cooperation and the sharing of cultural or creative ideas. They only reward individualist appropriations of the same. Cooperation, especially at the level of purposeful assembly ('crowds', 'mobs'), is still mistaken for something disruptive, needing control, rather than being seen as a potential agent of renewal. 'Creative destruction' of existing arrangements is prohibited, while the creation of adaptive and useful 'newness' out of group actions is literally unthinkable – there is no framework of law or organisation to bring it into conscious consideration. As a result, when citizens do exert a group will, the resulting 'disruption' impacts on governmental, legal and business arrangements as an exogenous shock, instead of being accommodated as part of an endogenous growth process.

The only mechanism available to populations as such is their own energy. Fortunately, this can be exerted competitively, especially among different cities and regions. Some cities achieve creative innovation 'spikes' compared with others. In abstract terms, cities are 'hubs' in globally extensive social-creative-information-enterprise networks, but in historical actuality, cities rise and fall competitively, and are at the heart of creative dynamics.

Individual citizens do not expect to collect a percentage of the gains made by their contribution to a creative city – they are not rent-seekers. Instead, the benefits of creating a vibrant, attractive and enterprising city flow to the group or deme. The 'we'-community benefits as a group; benefits are not regarded as property or rent. Civic pride can of course motivate spectacular acts of individual generosity (which is evidence of group-identification), but even here the beneficiaries are citizens as a whole, not the 'investor' in the infrastructure, hospital, school, artwork or fountain.

Now, with social media, civic benefaction is not confined to aristocrats and HNWIs (high net worth individuals). It can be practised by anyone, through congregation and association, assisted by technological novelties such as Kickstarter or Pozible, flash mobs, or supported by old-fashioned civic incubators like coffee shops (with free WiFi), where active citizens can congregate, mix, and push along the schemes that will form the future.

Creative destruction and social learning

It may seem unnecessarily complicated to propose a 'definition' of creative industries that requires four components, each at odds with the others. But simplification does not seem to be how the 'system of systems' works. To make matters more difficult for policymakers, technological and social changes are forcing the pace. In particular, the rapid growth of the internet and social media has had a disruptive effect, especially with the growth of consumer-created content. The existing, 'analogue' creative industries were themselves among the first to experience Schumpeterian 'gales of creative destruction', which followed the development of global online digital networks and their uptake by 'everybody'. The driver of the creative industries is transforming from copyrighted 'arts and media' to 'publish-yourself' digital networks. Examples include YouTube, Facebook, Wikipedia, Twitter and other social networking sites, which provide the platform for user-created content and 'social network markets' (Potts et al., 2008), and the popular, global medium of exchange for urban semiosis. Pretty soon, the same energies will spill over from the digital to the material world, as 3D printing shifts manufacturing from its current large-scale, firm-based form to DIY and micro-business forms.

All this leads us to assert that despite the awesome technological inventions and the impressive rate of growth (Moore's Law), the most important 'invention' of the internet has been 'the user' (CI-3). Among the ensuing disruptions, the digital user is in tension with the analogue copyright-holder, a tension that is by no means resolved. The emphasis shifts from copyright (CI-1) to innovation (CI-3); from IPR (CI-1 and CI-2) to emergence (CI-3 and CI-4). While creative industries require strong copyright enforcement by global agencies like WIPO (World Intellectual Property Organisation), a creative culture operates on the axiom that 'knowledge shared is knowledge gained'. WIPO maintains a strong interest in the creative industries, especially in developing countries.[2] But such regulatory interventions do not drive creative enterprise; group-action (social media) and city life do that.

Given the importance of users as producers, learning and experimentation are vital elements of creativity, but they are missing from standard creative industries models. New ideas may come from outside the industrial context of expert specialisation, to include learning among myriad users, and learning from networks-as-agents. This kind of networked and creative learning is informal, distributed, peer-to-peer, just-in-time and imitative. For the general population, it is often associated with entertainment formats rather than the formal education system. But that population is now a productive resource in its own right. Thus a prerequisite for further economic growth is *education* – formal and informal – for the growth of creative productivity and interaction among users.

However, as for creative industries, so for education: it isn't the 'provider' that matters so much as the 'user.' Cities with high student numbers lead global creativity tables, and those students lead diversification. According to Malcolm Gillies (2013), 100,000 of London's half-million students are international students, and a 'majority of undergraduates studying in London declare themselves to be other than "white British"'. Students are global mixers, early adopters, have relatively high disposable income (spare cash for novelties), are mobile, experimental, flock to special events, festivals, and colonise neglected quarters with low rents, frequently reviving them in the process. Thus, they perform a *social learning* function for cities. This is not a job for higher education and schools; it is conducted informally in the 'clash of systems' that people experience as part of urban life. In fact, people need to cluster, both physically and online, just as much as producers do.

In such a lively environment, creative innovation accelerates both formally (education and the arts) and informally (participation and the media). Innovation itself can now be seen as both 'elaborate' production by expert organisations (CI-1 and CI-2), and 'emergent' meanings arising from distributed, self-organising social networks (CI-3 and CI-4). What links them all is ideas. As John Howkins (2009) puts it, 'ideas are the new currency'. This kind of currency is not always monetised. Some ideas circulate entirely outside of the market, operating in social networks and in economies of attention. For others, many creative artists and start-up businesses make the point that 'emergent ideas' and making money, especially Cooke and

Lazzeretti's (2008) 'criminally large amounts thereof', may be separated not by sector but by time – today's YouTube video from the bedsitter may be tomorrow's HNWI (high net worth individual) in the tax haven.

What to do about it?

In practice, a combination of CI-1 creative clusters, CI-2 creative services, and CI-3 creative citizens, is part of the intellectual infrastructure of a creative city (CI-4), bringing into one place the energies of:

- Producers/consumers;
- Intellectual property/intellectual capital;
- Elaborate/emergent creativity;
- Work/leisure;
- Supply/demand;

> (the slash in each pairing denotes both clash and connection).

The creative city is a 'medium' (in the art sense) in which population-wide creativity is mixed and circulated. With broadly distributed digital creativity, the extent and rate of experimentation and adaptation accelerates for the entire economic–cultural system, as does the potential for distributing solutions that can rapidly scale up from 'garage' start-ups to global applications (e.g., iTunes app store). This expanded and accelerated notion of creativity as a broad-based 'innovation culture' (CI-3) means that cities will need different policy settings compared with those that see the 'creative industries' merely as a sector of the economy (i.e. CI-1 and CI-2).

The creative economy can be understood as *enabled innovation*, where industry clusters (real estate) are only the first stage. Rapid adaptability among 'the clash of systems' is required for survival, and innovation needs to be modelled as 'scale free' in order to link bottom-up agency to top-down, globally distributed applications (both cultural and economic) via digital media and online social networks. Rethinking creative industries as *enabled social innovation* precipitates changes in city policy settings:

Creativity

- Cultivation of urban semiosis and the productive clash of systems;
- Shift from producer to consumer; from experts to users;
- Networks as productive 'places' within cities;

Urban planning

- Shift from real-estate to human resources;
- Emphasis on enabling and improving social learning;
- From provider planning to evolving networks ('urban emergence': Hélie, 2012);

Economics

- From industry sector to adaptive, complex, open systems;
- Interaction of culture and economy;
- From copyright to innovation; IPR to emergence.

In terms of physical infrastructure, it will be important to focus not on production plant but on relationship-formation, shifting attention from real-estate solutions to social networks and places to mingle, typically creative 'quarters' of cities (Roodhouse, 2010). These include 'scenes', festivals, incentive competitions or awards, and venues that allow the integration of cultural and economic approaches to creativity, the mixture of ideas, and a rich interaction between productive, 'entrepreneurial consumers' (Hartley and Montgomery, 2009) and creative enterprise (see Figure 6.2).

Constructing a creative city requires nurturing all three columns of attributes in Figure 6.2: *culture* for 'emergence'; a *place* for 'mixing'; and *economy* for coordination and scaling. Figure 6.2 also shows how the middle column, the city, acts as the medium between culture and the economy, bringing the different values, actors and knowledge of cultural and economic systems into productive 'marriageability'.

CULTURE	PLACE	ECONOMY
Consumption	Mediation	Production
Demand	Platform	Supply
Novelty bundling	Urban connections	Institutions and firms
Intellectual capital	Community context	Intellectual property
Identity	Knowledge	Growth
Play	Mix/Move	Work
Scene/Festival	City Quarter	Industry Cluster
Creative culture	Creative city	Creative industries
social ...	network ...	markets (Potts et al., 2008)

FIGURE 6.2 Urban semiosis: cities as incubators of social network markets

Abandon the term? From creative industries to creative economy

Marriage sometimes brings a name-change. Whether or not this is advisable in relation to personal identity, it is certainly warranted in relation to the science of creative culture. It may be time to abandon the term 'industries' and, when a generic term is required, to refer instead to the 'creative economy' (Hargreaves et al., 2013). This term is itself too narrow – in our view creativity belongs to culture, not just to the economy (see the discussion at the end of the previous chapter) – but because 'the economy' is more developed as a formal system that can be modelled and analysed than culture (currently) is, we accept that 'creative economy' is preferable for formal purposes, e.g. public policy-making, private business strategy and scholarly research. It does not *encompass* the levels of CI-3 and CI-4 (creative citizenship and cities). However, it does allow analysis of how cultural values have converged so thoroughly with economic ones that the two are now 'integrated systems', each co-constituting the other. In the present state of knowledge, this is easier to observe with the tools of 'the economy' than with those of 'culture', although the direction and even purpose of the analysis may be to show how creativity exceeds economics, rather than being defined by it or confined to it. One of the implications of this shift is that the term 'economy' needs to be expanded to encompass microproductivity and the productivity of social networks, extending also the possibility of applying economic analysis to units smaller than the firm.

Notes

1. See www.ipo.gov.uk/about/press/press-release/press-release-2013/press-release-20130510.htm.
2. See, for example, www.wipo.int/copyright/en/creative_industries/; and www.wipo.int/ip-development/en/agenda/flexibilities/resources/studies.html.

PART II

FORCES AND DYNAMICS OF CHANGE: THE THREE BIGS IN ACTION

EVERYONE

7

TECHNOLOGY

Universal connectivity will bring together all the information and services you need and make them available to you regardless of where you are, what you are doing, or the kind of device you are using. Call it 'virtual' convergence – everything you want is in one place, but that place is wherever you want it to be, not just at home or in the office.

(Bill Gates, 1999)[1]

Universal?

In 1963, when Ted Nelson developed *hypertext*, central to the internet we see today, he saw it as a revolutionary technology of knowledge production and distribution, promising to enable everyone to act as a creator. As he envisaged it:

> It would be a universal publishing system where every interested person has direct access to humanity's accumulated knowledge – in effect, the ultimate system where each person is both contributor and user. (Cited in Stockwell, 2000: 168)

Half a century later, the increasingly distributed means of media production has led to a surge in 'mini-media producers' (Leadbeater, 2006) and the rise of the 'writing public' (Hartley, 2008). Content-creation has become an increasingly globally distributed user-created system. We are beginning to see the promise of the internet taking shape on the horizon. Pioneers are often attracted to 'universal' notions. Another such is Jimmy Wales, co-founder of Wikipedia. Writing in 2005, he expressed his ambition for it:

> Wikipedia is first and foremost an effort to create and distribute a free encyclopedia of the highest possible quality to every single person on the planet in their own language.[2]

This universalism has been criticised as a kind of Californian utopianism that thinks there's a technological solution to everything (Morozov, 2011, 2013). On the other hand, it is in fact the case that digital connectivity, now extended from computer devices to mobile telecoms, is accessible to and used by billions, across all types of society in all states of economic development. It's not quite 'every single person on the planet', but it is beginning to look like what we might call a 'zeroth order of approximation' to that (see Chapter 3). So, among other pertinent questions, one that is worth considering is this: to what *uses* do ordinary people – the people formerly known as consumers – put their new-found access, knowledge and creative opportunities? This chapter cannot offer a comprehensive answer to that question (we're not speaking about 'every single person on the planet'), but it will attempt to provide an emblematic one (to a first approximation). Our emblems take the unlikely form of 'Shouting Beast' and 'Corndog'.

'It's our turn to get famous!'

In 2002, a series of parody videos went viral. The videos, later known as *The Big History Trilogy*,[3] were created by Chinese television professionals for their in-house New Year party. They repurposed and redubbed scenes from old revolutionary movies for self-ridicule, with a satirical take on current affairs and mockery of official rhetoric. These were pre-YouTube days, and video-streaming sites were still a couple of years away, so information about the *Big History* videos was shared on bulletin boards and internet forums, while the videos themselves circulated mostly through BitTorrent software or hard-disk offline, via personal networks among those who could afford expensive gadgets.[4]

Jiaoshou, or *Shouting Beast*,[5] the main protagonist of this chapter, was 18 at that time and had just been introduced to the internet. He loved the *Big History* series and wished he could make videos of his own. He would later become a prolific video blogger, imitating the *Big History Trilogy* in most of his early videos.[6] However, at the time, video-creating equipment and software were off-limits for him, like most youngsters of his age. Being a high-school student his top priority was to fight fiercely for a place at a good university. But during his years as a civil engineering student he began to experiment with online writing, learned to dub internet videos, and became a part-time net jockey. In 2006, when video-streaming became popular in China and editing tools were readily available online, Jiaoshou started to convert his writings into videos in his spare time. These videos, known as the *Shouting Beast* series, won him a big following among other user-creators. In 2009, he was voted the Most Popular Blogger in the *Tudou Video Festival*, an annual industry event.[7] Tudou, literally 'Potato-Net', named in ironic homage to couch potatoes, is a major video-sharing site in China, launched at roughly the same time as YouTube.

During the festival he met Corndog, who had happened to go to the same primary school as he had attended. Jiaoshou collaborated with Corndog on a few occasions. Corndog himself went on to win the 'Golden Potato Prize' at the Tudou Video Festival in 2010, where he made the famous statement, 'It's our turn to get famous!'[8]

Jiaoshou's popularity began to win him business contracts. Tudou invited him to create an internet mini-play series for its advertising clients, including *Master Kong*, a popular Taiwan-owned brand of noodles, bottled beverages and pastries.[9] The success of these videos changed his career path. In 2011, after almost a year of contemplating and preparation, Jiaoshou quit his job as project manager in a construction company in Central China and started up his own company, Unimedia, with other video creators and senior managers from Tudou. In 2013, in partnership with YouKu, it launched a mini-play series called *Totally Unexpected* (also known as *Surprise*), targeting people on the move. The first season of the series includes 15 episodes, each of them 5–6 minutes long, short enough to finish viewing while waiting for the bus or sitting on the toilet. The series was a huge hit and attracted more than one billion views by August 2014. The second season, released in June 2014, garnered 30 million views within a week.[10] It went on to create a New Year series together with the hugely successful Hunan TV, which aired both online and through Hunan's cable network. At roughly the same time as Jiaoshou, Corndog quit his job too, and began to experiment with online video advertisements.

Jiaoshou and Corndog are among the millions of the 'everyones' who have found their voices, honed their skills, experimented with their creative productivity online, even carved a career out of it, enabled and facilitated by affordable ICT and increasingly ubiquitous internet access.

A moment of opportunity

The emergence of the concept of 'everyone' as a viable description of media producers (just as everyone produces language) provides us with an opportunity to rethink entrenched ideas about popular culture, productivity and the creative industries. As we discussed earlier, we believe that culture is based on communication within and among groups, and creativity is a group-made common resource, generated from interactive participation between and among users. Thus the process of communication is also the process of production of culture and creativity. To begin a detailed answer to the overarching questions of this book – where creativity comes from, how it connects people, and what it is used for – we need to start with the process of *cultural production*, that is, the making of groups and the negotiation of meaningfulness, identity and relationships.

In what follows in this chapter, we analyse at the micro-level how groups (demes), identities and subcultures come into being. The two cases we use to illustrate the process are Jiaoshou and Corndog. As culture works at the level of groups rather than that of individuals, the focus is not about their individual talent or artistic skills. Rather, the emphasis is to understand the *making of* Jiaoshou and Corndog, in order to tease out the mechanisms of group-formation and cultural co-production.

Oil Tiger Machinima Team and the making of Corndog

Corndog became famous overnight with the distribution of a widely acclaimed internet video, *War on Internet Addiction*.[11] However, in contrast to the trope of a lone hero making a hit video singlehandedly in his bedroom or garage, Corndog has a team behind him. It is a self-organised group of gamers and machinima fans called *Oil Tiger Machinima Team*, or OTMT.

OTMT is active on the fringe of a self-organised WoW (World of Warcraft)[12] fan forum called NGA (National Geographic of Azeroth), where the team recruits most of its members.[13] These are largely handpicked by Corndog, based on the skill profiles and congeniality of potential members. During his time off work Corndog serves as webmaster on the video panel of the NGA. Membership is by invitation only and decided by a deliberative process among the group. The team had 53 members at the time of co-author Li's phone interview with Corndog.[14] Some of them are good at music production and singing, others at graphic design, still others at video-postproduction. The members are geographically distributed, and play games on different servers. What bound them together is their shared interest in both the WoW game and the NGA Forum. Communication among the team is through QQ Group, a messaging tool for Chinese internet users provided by Tencent, a successful internet portal based in Shenzhen. Co-author Li asked if he could observe their intragroup communication, but Corndog turned down that request after consulting group members: 'They don't agree, saying they would feel weird'.[15]

OTMT doesn't have a group ID or collective representation on NGA forum. Its members are active on their own there. OTMT exists as a trademark for the co-creations of the team.

The co-creation of *War on Internet Addiction*

War on Internet Addiction (*WIA*) is the third video produced by the team. Both of the previous two are machinima videos, but neither of them travelled as far as *WIA*.[16] The content of these videos and the reasons for the wild popularity of *WIA* is of great interest. However, for the purposes of this chapter we will focus on the collaborative way in which the videos were created, with a view to shedding light on practices of group-building and cultural production.

The first video under the trademark of OTMT was *Song of the Skeleton Party*.[17] Private Ryan,[18] one of the core members of the team, initiated it, and Corndog worked as his assistant, co-authoring the script and co-directing the shots. The video was well received on NGA. More important, the video introduced a popular Tauren character called *Kannimei*,[19] which was to become the name of all the three videos created by the team. *War on Internet Addiction* is the third of the Kannimei series, and the first to travel beyond the game community. It is 64 minutes long. According to Corndog in a textual interview with Phoenix TV, it took more than 100 users around 3 months to co-create, with no cost except a game fee.[20] Corndog took the leading role in the process, writing and directing the production, with Private Ryan as his assistant. The script was discussed and revised together with Private Ryan before it was circulated among the whole group to solicit ideas and tidy up loose ends. The core production crew was from OTMT, with roles and timing negotiated among Corndog and team members.

Collaboration and co-creation was not limited to team members. Corndog also crossed group boundaries for help with the creative process. One source of help was WoW guilds, where OTMT recruited gamers to perform minor roles.[21] 'I would go to a guild and shout out that I need people to run errands for my game video, and guild members who could find time just came and helped' (interview with Li). Gamers have done this for free. These gamers are not only voluntary participants but also a ready fan base for the videos in the pipeline. Many celebrity gamer-bloggers outside of OTMT were invited to work on the video, contributing to the whole creative process from the storyline to the post-production. The dubbing and music on the video is highly acclaimed. Well-known names such as Catherine Linlin, Loveqiaolin, tnnaii and babymavis are acknowledged at the beginning of the video.[22] Banyun⑨Ke, a video team active around Acfun, an anime fan forum, participated as a group in the production of the video, offering suggestions on script lines and taking over some dubbing work.[23]

The list of participants would be too long to be given exhaustively, a point Corndog made meticulously in his introduction to the *WIA* on NGA forum (interview with Li). We have emphasised here the collaborative practice among and across network boundaries, in the belief that the cross-boundary collaboration of the sort we see in the production of *WIA* taps into the best of the 'collective intelligence' (Levy, 1997) of internet user networks and brings about better content. By enlisting the help of a diverse range of gamer-users and involving them as part of the production, Corndog made all participants owners of the video. This has not only made *WIA* a better video, but it has also helped the video travel further, reaching more diverse user networks and getting more popular along the way. The sense of co-ownership is not related to copyright. Rather it comes out of participation.

Also commendable in the co-creative process is the level of trust that is demonstrated among participants. Corndog cited an example of this in co-author Li's interview with him. The shooting of the video needed several dozen gamers to be online at the same time and to follow instructions from Corndog, issued through the group chat functionality afforded by Skype voice. In the process of shooting, some might need to get food or have a break, others may need to get to work, and this could slow down the whole shooting process. Their solution was to borrow the accounts and passwords of those who couldn't stay online and give them to others who could, returning these accounts to their owners when they needed them back.

This is the sort of 'thick' trust that is generally associated with close-knit communities enjoying intensive and daily contact (Kavanaugh et al., 2005; Diamond, 2012). While OTMT is a close-knit and relatively stable network, the network of participating users in the production of *WIA* was more ad hoc. In a world where both institutions and individuals are still grappling with identity-theft, particularly online (Sullins, 2006; Wang et al., 2006; Whitson and Haggerty, 2008), the high level of trust shown among the ad hoc user network in the co-production process is worth noting: it signals a 'we'-community or deme, which is another way of describing a culture.

The success of Corndog is the success of OTMT and the user community beyond. The production of the famous video is based on effective communication and interaction among and beyond the group of OTMT. Thus not only the video but also Corndog himself are creative *products of* that community, originating not in the talent of Corndog himself, or that of any other single individual. What follows is another co-creative process that is embedded in co-production of videos, and cultures: the co-creation of identities.

Identity performance, creativity and the rise of Jiaoshou

Part of the experience of 'liquid modernity' (Bauman, 2000), an age when 'uncertainty, flux, change, conflict, and revolution are the permanent conditions of everyday life' (Deuze, 2008), is the transient nature of identity and the disorientation of the self. As Sean Redmond (2010) observes,

> The body and mind have been rendered borderless and open, on a more apocalyptic note, to invasion and continual disorientation. The self in one reality, one time zone, with one set of spatial coordinates has been torn asunder.

The ubiquity of virtual networks afforded by advances in information technologies, however, has at the same time facilitated the 'shape-shifting' of identities, affording us the opportunity to formulate 'decentered and multiple' identities (Turkle, 1997), and to produce and distribute 'copies' of ourselves (Senft, 2008). In this process of identity redefinition and re-creation (Butler, 1990), the individual doesn't necessarily need to be the disenfranchised object suffering from 'a traumatic sense of fear' (Redmond, 2010). Rather, as we will show in the case of Jiaoshou, they can negotiate and experiment with multiple identities among the groups in which they are embedded. This process is not a lone journey, more of a group adventure, where not only individuals but also groups around them rediscover or *remake themselves.*

Jiaoshou's real name is Yi Zhenxing. The online Jiaoshou was once called *Stupid Dad,* an innocuous term in a local dialect of Hunan. His first video was a video-game commentary, in which he called himself a professor-class game commentator. He then played with the word 'professor' and made a series of game videos in the name of Jiaoshou, literally 'shouting beast', homophonic in Chinese with the word 'professor'.[24] Jiaoshou was adopted as a username to replace Stupid Dad in mid-2008, for two reasons: he didn't want his ID to sound as though he was taking advantage of other internet users; and, more importantly, users preferred to call him Jiaoshou (2010). In this sense, Jiaoshou is a user-co-created name.

Jiaoshou is famous not only for his videos, but also for the signature mask he wears whenever he is shown online. The mask is also a co-creation.

In co-author Li's interview with him, Jiaoshou acknowledged that he had drawn upon a funny comic series by *Ludougao* (literally Green Bean Cake) for the mask. The series, known as 'face paralysis', attracted a large following and became a fad among internet users in early 2007.[25] Although there had been popular video bloggers in Japan and Shanghai wearing animal masks or medical masks, he was the first video creator to adopt a paper mask (interview with Li, 2010).

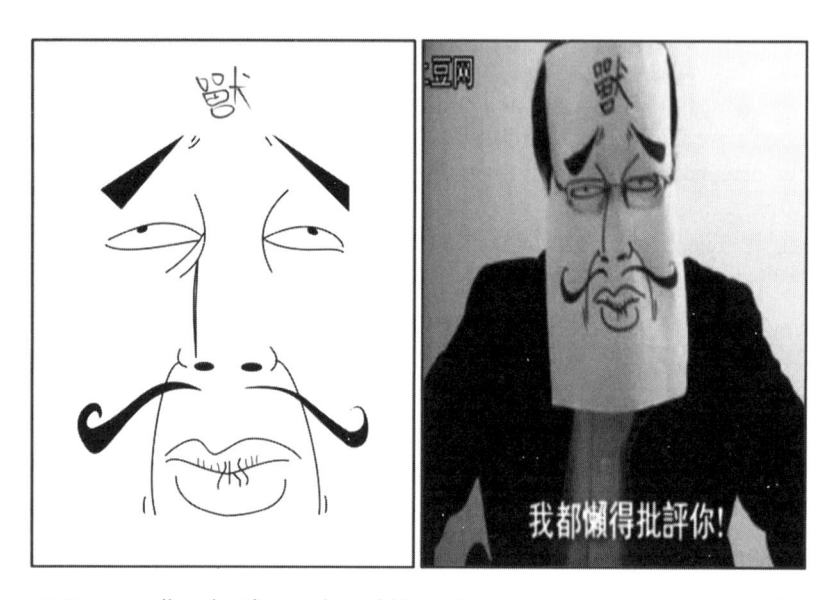

FIGURE 7.1 Jiaoshou's mask and his online avatar. The character on the mask is 'beast' and the line reads: 'I can't even be bothered to tell you off'

Jiaoshou has multiple identities. He is at once a popular video creator and a persona in the videos he creates. By this Jiaoshou has become an avatar, a 'performed character' not limited to a fixed corporeal self (Goffman, 1971). He can be both and one at the same time, speaking to and connecting with users across age, educational and cultural boundaries, though users don't need to make distinctions between these two identities. To a certain extent, the identities have afforded a 'third space' (Winnicott, 1971) for Jiaoshou and his fan-users, a space where reality is intermingled with fantasy, making possible multiple modes of interactions. When asked about his purpose behind these multiple identities, he said:

> Well, [Charlie] Chaplin was a movie-maker and actor at the same time; he was at once the clown with a moustache on the screen, the director with a loud-hailer in his hands, and the grey-haired old man off the screen. Multiple identities are very common ... for people with a strong sense of self-presentation ... For me, my main purpose is to build my own brand, my own identity. I want my audience to recognise my videos at first sight.

> So I have tried to be consistent with my mask. Even if I (the video creator) am absent from the video, I want (the persona) to be there. (interview with Li, 2010)

In what follows we discuss how Jiaoshou has negotiated these identities, and maintained the balance between the online and offline, private and public aspects of these identities through his interaction with users.

Masquerading and group-making

As Lawler (2008) observes, it is an old and widespread theme in storytelling that we need to wear a mask to show our true selves. Jiaoshou wears two masks: the facial mask he uses as part of his online avatar; and the other, invisible mask which he – as well as anybody else – wears to project a more favourable self-image. According to Erving Goffman, that mask or, rather, masquerade, is what makes us as we are socially. In *The Presentation of Self in Everyday Life*, Goffman compared identity to theatrical performance, during which actors tailor self-presentation to foster favourable impressions based on audience and context. The self and identity emerging out of this process is 'a product of the scene that comes off' (1971: 245), a project of collaboration and interaction between the performer and his audience. Thus identity is inherently a group production and product.

Terri Senft (2008) has conceptualised identity formation in the internet space in a Goffmanian fashion. She proposes to approach it through the lens of 'micro-celebrity', which she defines as a style of performance that 'involves people "amping up" their popularity over the Web using techniques like video, blogs, and social networking sites' (Senft, 2008). These techniques are 'strategically' *interactive* in nature, because, as she observes, 'On the Web, popularity depends upon a connection to one's audience, rather than an enforced separation from them' (2008: 26). Thus in the online setting, as in the offline world, identity performance is a *group act*, a collaborative, interactive and continual process, constantly co-creating and re-creating at the same time. It is conducted on multiple platforms (SNS, blogs, BBS, etc.), and by various means (textual, visual, audio, etc.).

Jiaoshou knows very well the importance of connecting with his users. He has tried to build a sense of 'ambient affiliation' (Zappavigna, 2011),[26] togetherness and co-ownership with his users, making them part of the creative process and appealing to shared experience with them. In his acceptance speech for 'the Most Popular Blogger' in the 2009 Tudou Video Festival, he acknowledged users as essential to his creativity: 'Were it not for you, I would not have bothered to make videos'.[27] Indeed, Jiaoshou doesn't make videos for his audience, he makes videos *with* them. He has a good sense of how 'new media' works and has invited his audience to participate in the creative process:

> I place great emphasis on communicating with fellow internet users, and I take their opinions seriously. I think this is the biggest difference between old and new media. I constantly adjust my production according to the majority opinion of my audience. (interview with Li, 2010)

As his connection with his users and his identity performance are enacted and reinforced through co-creative storytelling, Jiaoshou has consciously and conscientiously chosen the right formats to tell the right stories. As he says,

> As you can see in my videos I use some anime footage from mid-1980s classics, some from post-2000s popular ones. My purpose is to invoke the nostalgia of the post-1980ers and appeal to the novelty craze of the post-2000ers at the same time. My fans are generally in the age group of 14–24. I choose this footage on purpose, partly to accommodate my audience, and partly to entertain my own interests. (interview with Li, 2010)

Jiaoshou also communicates with users on multiple social-media platforms. He calls himself 'Pope of Vulsar' (猥琐教主, literally 'Pope of the Religion of the Vulgar'), a group with a sizeable membership on mop.com.[28] He has a video-blog with tudou.com that is constantly updated.[29] He posts his new videos there, shares stories behind and beyond those videos, and constantly communicates his new plans and new ideas to users. He has a blog with sina.com, largely to share and recommend videos by others,[30] a BBS on Baidu.com initiated, maintained and populated by his user-fans,[31] and his own website that integrates all these links.[32] These platforms are interfaces between Jiaoshou and his users, and among users themselves. Since some of the users are active across platforms, stories and ideas posted on one platform are quickly shared and distributed among the whole network of interested users.

As instant messaging tools can't accommodate group talk among big teams, Jiaoshou has turned to 'web chat' (版聊) to communicate at once with large groups of fan-users. He uses the commenting function of blogs and BBS to conduct these group talks irregularly at the request of users (interview with Li, 2010). He usually posts a notice on the time and venue of the chat before it happens. The chat we observed happened on his Sina blog in late April 2010.[33] After the chat started, substantive content was relayed to his Baidu forum simultaneously by interested users,[34] where comments were exchanged on the chat. The chat lasted about 2 hours and generated 800 posts at the blog. Among these 800 posts more than 300 were relayed to the Baidu forum.

These posts, mostly casual talk and gossip, serve an important social function by being 'community-constituting' (Baym, 2000), reinforcing connections and social bonds; as Li Shubo (2010) observes they 'play an important role in building up trust and a shared common sense within online communities.' Moreover, when these chats and comments are shared across platforms, they become archived information accessible to users both present and absent,[35] thus helping to create an ambience of 'connected presence' (Licoppe, 2004), or 'presence-in-absence' (Howard et al., 2006), among distributed user-fans and so contributing to a feeling of shared experience and collective identity. As Lisbeth Lipari observes, 'We become one when we listen together – to the voices of god, to a singer, to a speaker, to the wind blowing through the trees… Thus, in listening, we *become*' (Lipari, 2010, original emphasis).

Of course, shared collective experience is shaped and formed not only by means of chats and video formats, it is also, and maybe more importantly, done through the content of the videos themselves. After all, the users are attracted to Jiaoshou in the first place because his videos make them laugh, and think, as is attested in messages left by users:

> Hi, I am a 90er from Taiwan. Your videos can really take away people's stress. Hope to see more of them, Jiaoshou. (lineage205ph, a Taiwanese user)…

> Really the works of Jiaoshou are deep and profound … he doesn't want to show that because that would appear shallow … I hope we don't stop at the vulgar look of his videos … I have just blurted out my feelings. Ha-ha. Jiaoshou is matchless.[36]

The Shouting Beast beyond Jiaoshou

The multiplicity of Jiaoshou's identity has made it possible for him to become independent of a corporeal self and to become a symbol and character. Two markers of this independence are the fan journal featuring Jiaoshou and the commodification of his facial mask.

In May 2009, an ad was posted for the sale of a Jiaoshou facial mask in a BBS of Jiaxing, a city in the highly successful commercial province of Zhejiang. The ad reads, 'Facial mask of Cyber-celebrity Jiaoshou for sale, professionally made'. The seller quoted ¥5 RMB per mask and provided a delivery service for local customers.[37] It is impossible to know the number of masks sold, or even whether the ad itself is a spoof or a truly smart business plan. However, the very idea that Jiaoshou can be a sellable product shows that Jiaoshou as a character can stand on its own, more of the persona who pops out in the spoof videos to tell people off than the person who creates these videos. Here identity formation and production, usually regarded as a *cultural process*, becomes a conspicuously *economic activity*.

Jiaoshou as a stand-alone persona is more outstanding in a fan-created comic journal called *Jiaoshou Weekly* (see Figure 7.2). Edited by a user called 'the King whose ID gets blocked' (被封号的国王, hereafter *King*), the journal was a fan co-creation. *King* set up several QQ groups, such as the Comic Group, the PS group, and the GIF group, to solicit ideas and enlist help. Unlike Corndog's QQ group for his gated community, *King*'s QQ groups were open to any interested fans. The journal had an official website,[38] which spoofs the news agency Reuters and calls itself *Toulushe* (透露社, literally *Disclosure Agency* – it is the Chinese translation of Reuters read backwards). The journal was not published on a regular basis and only three issues are available. *King* has cited censorship for the dysfunction.

FIGURE 7.2 Cover pages of *Jiaoshou Weekly*[39]

The three issues of the journal have roughly the same structure, including columns such as Genesis, Special Report and Shout Weekly. At the beginning of each issue there is a statement claiming that the journal is authorised by Jiaoshou, though Jiaoshou himself admitted not knowing *King* well, having only chatted with him several times online (interview with Li, 2010). In the journal, Jiaoshou becomes a comic character born out of an egg, an omnipotent manga icon that spices his talk with profanity, fights all evils and ignores all established social norms. In issue three, this persona even fights *Kongfu Bunny*, a comic character created by Vincent, a lecturer and an anime professional at the Communication University of China. The journal also incorporated in its offerings new developments in the Chinese cyberspace and commented on social issues through the comic Jiaoshou. On the cover page of the second issue, the two animals leading the Santa Claus sleigh are not reindeers, but Grass-Mud-Horses (see Wikipedia), a legendary animal created by internet users to mock government talk and vent frustration caused by censorship.

In the editorial of the second issue, the creators complained about censorship and included a page showing the grave of *Toulushe* (see Figure 7.3). The epitaph reads: 'Harmonise your harmony, but don't be harmonised by harmony. Buried here are comrades from *Toulushe*'.[40] After burial, the group created the third issue in February 2010, and that seems to have been the end of the journal. Although short-lived, it is significant as a cultural creation. If the activities of Jiaoshou the spoof creator connect him to 'personal branding' (Marwick and boyd, 2011) and 'micro-celebrity' promotion (Senft, 2008), where social media are employed to assure immediate and proximate access to personal information, private thought, mundane routines as well as the spectacular activities of the would-be celebrity, then the creation of Jiaoshou as a comic character by his fan-users, while it confirms the effectiveness of Jiaoshou's strategy, is a process of negotiation and co-ownership, and an initiative of active participation, appropriation and re-creation. It is act of *co-branding* and *wiki-celebrity,* where users apply social media and digital technologies to co-create a pop icon by and of themselves. Everybody can participate and tweak it the way they like, and own it. Jiaoshou and the co-created journal provide a glimpse not only into the ways that spoofing culture emerges and grows, but also, more broadly, into how creativity and innovation take place: how ideas come into being and travel, how they are modified by experimentation and tweaking, and how they are accepted or rejected, renewed and retained, to start a new cycle of dissemination and innovation.

FIGURE 7.3   The tombstone of *Toulushe* (Disclosure Agency)

Collaborative creativity and the scaling-up of microproductivity

Like Corndog, Jiaoshou represents the figure of 'everyone' in the sense that he is a DIY creator, using affordances to hand, rather than a trained professional or authority. However, as we have tried to illustrate, the co-production of his identity in social networks demonstrates that 'everyone' is not a solitary or self-sufficient figure (or entrepreneur in waiting), but an outcome of 'we' groups in communicative interaction. 'Everyone', then, is a social-network or system concept, not one based on the 'possessive individualism' of Western philosophy (Macpherson, 1962). We have elaborated on the communicative strategies and group-making practices of Corndog and Jiaoshou with a view to driving home (with micro-level examples) two of the main points of this book: (1) culture (identity, meaningfulness, sociality) is a process of group-creating communication, and (2) creative productivity (which can also be called knowledge) is the outcome of that commutative process. Thus, the extension of tools for group-communication and creative productivity to encompass whole populations, via the internet, digital media and social networks, creates an entirely new dynamic for cultural, communicative and creative systems in general, and thus for the growth of knowledge. Now, culture, creativity and knowledge can be made, distributed and innovated by anyone, anywhere in the system, not just by organised agencies like firms, authorities or agencies. Thus innovation or experimentation can originate anywhere in the system. In principle (assuming access), anyone can join in, but not as free agents; only within the rules, connections and capabilities offered by the system and institutionalised clusters within it.

Neither Corndog nor Jiaoshou were media experts; however, through the participation of and interaction with peer users they became heroes among online communities and have created productions as popular as, if not more than, those of media professionals. They are what their groups have made them. Although the groups of Corndog and Jiaoshou are different from each other, they do share properties typical of the new modality of cultural production, or what Yochai Benkler calls 'commons-based peer production' (2006), made possible by advances in communicative technologies: collaborative and non-proprietary, based on sharing rather than competition; distributed, decentralised and autonomous, relying on self-organisation rather than market signals or managerial commands.

The democratisation of production and the scaling up of the microproductivity of 'everyday' users can take many forms. Though on the surface chaotic, the process generates 'heroes' such as Corndog and Jiaoshou, and grows and sustains big companies such as YouTube and Tudou Youku. Even more important, it contributes to the formation of a knowledge-space where the costs of and barriers to entry are radically lowered for the majority of people alive today, to include unprecedented numbers of contributors. If, instead of leaving it to trained elites (expert pipelines controlled by firms, IP law, etc.) *everyone* plays a part in boosting the growth of knowledge, and its more efficient distribution and uptake, then this is surely a new or emergent phase in creative productivity – a phase where knowledge, the noösphere, becomes a planetary force. This is what we mean by 'everyone'.

In *Collective Intelligence* (1997), Pierre Levy imagined an intricate connected, all-encompassing knowledge space for all of humanity, where a community of researchers, thinkers and artists would search, explore, connect and consult. It is a space at once universal, pluralistic, collaborative and evolving. This imaginative space is indeed taking shape, we argue, except that it is not reserved for those 'researchers, thinkers and artists' as separate professions, but for each and every one of us, acting (from time to time) *as* researchers, thinkers, artists … and as entrepreneurs, teachers, mediators, scientists and investors (crowd-funding), etc. This space is at the same time a social network market (Potts et al., 2008), where new ideas and innovations are mooted, made and marketed, and one where 'clouds' of expertise and debates are formed and interact, and campaigns launched (Leadbeater, 2010).

Notes

1. Bill Gates (October 1999) 'Everyone, Anytime, Anywhere: The next step for technology is universal access'. Available at: www.microsoft.com/presspass/ofnote/10-04forbes.mspx.
2. See http://lists.wikimedia.org/pipermail/wikipedia-l/2005-March/020469.html.
3. The videos are available at www.youtube.com/watch?v=3i_9Ildo610 and www.youtube.com/watch?v=tIrqMgIRi7k&feature=related.
4. Flash discs were formidably expensive and without enough storage capacity for the videos.
5. Jiaoshou, literally 'shouting beast', is homophonic with 'professor' in Chinese. It is often used online to refer to university teachers, an indication of the damaged reputation of the whole university sector, not least because of academic and moral corruption. This kind of wordplay is commonplace in the cyberspace of China.
6. Co-author Li interviewed Jiaoshou in 2010. Further references to this interview are noted in the text.
7. See www.tudou.com/home/user_viewDiary.php?vlog_id=1448715.
8. For the live video of the prize awarding ceremony and Corndog's acceptance speech, visit: www.tudou.com/programs/view/0BfPzP5VMIw/.
9. The ad series is available at www.tudou.com/programs/view/zePGKI5bCOc/.
10. More information is available in a report on Unimedia: Totally Unexpected, at http://renwu.people.com.cn/n/2014/0729/c357679-25362229.html.
11. The video is available at www.tudou.com/programs/view/qe-lW8lffVY/. YouTube has a version with subtitles at www.youtube.com/watch?v=emVhTjBYchs.
12. WoW is a massively multiplayer online game developed by Blizzard Entertainment. The game entered China in 2005. For more information, visit its official site at www.worldofwarcraft.com/info/beginners/index.html.

13. With more than two million users NGA (http://bbs.ngacn.cc/) is more popular in China than the official WoW site. It was incorporated in 2009 into 178.com, a game portal based in Beijing.
14. The interview was conducted by Henry Siling Li on 16 March 2010, with Skype voice functionality.
15. Corndog was interviewed by co-author Li in 2010. Further references to this interview are noted in the text.
16. The other two videos, are *The Song of Skeleton Party* (骷髅党之歌) at www.tudou.com/programs/view/_iBhnbCfW3g/, and *To be Released on Another Day* (择日再) at www.tudou.com/programs/view/dTDyF1M-st4k/. Corndog has a video blog on Tudou.com where videos by the group and Corndog himself are posted, at www.tudou.com/home/item_u13680759s0p1.html.
17. See: www.tudou.com/programs/view/_iBhnbCfW3g/. Skeleton Party is a term in NGA forum that refers to users disciplined by webmasters. According to the rules of the forum, rule-breakers lose reputation points and users with a reputation point below zero lose their avatar and get a generic skeleton. The rules, however, are largely at the discretion of webmasters. As a result their rulings are very arbitrary. *Song of the Skeleton Party* is a video of ridicule and self-amusement.
18. ID in NGA forum: Ryan, 1942.
19. Tauren is a race in the WoW game. For more information about it visit www.wowwiki.com/Tauren. Kannimei, literally 'look at your sister', is a name of an ID on NGA forum. It can also be used as a curse.
20. Lu Qiuluwei's (2010) interview with Corndog [in Chinese]. Available at http://blog.sina.com.cn/s/blog_46e9d5da0100h9zo.html. The television interview is available from Phoenix TV, at http://v.ifeng.com/society/201001/e433c136-a77f-4381-a62a-3dba4b418b7d.shtml. In the interview, Corndog's opinion was read out by a presenter from Phoenix TV because he was very fearful of being hunted down by the authorities, and thought it better to remain anonymous.
21. According to Anne-Mette Albrechtslund (2010), guilds are player-generated teams and they 'vary greatly in size, ambition, and demographics'. 'Guilds have a leader and, usually, officers who have the authority to decide on important issues such as the recruitment and eviction of members. Often, guilds explicitly label themselves after their preferred playing style, such as raiding guilds, casual guilds or role-playing guilds'.
22. Music featured in the video includes *Ain't No Rest for the Wicked* by the American rock band Cage the Elephant; *Maybe I Love You* by Girlfriend; and a cover version of Karen Mok's *All of a Sudden*, by Catherine Linlin (www.yyfc.com/1771771/), who is a WoW gamer and an acclaimed cover singer in the game community. Both Loveqiaolin (www.tudou.com/home/loveqiaolin) and babymavis (www.tudou.com/home/_3944055)

are popular v-bloggers; tnnaii (http://u.youku.com/user_show/id_UMTQ4MzgxNTky.html) is a character voice talent.
23. Banyun⑨Ke has a video list on Tudou.com at www.tudou.com/playlist/id/7240262/.
24. It should be noted that 'shouting beast' circulated on the internet as a derogatory term to refer to university teachers long before it was adopted by Jiaoshou as his user ID.
25. *Ludougao* has a blog (http://blog.sina.com.cn/lvdougao) where a lot of similar funny comic pictures are available. The 'paralysis' series is available in many forums and BBS, for example, at http://tieba.baidu.com/f?kz=370949019, and http://dzh.mop.com/topic/readSub_7888162_0_0.html.
26. Leisa Reichelt (2007) uses a similar term, 'ambient intimacy', to refer to this type of bonding. She explains, 'Ambient intimacy is being able to keep in touch with people with a level of regularity and intimacy that you wouldn't usually have access to, because time and space conspire to make it impossible': www.disambiguity.com/ambient-intimacy/.
27. The speech is accessible online at www.tudou.com/programs/view/p4h68mr7oVs/.
28. According to Jiaoshou, Vulsar is one of the biggest groups on mop.com. Formed around 2002–3, the group is still affiliated to mop.com but has also established its own website at www.vulsar.com/vcode.htm. 'Vulsar' sounds similar to the Chinese word for 'vulgar'. It is common on the net in China to playfully call a group, a belief, or a pattern of behaviour a 'religion' (教). For example, Li Yuchun, the winner of the 2005 Super Girl talent show, jokingly called 'Brother Chun' on the net, is spoofed as the Pope of 'the Religion of Brother Chun'. A lot of stories have appeared online as to the omnipotence of 'Brother Chun', of which the catch phrase is, 'Believe in Brother Chun and become immortal'. They even have versions of the 'religion' in different languages (www.hudong.com/wiki/%E6%98%A5%E5%93%A5%E6%95%99).
29. www.tudou.com/home/yzx119/.
30. http://blog.sina.com.cn/jiaoshouxiaoxing.
31. http://tieba.baidu.com/f?kw=蠢爸爸.
32. www.jiaoshoutv.com/.
33. See http://blog.sina.com.cn/s/blog_64d63a8c0100ifh5.html.
34. Visit Chunbaba Forum on Baidu at http://tieba.baidu.com/f?z=756066150&ct=335544320&lm=0&sc=0&rn=30&tn=baiduPostBrowser&word=%B4%C0%B0%D6%B0%D6&pn=0.
35. In the Baidu forum, users are constantly advised to refer to archived chats for information.
36. Quotations are taken from the comments area at Jiaoshou's tudou.com blog at http://www.tudou.com/home/yzx119#comment_area.
37. See the ad at http://bbs.sogou.com/179396/elbbGEWIt8VIBAAAA.html.

38. See http://www.tlshe.com/.
39. The three issues of *Jiaoshou Weekly* are available respectively at http://tieba.baidu.com/f?kz=681022052 (issue 1); http://tieba.baidu.com/f?kz=685630038 (Issue 2); and http://tieba.baidu.com/f?kz=707741349 (Issue 3).
40. As shown in the picture, the epitaph is in Chinese:'和谐你的和谐,不要被和谐所和谐'. The translation is by H.S. Li.

EVERYTHING

8

ECONOMY (1) MAKERS

> WILLIAM MORRIS, the father of the Arts and Crafts movement that briefly flowered in the late 19th century, would have approved of Etsy.
>
> (The Economist, 2014)[1]

Creative communities – demic microproductivity

This chapter, and the following one on 'scenes', addresses – in order to extend – a familiar issue in the study of creativity, namely the question of whether there is a specific 'creative industries' sector, or whether creativity should be understood as belonging to the whole 'creative economy', i.e. to 'everything'. Our position, as explained in the first few chapters of this book, is to expand the concept of creativity, not only across the economy, but also further than that to include culture as well, but to keep the two connected by conceptualising culture as a source of newness, a site of microproductivity and group-made knowledge (via social networks), and thence an important influence on economic life; just as economic values are an important influence on cultural life. In this situation the question doesn't need to be resolved, because creativity is produced along the edge of these two systems as they grate against each other, continually, as a dynamic process that links meaningfulness and money (cultural and economic values) among very large-scale groups. The question of where the creative sector extends *within* the economy only arises if 'creativity' is first reduced to one of two things: either an *output* of an industry (value generated from intellectual property), or an *input* into many industries (a professional occupation or skill that adds value to existing economic enterprises on a service-delivery basis). We don't think either of these propositions does justice to the concept of creativity that we derive from our approach to culture as a source of newness. In this conceptualisation, creativity is a kind of irritant that generates novelties along the clashing border between culture and economy, along the edges of dynamically interacting systems (culture and economy), such that these new ideas become candidates for adoption and thus innovation. In this conceptualisation, the 'creative industries' or 'creative economy' are those where *innovation is the output* (Potts, n.d.).

Thus we do not confine our economic interest to the *ownership* of creativity. We do not see it as a property belonging to firms or to long-trained artists and specialist producers. Instead, we see it as systemic: it can belong to anything and everything that is made or traded. Creativity can be found wherever production occurs. If its output is innovation, it's a stimulant to any industry. Many firms and sectors have begun to prioritise 'design thinking' or 'creative innovation' in order to benefit from it. Many traditional industries employ 'creative' personnel to signal their 'newness' in new ways. Further, this trend is not confined to advanced economies; these same influences can be discerned in the common culture of both affluent and developing countries, in the use of technologies and networks for 'vernacular' creativity (Burgess, 2006).

Quite clearly, creative, aesthetic, cultural and mediated values intersect directly with technological, engineering or manufacturing processes, and with the delivery of services. The design of aeroplanes and cars, of phones and computers, of holidays and education, cannot be understood without recognising the *economic* importance of creativity and culture. It works both ways: Samsung and Apple (whose products are stuffed full of clever technology) are well known to have flown high on the wings of design; while the Airbus A380 – the world's largest passenger airliner – 'looks good' because it's well engineered. Services like tourism tend increasingly to be tailored to lifestyle, where a beautiful experience – or an extreme one – is more important than the lowest cost.

Another way of tracking the mutuality of creative industries and the rest of the economy is to observe that many creative occupations (writers, artists, filmmakers, designers, etc.) work directly for 'non-creative' organisations – government departments, transport services and the like, not just for media companies or architectural practices (see Cunningham and Higgs, 2008, 2009; Hartley et al., 2013). Indeed, many policy professionals promote 'creativity' as a necessary ingredient for bringing underperforming companies out of the doldrums, noting that innovation is often sadly lacking in well-established firms, even those that know what they're doing and do it well, because they are apt to find that some upstart has overtaken them and the market has changed beyond their capacity to serve it. In this sense, then, the whole economy must indeed be understood as creative, because not to do so will lead to the extinction of those who fall behind – those who don't produce innovation as an output.

However, as we have argued, this is not the whole story. There is an even larger context in which it is important to consider creativity's economic significance. Current cultural and creative policy is (quite properly) focused on *firms* – the smallest unit of analysis in economics. Apart from the choices they make as consumers or entrepreneurs, individuals don't 'count' in economics (they're too 'micro'); and nor do large-scale systems. Sociality and culture are beyond its scope (they're too 'macro'). The way that people clump into groups, what they do with their time, with each other, and with the 'affordances' of contemporary urban life, is not thought to be *productive* in economic terms. Large, disorganised, uncoordinated social groups are 'dark matter' for economics – everyone knows that they're there, but the analytic apparatus that's designed for identifying firms simply can't 'find' them.

This doesn't pose a problem when there is a clear distinction between producers (professionals, experts, specialists, in firms or other institutional agencies) on the one hand, and consumers (amateur, inexpert, unfocused, unorganised) on the other. Since the emergence of ubiquitous digital technologies, the internet, social networks and DIY culture, however, it has become clear that this distinction is under attrition. Consumers are also producers and users. What they make or say is not necessarily 'professional' in the sense that it is done according to a trained procedure and intended for sale, but it may nevertheless be just as creative as anything produced by a high-investment studio. Furthermore, those clumps or groups of otherwise uncoordinated agents can now be 'mapped' as 'social networks', which themselves – as groups – are productive of new knowledge, new ideas and applications.

Doubtless this has always been the case, but the emergence of trackable 'big data' has meant that what people make, do and say for themselves can at last be 'seen' – both by policy analysts and by existing firms. Naturally, there's a scramble among incumbent organisations to exploit this new source of knowledge, but that's not where this chapter is heading.

Instead, we return to the question of how 'everyone' (as characterised in the last chapter) is *productive*, and how that may be directly significant for the economy, not simply by leaving a clickstream or other trace that can be exploited by 'big-data' miners, but also for what users create for themselves, and in concert with others.

The implication is that the boundary of what counts as 'the economy' needs to be extended. There is practical good sense in thinking seriously about this. As we've mentioned, among the most important economic 'outputs' of the times is innovation. But what is the *source* of innovation? Many economists (Herrmann-Pillath, 2010; Hutter et al., 2010; Potts, 2011) recognise that the 'source of newness' is culture, and that innovations come from the *uses* of new ideas whencesoever they may be sourced, not just from corporate labs and think tanks.

Both informal social networks ('connectivity') and user-created content (consumer co-creation) can generate innovation, and because there are billions more users than there are firms, the ground from which new ideas can emerge is radically extended (Banks and Deuze, 2009; Gauntlett, 2011). It is well known that certain innovations came from consumers and users rather than from design studios or developers. Texting is a classic example (invented by impecunious teen users not phone manufacturers). Computer games rely on elite gamers to test and refine their products, resulting in co-created games (Banks, 2013). Creative productivity can be scaled up, straight from the inventor's garage, coffee shop or bedroom to a global market of billions. This is familiar in creative writing, where someone can be an unemployed single mother living off benefits one day, and J.K. Rowling the next. It is also familiar (although somewhat mythologised) in the tech sector, where a clever algorithm, app or device can be a student doodle this week and a global corporation next.

Thus the question of whether the 'whole economy' is creative is not really the right question, if what is understood by 'the' economy is not revised. The whole economy includes the *microproductivity* of millions, potentially billions, whose actions and efforts, ideas and applications, which would once have been discounted, are now an important source of creativity, newness and innovation. As far as the economic potential of creativity goes, '*everything*' ranges across a wide range of players, including those who are creatively active but not 'in it for the money', thereby adding community and social enterprise to economic calculation. This is especially important in directly creative pursuits, where self-expression, community identity or solidarity, and social connectedness are at a premium: people crave meaningfulness, attention and approval as part of well-being, so 'semiotic affluence' (Sahlins, 1974)[2] and 'the economy of attention' (Lanham, 2006) are just as important as wealth-creation.

The remainder of this chapter, together with the following one on 'scenes', sets off in pursuit of some grounded examples of creative activity that link 'everyone' with 'everything' – everyone understood as 'makers', and 'the economy' understood as 'scenes'. The take-out message is that cooperative creativity pervades society (Sennett, 2012) when productivity is DIY (makers) and when symbolic or meaningful connectedness is directly expressed (scenes).

The 'Year of the Maker'

'Maker culture' is probably as old as humanity. It persists (without being labelled as such) in the home, on the street corner, in hobbies and play, in workshops and in the garage or shed. But it has gained a contemporary dimension, amounting to a 'Maker Movement', in recent years. This innovation can be traced back to Apple co-founder Steve Wozniak, who built a little blue box for making free calls after reading an article about a device that could crack phone networks. The DIY ethos became widespread among US West Coast garages – the legendary home of the start-up tech company. It has even been celebrated in fiction, in Cory Doctorow's (2009) novel *Makers*, a science fiction story that, he says, 'predicts the present'.[3]

The 'maker movement' idea was captured by *Make Magazine*, launched in 2005 to 'celebrate your right to tweak, hack and bend any technology to your will'.[4] Later on, that magazine launched a public annual event, the Maker Faire, as further celebration of 'arts, crafts, engineering, science projects and the Do-It-Yourself (DIY) mindset'.[5] The first Maker Faire was held in San Mateo, California, in 2006 to provide a stage for makers in America to exhibit their work, exchange ideas and seek business opportunities and partners. In the same year, the open-source hardware *Arduino* was born, which was designed to make interactive objects or environments more accessible. This was a real curtain raiser for the maker movement. The Maker Faire has also grown into a global movement with thousands of enthusiasts gathering to present their creations and to share new techniques (see Figure 8.1). In 2013, there were 100 Maker Faires held all over the world. The 2013 'Flagship Faire' in New York hosted 650 stalls and attracted a crowd of 75,000 people. So-called 'Featured Faires' were produced in collaboration with *Make* magazine in Detroit, Kansas City, Newcastle (UK), Rome and Tokyo. Nevertheless the best part of the story must be the 93 local 'Mini Maker Faires', based on local communities at smaller scale.[6]

The USA is still the biggest host of the Maker Faire. In February 2014, the White House announced that its own first-ever Maker Faire would be held there later in that year, which indicated a 'clearest sign yet that this is a trend that has advanced beyond the insular world of geeks and tinkerers and has made it to the most hallowed halls on the planet'.[7] Europe is the place where the Faire is growing most rapidly: the number increased from 5 to 20 in 2013. The biggest one, held in Rome, attracted 200 makers and 35,000 visitors. The frenzy has also travelled to South America (Santiago), Australia (Adelaide and Sydney) and Asia (Jerusalem, Seoul, Tokyo, Taipei, Hong Kong and Shenzhen). Dale Dougherty, one of the founders of Maker Faire, launching the first Maker Faire in Norway (January 2014), announced that this was the 'Year of the Maker'.[8]

Makers

Makers are defined by *Wired*'s Chris Anderson (2012) as groups of people using the internet and the newest industrial technologies to make individual manufacturing products. Sometimes they are also identified as tinkers, hobbyists, enthusiasts and amateurs. They engage in 'microproductivity', producing highly customised outputs in boutique quantities for a highly localised market – but using internet connectivity in such a way that a successful line can be scaled up to global quantities very quickly, or a technique not

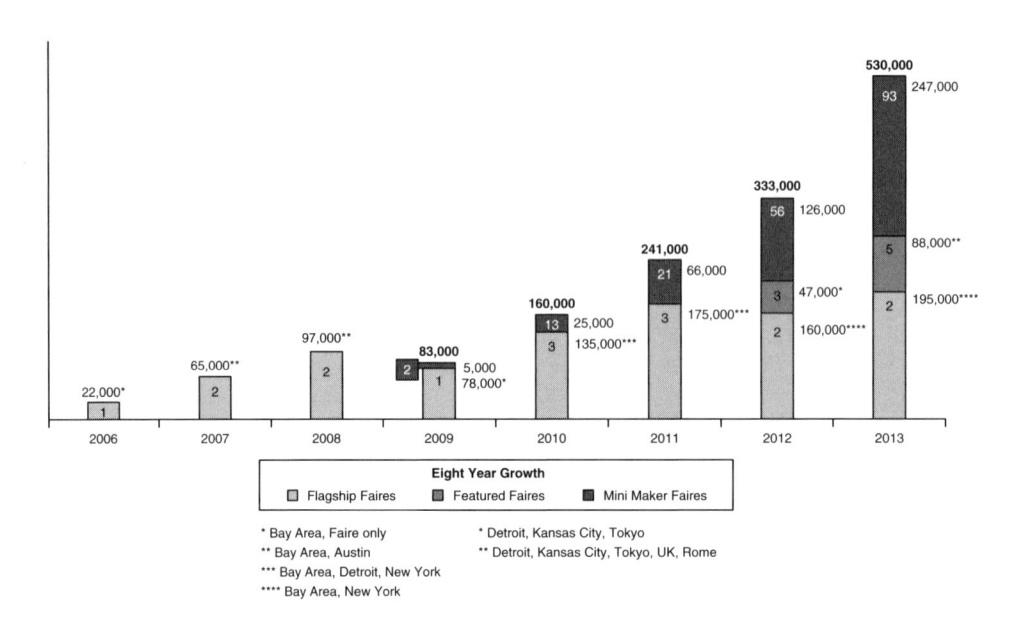

FIGURE 8.1 Growth of Maker Faires. Adapted from http://makerfaire.com/new-york-2015/call-for-makers/

available locally (say, 3-D printing in a precious metal) can be realised using assets that may be physically located on the other side of the world.

The two characteristics of makers, according to Anderson, are: (1) they usually make things combining software and hardware ('digital DIY'); (2) they are usually involved in an online community, sharing not only their stories of making, but also source code, prototype and copyright (open-source and 'DIWO' – Do It With Others).[9] Thereby, they are no longer lone inventors in a garage, but are connected to the web, i.e. to social networks and social network markets, which in turn become the engine for makers to participate in what Anderson sees as 'a new industrial revolution' (2012). His claim is not so far-fetched, if Joel Mokyr's analysis of the original Industrial Revolution is accurate. Mokyr (2009) argues that the reason why that process took off rapidly in Britain, before other countries, was because of the widespread presence of myriad anonymous craftsmen, engineers and artisans, who tweaked and tinkered with the headline inventions (steam power, etc.), finding innovative uses for them in specialised applications emanating from sheds up and down the land. In short, the Industrial Revolution itself was essentially a 'maker movement'.

Makers are different from the traditional image of inventors. Inventors seek radical innovation, and dedicate themselves to new technologies, materials and products, while makers often focus more on tweaking and spreading an existing technology or finding new applications. Their work is more likely to result in incremental innovation; the mission of the maker movement is to promote *wide participation in innovation*, and to bring new technologies to people's daily lives.[10]

From a broader point of view, the Maker Movement is not confined to technological tinkering. *Make* magazine includes categories of Crafts (sewing and knitting, etc.) and Art & Design. As Chris Anderson put it, the one who loves cooking is a maker in the kitchen, the one who loves gardening is a maker in the garden!

Makerspaces

In addition to Maker Faires, makerspaces (makerspace.com/), following the prototype of 'hackerspace', have mushroomed in cities. In fact, 14 out of the 100 Maker Faires have been sponsored by makerspaces, while others are sponsored by museums or libraries, which are running or supporting makerspaces.[11]

The first hackerspace, C-base, was founded in Berlin in 1995; along with Metalab founded in 1996 in Vienna. These European tech communities directly influenced the creation of hackerspaces in the USA. In 2006, Tech shop,[12] the first commercial chain of spaces, was launched there. Later, three more were launched in California, one each in Michigan, Texas, Arizona and Pennsylvania, and one each planned for Virginia and New York.

It is not always easy to tell the difference between hackerspaces and makerspaces nowadays, as the terms have begun to be used interchangeably. 'Hackerspace' once referred to the places where the DIY hobbyists could meet and share their experiences in using existing technologies to crack open the expensive, monopolised service resources; but now it is more likely to be 'a community-related physical space where people can meet and work on their projects'.[13] *Make* magazine rephrased it to 'makerspaces'; thus generalised, more than 1000 active makerspaces/hackerspaces have been recognised around the world, and the number is increasing. Universities, schools and libraries have followed the trend. As community resources, they have routinely offered workshops on arts and crafts activities, from paper cutting to model aeroplanes; some for children and others for adults. Now, they are augmenting this time-honoured function with a stronger technological focus. However, most makerspaces still grow from the grassroots, rather than from institutional providers, some staying in loosely organised tools- and space-sharing communities, while others develop new business models for sustainability and growth. The common thread is that they are all united in the mission to provide and improve access to knowledge, and they represent the 'democratisation of design, engineering, fabrication and education'.[14]

Lacking a personal garage means that sharing space and tools is even more important in China (although some might tinker in their apartments). China is not short of top-down (official or property-development) examples of 'creative clusters' or 'creative parks'. Some of these have been criticised for their empty buildings, lifeless environment and dull businesses, the product of zoning aimed at boosting property prices in the surrounding district – in short, that they are not creative at all. Nevertheless, China does boast successful clusters, including 798 Art District in Beijing, Tianzi Fang in Shanghai, and OCT Loft in Shenzhen.

Another good example is Shanghai's Xindanwei (literally meaning 'new work unit'), which offers office space, meeting rooms at reduced prices and a tutoring programme for start-up members. The trendy location (Xindanwei is located at Yongjia Rd in the French Concession area), the art deco style, the coolest cafés and workshops have made Xindanwei the darling of the 'creative class' and bourgeois citizen-shoppers alike. Since 2010, it has also recognised the trend towards micro-manufacturing facilitated by open-source networks, and has established a new category called 'xinshanzhai' or 'New Shanzhai' (the 'shanzhai' phenomenon is discussed in more detail on pages 114–15 below). The first workshop was co-organised with the then newly established XinCheJian ('New Workshop'), a non-profit organisation with a mission to support, create and promote physical computing, open-source hardware and the Internet of Things. Thereafter, XinCheJian has become the symbol of China's maker movement. Talks, workshops and demonstrations of new techniques are held in XinCheJian. It also organises members to participate in international competitions. To sustain its running costs, members pay ¥100 RMB ($16) monthly for using the space and tools, and workshops and tutorials cost ¥100-300 RMB ($16-48) with materials provided – so you can take your DIY work home. For instance, there was an Arduino Workshop for Beginners, and hands-on teaching of how to build an aquaponics system for fish and vegetables at home, etc. Wednesday nights are usually open to the public.

International figures have played a crucial role in initiating makerspaces like XinCheJian and Dim Sum Labs in Hong Kong.[15] Meanwhile, more home-grown makerspaces can be found in cities like Chaihuo in Shenzhen and Maxpace in Beijing.

Compared to fancy labs (like The Edge in Brisbane) and bourgeois (*xiaozi*) offices and cafés, which are the favourites of the creative economy, makerspaces are more likely to be a shelter for geeks, hobbyists and amateurs. Instead of a shiny or nostalgic look, makerspaces are often characterised by tools and electronic kit spread out on tables. They do not sponsor live music performance, or a poetry theme party, but they do organise DIY workshops and inspiring speeches on new techniques and entrepreneurship. It is a cosy community for makers. They may come from all walks of life, but they are united in one purposeful (demic) identity – makers.

The maker movement has sparked official interest in China. Not long after the opening of XinCheJian, the Shanghai government announced a plan to fund 100 'innovation houses' throughout the city. It was reported that six had opened by March 2013.[16] Similarly, in the USA, the Obama government planned to introduce makerspaces equipped with 3D printers and laser-cutting tools, etc. to 1000 schools and universities in the four years from 2012. Government agencies are involved in organising Maker Faires. For instance, the bureaus in charge of business in Anchorage, Louisville and McAllen in fact initiated their local Maker Faires, and many exhibitions are sponsored by government.[17] This indicates a new strategy of government to invest in innovation, with the hope that the next ground-breaking technology will emerge from one of the makerspaces.

Economics of making

The poster child of commercialising makerspaces, TechShop, posted (a symbolically numbered) *798 percent revenue growth* over three years (2009–12), and was named in *Inc. Magazine*'s 2013 list of the fastest-growing private companies.[18] TechShop's income comes mainly from two sources. One is a membership fee of $125 USD per week, raised from over 4000 registered members. The other is training fees. TechShop hosts over 150 courses per month, and charges $50–100 USD per course. Further income comes from selling tools and materials, and customised manufacturing services to individuals and small enterprises. TechShop calculates that a branch will reach a balanced budget when it owns 400–500 memberships. The first shop took 3 years to reach 600 members; the San Francisco branch took 8 months; the San Jose one took only 6 months; and the Detroit branch was *opened* with 500 members. According to the CEO Mark Hatch, each branch can support a maximum of 2000 members.

Even though such expansion is small beer when compared with global franchises like KFC and McDonald's, nevertheless it astonishes the world by hatching a series of successful projects and by attracting big-shot partners, such as the Ford Motor Company, Defense Advanced Research Projects Agency (DARPA), the US Department of Veterans Affairs, and AutoDesk. TechShop receives support from these entities because it provides diversified and advanced prototype tools to them, together with the chance to meet other makers and work together. DARPA encourages its funded R&D researchers to become members of TechShop so as to use their equipment and speed up the innovation process. Veterans Affairs purchased 2000 memberships with three courses each year to offer to veterans in need.[19]

Many other makerspaces have followed this gym-style approach, except that members may be more interactive with each other and seek cooperation. Most of the makerspaces are less commercialised and closer in style to a non-profit community. The fee charged by XinCheJian, for instance, 'can barely sustain its operation', so it says.

Some other micro-economic activities are taking place in the maker movement. For instance, the work of makers is for sale – all sorts of technological craft goods are displayed on the shelves. They can be purchased individually, or customised and ordered in batches. They can go to online shops, from general emporia like Amazon.com or Taobao.com to specialist professional outlets.

Thus, for instance, *Seeed Studio* not only founded a Chaihuo hackerspace to keep equipment and hold meet-ups and activities, but it also connected members and their products with other makers on its online platform.[20] The services it offers are in three categories: Bazaar, Propagate and Wish. *Bazaar* is the place where you can find designed module electronics for quick prototyping, small-scale projects and inventories of makers. Bazaar helps with sales. *Propagate* is a service to facilitate the manufacturing part of the hardware: makers send prototypes with manufacturing files, and the engineering team of Seeed will validate and integrate the design into small batch production lines. When the inventory is sold out, any profit will return to the maker after deducting manufacturing costs. *Wish* is the place where the popularity of a prototype or an idea is estimated by the vote of community – people can also comment on and even join a project.

The Seeed website is quite similar to a crowd-sourcing website, but on a smaller and focused scale. The dominant crowd-sourcing websites, such as Kickstarter, Pozible and Indiegogo, have become emblematic as a DIY and maker business model. Kickstarter is the world's largest funding platform for creative projects. With categories of arts, comic, fashion, music, film and TV, design, technology, publishing, and food, it is a dream studio of makers. In 2014, it announced: 'Thanks a billion!' – that is, a billion dollars had been raised via this website since its inauguration. It is not just about the money, of course. Posting a project in the website can also function as market research; meanwhile, makers can make contact with potential customers and form a trusting relationship before the product is produced, and they may get unexpected help from the 'audience'.

Some accuse Chinese makers of relating their work to money too directly. A more considerate comment would be to note that they are under too much pressure and 'they can't just enjoy making'.[21] Mr. Li, the co-founder of XinCheJian, said some of the best hackers in XinCheJian are 'second-generation rich' – because they do not need to worry about money. They are *economically* free to experiment.[22] But a majority of people (including local governments) think this is a real chance for entrepreneurship and, more seriously, for a new industrial revolution. Still, Eric Pan, founder of Chaihuo, believes that 'developing a culture where making can be fun is a key piece of the creative process that leads to commercial innovation'.[23]

Naturally, people can just enjoy making and make something exclusive, for their own use or for their loved ones. Thus, in January 2013, a news report attracted massive attention: a father (who was named 'King of Making'), working with a team over 18 months, made a mini-racing car for his boy. This car can reach 130km/h ... but of course the father set the limit at 5km/h. This is in the maker spirit, where, in Adrienne Jeffries' words: 'it is more about encouraging empowerment, that is, skill over money, building over buying and creation over consumption' (2013).

But at the same time it is not a crime for people to want to distribute their work widely, and to make a profit. Here, the economics of making spring from selling individual goods, small-scale production, larger orders and start-ups. Some makerspaces include a concurrent venture-capital fund. One, founded by Cyril Ebersweiler and Sean O'Sullivan, is called HAXLR8R.[24] It is an 'accelerator' for maker projects with a focus on manufacturing hardware devices. It offers a 111-day hatching programme twice a year to selected start-ups, with funding, office space and mentorship. In 2014 it was running cross-regionally between San Francisco, USA, and Shenzhen, China, merging maker creativity with open-source manufacturing, facilitated by the enormous number of mini factories in Shenzhen.

In addition, the economics of making is organised by *network*:

- First, networks enable makers to *make things*. They follow technological recipes based on open-source data, as well as sharing their own techniques and experiences. Thus, open-source hardware like Ardunio or Raspberry Pi, etc. is important.

- Second, making usually encourages *cross-boundary cooperation* across networks. Engineers can find an industrial designer to help with the look and ergonomic functions of their creations; they may also help the designers to make their blueprints into real products. This happens in makerspaces and in Maker Faire, where makers face a wider group of suppliers, potential customers and audiences.

- Finally, network is the platform of *crowd-sourcing*. Makers usually do not aim to replace the major manufacturers, but to complement them, offering more candidates for ideas and solutions.

Made in China 2.0 – *Shanzhai* as open-source innovation

The world centre of maker culture right now, other than the Bay Area, is Shenzhen.

(Tom Grec, Dim Sum Labs member)[25]

Somehow, Shenzhen, 'the beating heart of the world's electronic supply chain',[26] has become a centre of maker culture. Shenzhen is the first Special Economic Zone of China and the central city of the Pearl Delta Region. The small fishing village of the 1970s is now experiencing the most vigorous economic growth in China. It hosts the plant of Foxconn, well-known as the manufacturer of BlackBerry, iPhone, iPad, Kindle, Xbox, etc. Huawei Technologies, which announces itself as 'the leading global ICT solution provider', is also based in Shenzhen. Nevertheless, what made Shenzhen home to the maker movement is its complete electronic supply chain. In the Huaqiangbei Electronic Market, makers can find whatever kits they need. What's more, thousands of mini-manufacturers can help them to realise any scale of production.

We cannot talk about the maker movement in Shenzhen (or elsewhere in China) without discussing *shanzhai* culture. *Shanzhai*, literally 'mountain stronghold' (i.e. outlaw's castle or pirate's den), is the name given to 'copycat' manufacturing, where electronic goods are copied and reproduced in low-cost, family-based factories for sale as 'no-brand' alternatives to branded versions. *Shanzhai* has attracted adverse publicity (especially in the West), accusing it of aggressively ripping off others' intellectual property to produce inferior copies. To outside observers, it comes across as Chinese-style innovation with a peasant mindset.[27]

On the other hand, many Western observers recognise that *shanzhai* represents more than piracy: it is a form of shared or crowd-sourced innovation (similar to copying in Classical music or fashion design); and also a development phase for new companies and markets before they reach maturity (repetitive exercises today may result in world-beating performances tomorrow). According to a German resident of China, Rainer Wessler, there are lessons here for the world – including the lesson that Western IP regulation is itself flawed, not a guarantor of innovation as its enforcers like to claim:

> *I appreciate that this thought [shanzhai as creative sharing] seems incompatible with the way we handle intellectual property in the international business world – though many agree that current IP law practice feels increasingly absurd, inhibiting innovation rather than protecting it. The Shanzhai don't worry so much.*[28]

Thus, when 'Obama' cell-phones can sell in Kenya with the slogan 'Yes We Can' with Obama's name on the back, *shanzhai* culture can surely be said to have made its own way in the world; and indeed, rather than seeing it as alien or outsider piracy, it would be better to see it as part of the larger and normal pattern of innovation, reproduction and distribution, speeding it up and integrating new players into global systems.

Double standards apply: *shanzhai* initiatives and innovations are criticised, even when they are out-competing Western or mainstream ones. For example, long before Nokia released its first dual sim card handset (the C1-00) in 2010 and its WP8 dual-sim phone series, dual sim cards had been a pervasive specification in the *shanzhai* phone markets. As for the 'Obama' phones, how is the ingenuity and sense of humour embedded in the product different from the single-serving site barackobamaisyournewbicycle.com created by Mathew Honan, the San Francisco freelance writer and *Wired* contributing editor, in February 2008?

To some extent, maker culture, in which customised products are made using open-source hardware, is part of *shanzhai* culture, supported by the *shanzhai* supply chain in turning prototypes to products. Notwithstanding safety concerns (products are not necessarily tested) and copyright disputes (intellectual property rights are not always respected), such making and remaking is a source of innovation. In the first China Maker Roundtable Conference in April 2013 (as part of the 7th China Inventors Summit), maker representatives discussed copyright issues. A possible resolution considered was to build a 'patent pool' where resources are open to copyright owners. This sounds similar to Creative Commons, which provides a flexible range of protections and freedom for creators, with 'some rights reserved'.[29] But open-source sharing has been and will continue to be the core of Maker Movement. Makers merely use mini-manufacturers to make their products. The Shenzhen-based Seeed Studio came from this environment, and thereby gained a competitive advantage over makerspaces in other regions.

Though the significance of the maker movement is widely praised, participation has not yet reached the level of mainstream manufacturing. Nevertheless, local governments are expecting maker sparks to strike a fire of innovation. It is hard to predict when the 'new industrial revolution' will mature; what is important now is that people are applying internet intelligence to the physical world, or in Chris Anderson's words: 'the Web generation [is] creating physical things rather than just pixels on screens.' This is worth noticing in the creative economy.

One of the troubling implications of our analysis is that the existing concept of *ownership* in the economic context (i.e. intellectual property) is radically undermined and in need of a makeover; one that recognises the importance of *sharing* or a 'commons' rather than a 'property' basis for productivity. Instead of privately owned or corporately controlled *information,* our analysis leads to a consideration of group-created and circulated *knowledge,* for which the model is more like shared language than economics.

Long-tail theory, Jugaad innovation and the informal economy

Chris Anderson's long tail theory applies here, indicating that innovation advanced by makers is as important as innovation from high-investment public or private R&D labs. Anderson (2006) described long-tail theory before the maker movement caught his eye. As the foundation of Web 2.0, long-tail theory works in a network economy when the cost of manufacturing and marketing niche products decreases substantially, making it economic to sell to niche rather than mass markets. Makers are sitting somewhere along the infinite tail of the curve. It is a step forward from 'selling less for more' to 'making more by using less'. Here, though, the growth of TechShop is outstanding, showing that the maker ethos can migrate 'up' the tail to reach much more substantial scale of operations.

This model of innovation at the margins is also reflected in the idea of Jugaad Innovation, from India, which means to improvise and find ways around prohibitive rules and institutions (Radjou et al., 2012). A similar idea is shown in Charles Leadbeater's latest book, *The Frugal Innovator: Creating Change on a Shoestring Budget.* He elaborates the case that 'creative communities with a cause' are a chief source of innovation, making do/making up/ making on a shoestring – but for a purpose, often related to improving conditions for a marginal or stressed community: the 'cause' and 'community' are as important as the 'creativity' – and the results may be scalable globally (Leadbeater, 2014).

This relates, in addition, to the controversy between the open-source and copyright models of innovation. In his study on Nollywood, Ramon Lobato (2010: 337) argues that informal markets have played a significant role in creating an 'efficient and economically sustainable' media market in Nigeria. His work with Julian Thomas also argues that piracy – the 'grey economy' – has important generative features and opens up great opportunities outside the formal media industries (Lobato and Thomas, 2012). Witnessing an informal economy around the globe, journalist Robert Neuwirth (2011) believes that the people who work in the informal economy are entrepreneurs who provide essential services and crucial employment, especially in developing economies.

In Chapter 7 ('everyone'), we conducted a microanalysis on the creation of newness through group-making and identity negotiation. The maker movement we have discussed in this chapter showcases a way through which such micro-creative-productivity can pool and scale at the meso-level to be part of a larger-scale creative force. What we intend to do in the next chapter is demonstrate how such creative productivity can integrate into the complex system of a creative economy.

Notes

1. 'The Art and Craft of Business', *The Economist*, 4 January 2014. Available at: www.economist.com/news/business/21592656-etsy-starting-show-how-maker-movement-can-make-money-art-and-craft-business.
2. The idea of 'the original affluent society' – one based on producing meanings – is accessible at www.eco-action.org/dt/affluent.html.
3. Quoted in an interview/review in *The Guardian*, available at www.theguardian.com/books/2009/dec/07/cory-doctorow-makers-interview. Doctorow came to prominence with his tech blog Boing Boing; his books can be downloaded for free from his website at http://craphound.com/makers/download/.
4. See www.scmp.com/lifestyle/technology/article/1262979/hackjam-great-minds-tinker-alike.
5. See http://en.wikipedia.org/wiki/Make_(magazine).
6. '2013: A Year of 100 Maker Faires', at www.makezine.com.tw/1/post/2014/01/2013100maker-faire.html.
7. Daniel Terdiman, 'White House to announce its first-ever Maker Faire', at http://news.cnet.com/8301-10797_3-57618256-235/white-house-to-announce-its-first-ever-maker-faire/.
8. Daniel Terdiman, as previous note.
9. 'How far is it from "Everyone is a maker?"', at http://www.shenzhenmakerfaire.com/post/3841.
10. See www.leiphone.com/china-maker-startup.html.
11. '2013: A year of 100 Maker Faires', at www.makezine.com.tw/1/post/2014/01/2013100maker-faire.html.
12. See http://techshop.ws/.
13. See http://hackerspaces.org/wiki/Hackerspaces.
14. See http://makerspace.com/.
15. See http://dimsumlabs.com/.
16. See http://selamtamagazine.com/stories/made-china-20.
17. See www.shenzhenmakerfaire.com/post/4398.
18. See http://techshop.ws/press_releases.html?&action=detail&press_release_id=47.
19. See www.shenzhenmakerfaire.com/post/3803.

20. See www.seeedstudio.com/depot/index.php?main_page=about_us.
21. See http://selamtamagazine.com/stories/made-china-20.
22. See http://online.wsj.com/news/articles/SB10001424052702303722604579111253495145952.
23. See http://selamtamagazine.com/stories/made-china-20.
24. See http://haxlr8r.com/about.
25. See www.scmp.com/lifestyle/technology/article/1262979/hackjam-great-minds-tinker-alike.
26. See http://selamtamagazine.com/stories/made-china-20.
27. See http://en.wikipedia.org/wiki/Shanzhai.
28. See also http://designmind.frogdesign.com/articles/shanzhai-s-role-in-innovation-strategy.html.
29. See http://creativecommons.org/.

9

ECONOMY (2) SCENES

Early on in my research, I realized that 'the scene' was an important resource for articulating resistance because a significant amount of everyday interaction online was about local scenes.

(J. Patrick Williams, 2006: 184)

Making a scene

Maker Faires and makerspaces, as well as Hackathons, nowadays often focus on a social or an educational issue by creating useful software for community purposes. They have caught the eye of journalists as a new 'urban scene'. Nevertheless, except for this technological example, the dominant forms of creative output are design, music, media production, performance and writing. Each type generates its own kind of *scene*. Cities are where such scenes may overlap and mix, creating an attractant for newcomers – especially among the young – for whom style and peer connectivity are strong values.

Scenes, which traditionally referred to the settings of paintings, are not confined to art, but extend to scenes in which art itself is set and enjoyed. Thus there's the 'gallery scene', with opening nights, gatherings of art communities and public shows for all. The 'theatre scene' is not just about the stage set, but also about drinks before the show or a visit to the pub or coffee shop afterwards. The 'music scene', 'London theatre scene', 'poetry scene' and 'Goth scene' have all been described by journalists. In the academic field, the study of scenes is well developed in the field of music ethnography, and discussion of the *concept* of scenes in cultural and subcultural studies is fruitful. For one thing, scenes are geographically specific ('the local scene' is going to differ in different cities or districts of one city). Scenes are also economic, associated often with the 'night-time economy'. Thus to study scenes is also to study the extension of economic activity into local cultural systems – and vice versa.

Scenes are readily associated with geographic locations. However, they are also connected with other scenes and places – they are mediated, with an online or broadcast dimension as well as street presence. Thus, Bennett and Peterson (2004) identify three geographical types of scenes: 'local', 'trans-local' and 'virtual'. Local refers to the original concept of a musical community that is rooted within a specific geographic focus (Straw, 1991). 'Trans-local' refers to 'widely scattered local scenes drawn into regular communication around a distinctive form of music and lifestyle' (Bennett and Peterson, 2004: 6), sometimes characterised by the interaction between the local scene and global media. The third form, the 'virtual scene', can be observed in music reviews in fanzines and in the commercial music press (Hodgkinson, 2004); it also embraces the change of communication patterns brought by the internet, which reveals a more fan-based discourse. These local and trans-local frameworks sometimes lead to the formation of a specific genre of music – for instance, Chicago blues (Grazian, 2004). However, the classification is challenged by Taylor (2005: 1027), who argues that a scene 'can be extended via print, broadcasting, or digital technologies beyond itself into a larger network', though the locality is still important.

The economic significance of scenes is also explored, as the importance of the 'night-time economy' has been recognised for many cities. According to Bennett and Peterson, the organisation of music scenes contrasts significantly with the assumption that 'over 80 percent of all the commercial music of the world is controlled by five multinational firms' (2004: 1). Furthermore, scenes and industrial ways of making music today rely on each other: a scene is the origin of authenticity and new forms of musical expression; while the music industry provides technology, from the CD to the internet, expanding its impact and realising its economic value (Bennett and Peterson, 2004).

To put it simply, the fan in the front row of the latest club scene – if the band is lucky – might also be the A&R scout for a recording company.[1] In this context, the former asymmetry in the power of record companies compared with that of musicians has begun to rebalance. Based on a case study of an electronic music club in Berlin, Lange and Bürkner (2012) conclude that because of technological change and the electronic distribution of music production, value-creation has shifted from large-scale producer-induced media (record companies) to consumer-induced live performance and interactive soundtrack. Here, the development of culturally embedded values, such as taste-building, reputation-building among artists and producers, and local community-building, are becoming increasingly important in the economics of music production. Musicians can make a name on the scene and interact directly with fans online and at venues.

Will Straw identifies *webs of microeconomic activity* that foster sociality and link this to a *city's ongoing self-reproduction*. He counts *scenes* as a sixth form, after these prior steps:

1. The recurring congregation of people at a particular place
2. The movement of these people between this place and other spaces of congregation
3. The streets/strips along which this movement takes place
4. All the places and activities that surround and nourish a particular cultural preference
5. The broader and more geographically dispersed phenomena of which this movement or these preferences are local examples
6. … *Scenes* (Straw, 2001: 249)

This is similar to Elizabeth Currid's (2007) description of 'creative scenes', which follows the path:

- Formal and informal institutions and social events as consumption sites
    - → Nodes of creative exchange
        - → Social production system
            - → Creative scenes form in diverse, open, amenity rich neighbourhood (the model is Manhattan)
                - → Cultural economy (symbiosis)

First, *formal institutions* like galleries, museums and venues are highlighted as being the marketplace between creativity and commerce (Becker, 1982). In these places, social events such as exhibitions, openings and industry parties are organised both for the 'ostensible purpose' of selling art and for the chance to meet like-minded people, tastemakers and gatekeepers over cocktails, and for potential cross-field collaborations (Currid, 2007). Take the SoHo-based Deitch Project's opening of Os Gemeos, a Brazilian graffiti duo and David

LaChapelle's *Artists and Prostitutes* exhibition (2006) as an example. As Currid describes it, the works of Os Gemeos and LaChapelle were fabulous; however, the 'motley crew' in the gallery seemed less interested in the art and far more concerned with interacting with one another (Currid, 2007: 102).

Meanwhile, life amenities like coffee shops, lounges and clubs are also important places for creative people to get together. Informal communication and links are often considered to lead to a positive effect of clustering of the formal labour pool, firms and suppliers. However, in a creative economy, the informal social realm becomes the centre of action rather than a spillover from other formal production patterns.

Here, formal and informal institutions, social events and activities, act as nodes of creative exchange. This requires a 'concentration of creativity', which offers a vessel for creativity to ferment and become something serious when a 'critical mass' is reached. It is not just 'weak ties' (Granovetter, 1973) but the dense concentration of different industries and occupations that work to propel innovation and the diffusion of new knowledge. Knowledge is exchanged in the most casual but significant contexts. This is the process of social learning. Furthermore, loose communities are formed to help to 'execute' the ideas. Therefore, rather than viewing these places as consumption sites or seeing them as (tourist) amenities in attracting people, creative people use these places as ways to advance their own careers (Currid, 2007: 95).

Moreover, these different dynamics speak to a broader range of social synergies, networks and institutions that allow for knowledge, skillsets, projects and evaluation processes to interact in a flexible, informal and largely efficient social production system (Currid, 2007: 110). 'Hollywood' is another example. Productive people 'find' each other, and projects get made, without central control, and without any one ownership regime. In strict economic terms, there's no such thing as 'Hollywood' – it's not a firm, or even an industry, but a self-creating, self-organising and self-sustaining social network (complex system) in which individuals, firms, producers and the labour pool, across multiple disciplines and platforms, can operate via short-lived companies that form for a given purpose (say, to make a movie), and then disperse. Coordinating such a system generates new opportunities (for instance, booking a cast); and overlapping systems (music, movies, fashion) generate creative experimentation and hybridity that can lead to new forms, such as when someone from a punk-music and 'zine culture becomes an art director and thence production designer, carrying the dark aesthetic of punk into the narrative form of the feature film (thinking of Alex McDowell, now a professor at USC), and so creating entirely new production techniques (which McDowell calls 'world-building') that may migrate across transmedia platforms, generating new value propositions at every step. None of this is possible without a milieu – a 'scene' – in which people live, work, consume, mix, learn and compete.

Consequently, entire neighbourhoods become scenes for particular cultural realms – in NYC, Chelsea for art, SoHo for fashion, the Lower East Side for music and art, the Bowery for music. Increasingly, the geographic boundaries of neighbourhoods and 'hang-outs' become blurred as broader creative scenes that manifest themselves in diverse, open and amenity-rich places are observed. Thus the diverse people and institutions within the cultural economy operate in a broader symbiosis (Currid, 2007: 106–7), that is, 'creative ecologies' (Howkins, 2009).

Ben Malbon (1999) investigated the clubbing scene in late 1990s Britain from the standpoint of geographies, that is: geographies of young people at play and of clubbing (playful vitality and resistance); geographies of experiential consuming (the interactional order, identity and identification formation and amendment); and geographies of sociality and performativity, which spin off the first two. With 150 nights out of twelve months' ethnographic observation – as both a clubber and a researcher – Malbon argues first that the playful vitality experienced through clubbing is much less about rigid conceptions of 'resistance', such as that associated with student movements in the late 1960s (Hebdige, 1979), and 'if clubbers are resisting anything ... it may be other aspects of their own lives' (Malbon, 1999: 183; see also McKay, 1998). Second, clubbing experience is synchronously produced and consumed, constructive (Butler, 1990) and expressive (Goffman, 1971). Belongings and identifications are not generated spontaneously, but rather are constituted through skills, competencies and shared knowledge that requires repetitive participation. Third, a defining feature of clubbing experience is the fluctuation between self and crowd – as Goldman said, 'self-expression is less a matter of mood, energy, practice, and pep pills than it is of feeling that the people around you are with you' (Goldman, 1993: 286). In short, clubbing is 'we'-group formation in action.

Silver and colleagues (2005) identify three general values of scenes:

1. Legitimacy, the pleasures of will;
2. Theatricality, the pleasures of appearance;
3. Authenticity, the pleasures of identity.

Emma Baulch (2007) tracks how the reggae, punk and death metal music scene grew in Bali, Indonesia, under influences such as media globalisation, with its 'fragmenting, hybridising, and diversifying cultural consequences' as well as media regulation. She chronicles the creation of subcultures at a historical moment when media globalisation and the gradual demise of the authoritarian Suharto regime coincided with revitalised formulations of the 'Balinese self'. Similarly, Saefullah (2011) examines local punk scenes, arguing that these are becoming agents of democratisation in post-authoritarian Indonesia.

Field (2008) explored the internationalised dance club scene in Shanghai during the period 1997 to 2007. Besides investigating the clubs as the 'conduit' for dance and music to enter China and the importance of 'international people' in developing the clubbing scene, Field also observed the social stratification and inequality revealed in the choice of separate and distinct space by some clubbers, which is less evident in the Western clubbing scene. Nevertheless, scenes are burgeoning in some places called 'creative parks' or 'creative clusters' in China, for example, Ideal 166 in Hangzhou and OCT Loft in Shenzhen.

China scenes

Ideal 166 Creative Industries Park in Hangzhou is an initiative of a small but experienced advertising company. Around 30 creative individuals are gathered in an industrial heritage site of Gongshu district. The Me-Too Café and its sister Chinese restaurant Qing Tao are what make the place popular, as well as the stores and work studios owned by designers in a variety of fields. The 'scene' constantly features music performance, exhibitions and theme parties, which attract fans with similar interests. A cultural community is forming. However, the designers are restless and looking for opportunities to move to new places so as 'to keep the momentum going', expanding scenes across the city.

In Shenzhen, the OCT LOFT Creative Culture Park (hereafter *the Loft*) is hiding in the city centre amidst the natural 'scene' of trees and bushes. It is an initiative of Overseas Chinese Town (OCT) Group, a large-scale state-owned enterprise engaged in cross-sectors from tourism and cultural industries to real estate and electronic products. The Loft is another example of the high expectation that China puts on new sectors of the economy to climb up the value chain.

The Loft hosts 60 enterprises and 40 plants and occupies an area of 40,000 square metres of land converted from old warehouses and factories. The idea of the Loft was to simulate the natural growth of the city, starting from an addition to an existing warehouse to accommodate a new art centre. The empty lots between these buildings were gradually to be filled with galleries, bookshops, cafes, bars, artist studios and design shops, along with lofts and dormitories. These new additions were designed to set up new relationships between buildings by wrapping and penetrating the existing fabric. They also created an added layer of interconnected urban space and public facilities. The planning did not seek to define a clear boundary or to fix forms. Instead it tried to set up a dynamic, interactive and flexible framework that would constantly adapt itself to the new conditions posed by the vast changes of the city.

In January 2005, the OCT Contemporary Art Terminal (OCAT) was opened in the Loft. It set out to function as a hub – a supply centre and departure point for contemporary Chinese art, i.e. an 'international terminal'. In December 2005, the first Shenzhen and Hong Kong Bi-city Biennale Urbanism/Architecture was held, which then became a major activity of OCT Loft and the architectural designers there. With more and more designer companies, art institutions, cafés, conceptual restaurants and bars flocking in, the Loft has turned into a burgeoning creative scene with multiple scenes of music, arts and life style.

The cases of Ideal 166 in Hangzhou and the OCT Loft in Shenzhen indicate a new way of place-making, of 'urban emergence' (Hélie, 2012). Cultural scenes and economic clusters are not confined within distinct boundaries but are transferable. Spontaneous scenes accompany the formation process of clusters and are a sign of their popularity or success. For planned clusters, though usually developed with an economic ambition, a scene is also an essential element, to distinguish them from manufacturing clusters, and to determine whether a place is lively.

Richard Florida (2010) argues that location-based, genre-specific music scenes are less important than clusters that are reshaped by economies of scale and economies of scope. This is based on an economic approach. However, scenes are the origin of new creative forms, or are where the good music comes from, and scenes therefore decide whether the industrial aspect of music will develop robustly. Thus, we advocate a contrasting argument, that scenes are *more* important than clusters, because they form new communities which have both cultural and economic potential: 'clusters' of people, who are like-minded, interacting, mutually learning and purposeful, are more important than co-locating firms. Thus, creativity thinking (cultural) is changing cluster thinking (industrial) to produce a new economic model of innovation from below.

Production of newness and urban semiosis

The maker movement provides a strong example for the democratisation of creativity, in particular, from the virtual world to the physical world. The movement is most robust in the technological field. It takes open source as the innovation model. It closely relates to the ideal of frugal innovation, which is not only evident in technology, but also in business models. It can be seen as part of the informal economy, which is claimed to be dominant in developing economies, such as China, India, Brazil, etc.

The maker movement represents only one perspective on the social learning system in the city. It is by no means the most important economic component of any city. The same applies to scenes. We have focused on these as 'emergent' sources of creativity and newness based on microproductivity and 'we' community formation, which together with social network markets (Potts et al., 2008) are rewiring current R&D and even the economic system in a systematic direction that is not confined to 'virtual' or mediated creative industries – the direction of self-organised, self-creating systems of value creation in which cultural and economic values are co-produced, by agents who may not be organised along traditional commercial lines (firms).

Further, scenes that rely on and generate cultural and artistic creativity are an epitome of urban semiosis (Chapter 4). This means that creative cities are those where citizens make culture and culture makes economy, characterised by scenes that are sites for social meeting and mixture as well as friction and 'clash'. Scenes connect cultures and nurture diversity, tolerance and civility as well as the economy. They coordinate economic value (GDP, jobs) and cultural value (meaningfulness, identity, relationships, boundaries).

Hereby we can answer the question of what creativity is in economic terms. It is the production of newness in complex adaptive systems (organised through network-like maker movements and scenes); and new knowledge and innovation that allow systems to renew and change, for themselves, endogenously.

Note

1. 'A&R' = 'Artists and Repertoire'. See: http://musicians.about.com/od/musiccareerprofiles/p/aandrprofile.htm.

EVERYWHERE

10

GEOGRAPHY (1) – BRICS

BRAZIL, RUSSIA, INDIA, CHINA, SOUTH AFRICA

I am not sure that I have the answer to many of the current difficult questions, but I would argue that handing more power to the BRICS is a good place to start.

(Jim O'Neill)[1]

A planetary system of difference

Critics have worried that the very idea of the creative industries, and the creative economy following through, are intrinsically Western notions, a 'white' problem, a problem of affluence, etc. This is not surprising, as prominent policy initiatives and published research work have come from the UK and former Dominions (Australia, New Zealand, Canada, South Africa), and affluent Europe. However, some of the most enthusiastic applications of creative industries and creative economy policies have been in developing and emergent countries, especially China and Brazil, both of which have combined large-scale central-government investment with significant business enterprise investment.

In the SE Asia region, there's hardly a country without a sophisticated creative economy policy, a government agency devoted to its implementation, and ambitious cities anxious to be dubbed 'creative'. Indonesia (especially during the Yudhoyono Presidency), Malaysia, Thailand before the 2013 military intervention, the Philippines, Vietnam, Cambodia, Laos, even tiny but rich Brunei – which, uniquely, manages to maintain a creative economy policy (Lennon and Abdullah, 2013) and new draconian Sharia laws at the same time[2] – have all taken the creative path as part of development. Cities such as Bandung in Java, Cebu in the Philippines, Chiang Mai in Thailand, and many others, vie for creative status.

Thus we are left with a pattern in which the 'idea' of the creative economy has generated considerable critical discourse in the Anglosphere, but it is being implemented most vigorously in jurisdictions with development imperatives, young populations and – at least in the case of China – a balance of payments surplus ripe for investment in the domestic economy. It is time, in short, to extend the geographical scope of creative industries and creative economy studies to planetary dimensions.

This chapter provides a glimpse of the emerging creative economy, as traditionally measured by policy and state agencies, in developing countries, in particular the BRICS countries (Brazil, Russia, India, China, South Africa) and MINT countries (Mexico, Indonesia, Nigeria, Turkey), two acronyms for emergent-economies-to-watch that were both coined by Jim O'Neill, former chief economist with Goldman Sachs.[3] In some regions the creative economy is more developed, while in other regions the business potential of culture is yet to be explored. Cities are the direct hubs and destinations of creative people and activities. This conjures up a picture of the creative economy taking root globally, growing and blooming 'everywhere'.

Brazil

Brazil has long been established as a cultural icon of the Latin American region. Its multi-ethnic culture, the ebullient samba and bossa nova and the colourful chaotic Rio Carnival are only a few of the symbols of the nation. Fashion weeks in São Paulo and Rio de Janeiro now rank among the world's premier events alongside those in New York, Milan, London and Paris. Brazil is credited as the most fashionable country in the BRICS.[4]

Creative industries policy received a powerful boost when President Lula de Silva appointed Gilberto Gil as Minister of Culture in 2003. Gil, only the second black person to attain cabinet rank in Brazil, is a renowned singer and musician as well as political activist.[5] Among his many accomplishments, Gil sought to combine Brazilian forms (samba, bossa nova) with African and other influences such as reggae. He was also influenced by Eastern meditative disciplines. Gil brought this experience with him to the Culture ministry, and soon promulgated a new direction for the creative industries. The *New York Times* reported his views on the connection between youth culture and government thus:

> 'These phenomena [hip hop culture] cannot be regarded negatively, because they encompass huge contingents of the population for whom they are the only connection to the larger world,' he said in a February interview. 'A government that can't perceive this won't have the capacity to formulate policies that are sufficiently inclusive to keep young people from being diverted to criminality or consigned to social isolation.' ... Mr. Gil said, 'you've now got young people who are becoming designers, who are making it into media and being used more and more by television and samba schools and revitalizing degraded neighborhoods'. He added, 'It's a different vision of the role of government, a new role.'[6]

The official arrival of creative economy in Brazil occurred on Gil's watch (2003–2008). It was identified at the eleventh session of the United Nations Conference on Trade and Development (UNCTAD XI) held in São Paulo (2004), where a Higher Panel on Creative Industries was convened to discuss the role of creative industries in development. The establishment of an International Centre on Creative Industries was proposed, followed by a forum discussing the scope, mission and operation (under the guidelines of the UN) of the Centre in Salvador de Bahia (Gil's home city) in April 2005. However, there's no sign yet of the establishment of this Centre.

Nevertheless, the creative industries idea has been adopted as an appropriate concern for international agencies, and the creative economy is evident in other Brazilian initiatives, such as the National Conference on Culture in 2010 and the establishment of the Secretariat of Creative Economy (SEC) in 2011. *The SEC Plan: Policies, Guidelines and Actions (2011–2014)* identifies the objective of a 'Creative Brazil', and highlights 'cultural diversity, sustainability, innovation and social inclusion' as the four guiding principles for its work. Recognised challenges include: information and data survey; articulation and encouragement of the furtherance of creative companies; education for creative competences; infrastructure for creation, production, distribution/circulation and consumption/enjoyment of creative goods and services; and creation/adjustment of legal framework for the creative sectors.

A range of programmes and activities occurs at city level. Rio de Janeiro, the *Cidade maravilhosa* (the marvellous city) has been home for music scenes, from the samba and bossa nova to funk and electronic. Based in the western district of Barra da Tijuca, the Arts City (*Cidade das Artes*) is Rio's leading music venue. It includes Latin America's second-largest hall for opera and classical music, seating 1800 spectators, which has been redeveloped to function as a multidisciplinary cultural complex. Since 1993 the municipality has provided residents with large exhibition tents in which music, theatre and dance performances are offered, as well as various arts training, including capoeira, guitar and yoga, at no cost or for minimal fees. Aimed at tackling social exclusion and revitalising public space, the project has been developed as a way of democratising access to culture while at the same time promoting local artists and sharing the management of cultural venues with civil society organisations.

Rio is also the major centre of the audiovisual industries of Brazil. TV Globo, Brazil's largest media conglomerate, is headquartered there.[7] The Rio Film Festival is Brazil's most important. A company owned by the municipality, RioFilme, has invested in about 300 feature films and 130 short films since 1992. Its mission is to promote and develop Rio's audiovisual industry, recognising its cultural, social and economic value. In 2010, RioFilme opened the first 3D movie theatre ever to be located in a Brazilian favela: CineCarioca Nova Brasilia, which attracted an audience of nearly 200,000 in its first 33 months of operation.

The creative sector amounted to 4.1 percent of GDP of the State of Rio de Janerio.[8] To keep up the momentum, a 'Creative Rio' (*Rio Criativo*) programme was launched in 2010, with pillar projects such as creating incubators for creative entrepreneurs.[9] A leading focal point for the creative economy is the Genesis Institute hosted by the Pontifical Catholic University of Rio de Janeiro, with incubators for Technology, Culture, Jewellery Design and Community Social Development. These Genesis Cultural Incubators assist cultural and artistic entrepreneurship and offer methodologies and instruments for business development and management, with support from University professors. Like many others, the Genesis Incubators are labs for knowledge transfer between universities and businesses, to help the self-sustainable development of start-up enterprises, which are expected to make an impact on the cultural and economic development of their regions.[10]

The Football World Cup 2014 and Olympic Games 2016 seem to present great opportunities for Rio in terms of cultural, economic and urban development. The government's Growth Acceleration Program called for a total investment of $872.3 billion USD in infrastructure, energy, and social inclusion and safety from 2007 to 2014. Major projects assist the diversification of cultural resources by constructing new facilities or revamping old buildings. A new museum, the Rio de Janeiro Art Museum (MAR) has been created.[11] The Museum of Tomorrow, a flagship high-tech science and environmental museum, is planned as one of the anchors of Porto Maravilha. The *Morro da Conceiçao* – a popular housing district in the heart of the Olympic project – is being completed with the rehabilitation of old buildings and abandoned warehouses, in order to create the 'City of Samba'.[12]

Brazil's biggest city is São Paolo, which also hosts some of the country's leading TV networks, advertising companies and publishers.[13] In Paraná, a road show of workshops on the creative economy, creative cities and local development was organised by the Secretariat of Culture and the Secretariat of Tourism together with the Federation of Industries in 2012, as the first step towards a creative economy program. The Brazilian government announced it would put $4.3million USD towards the growth of creative industries within Recife's Porto Digital, one of the largest tech parks in the country.

Private institutions, like the Brazilian Service of Support for Micro and Small Enterprises (SEBRAE), play an active part in promoting the creative economy. As an institute partner with public and private institutions across the nation, SEBRAE's involvement is essential as SMEs represent 56 percent of the formal urban labour force and 26 percent of the aggregate wage/salaries bill. SMEs include 5 million formal enterprises and an estimated 10 million informal businesses. SEBRAE in Rio de Janeiro has long been working in the creative field, including handicrafts, cultural tourism and music. In the state of Minas Gerais SEBRAE has worked to raise awareness of the creative economy. In 2012, together with the State government, it announced the creation of the 'House of the Creative Economy' in the city of Belo Horizonte (UN/UNDP/UNESCO, 2013).

Creative development in Brazil is growing thanks to a growing economy. Brazil has become the sixth largest economy in the world. Over ten years, 40 million Brazilian people have entered the middle classes with disposable income. Economic growth and consequent affluence have had great impact on social media use, with the support of a government that is in favour of the easy accessibility of social media. Access to technology has been a massive driver for Brazil, with internet connectivity almost doubling over five years. The increase in internet access also facilitates access to education and knowledge in a country where the price of computers and access to mobile technology have been kept deliberately low by a government eager to educate its citizens in digital culture. Figures suggest that Brazil is now the second largest market after the US for Facebook use, with around 40.3 million people actively engaged with social media on a regular basis. Pay TV is also on the rise with 45 million subscribers, and 15.4 million smart phones were purchased in Brazil in 2012.

Brazil is already a major exporter of music and in TV soap operas (telenovelas). It is the world's 12th music market and opportunities for electronic and pop music can be found throughout the country. In the publishing segment the last edition of *Book Biennale* reached an audience of 400,000 people. Another success is the Writer's meeting in Paraty (PLIP) organised by Liz Calder, editor and founder of Bloomsbury.

Russia

Russia boasts the world's eighth largest economy, two places behind Brazil. It is often commented on in Western media as economically conservative, leading to a limited play of culture and creativity. Nevertheless, Russia's rich history of art and culture and its enviable cultural infrastructure are universally recognised.

Scholars who have looked into the cultural policy of the Russian Federation agree that the Ministry of Culture plays only a small role in cultural and creative industries development. This is evident in the lack of a clear policy line. Furthermore, challenges rather than opportunities are noted. These include: state regulation; the perception of cultural and creative industries as too close to high art and cultural heritage; state-owned cultural organisations being discouraged from involvement in economic activities; private cultural enterprises being unable to access funding; and a hostile business environment for SMEs (including excessive bureaucracy, corruption, a lack of seed funding or tax breaks, and no proper tutoring) (Ruutu et al., 2009; Council of Europe/ERICarts, 2013).

This is quite apart from the hostile central government attitude to creative dissent, as the case of Pussy Riot amply illustrates. Nevertheless, based on a cooperative project between Manchester and St Petersburg, Justin O'Connor (2005) looked into the 'cultural industries' in Russia, in particular in St Petersburg. The above challenges were also reflected in O'Connor's experience. Furthermore, the strong pride in high culture entails resisting the commercialisation of culture, as the latter is perceived as an approach aimed at 'catching up with the West', rather than 'finding a specific path'. This resistance even extends to disdaining the concept of a 'transitional economy', which in contrast has been welcomed in countries like China.

Among artists, however, fine art has not been a conservative force but one for expressing the spirit of freedom, recomposition and underground ideas during the transitional period between the Gorbachev and Putin eras.

For instance, the 'New Academy of Fine Arts' was founded in St Petersburg by Timur Novikov in 1989, and continues under his successors, including the multimedia computer artist, filmmaker and 'Neo-Academist' Olga Tobreluts, one of the first artists to use digital and computer technology in her work, which combines classical subjects and pop culture icons in wry mutual criticism. The New Academy has acted as a meeting point for artists, ideas and new forms of expression, straddling both nonconformist and official art scenes, and supporting creative practice with provision of studios, tuition and events.[14]

Thus, in practice, regions and major cities like Moscow and St Petersburg are interested in the creative industries, and many projects are developed with the collaboration of international institutions like the Council of Europe, EU, British Council and Calvert 22 Foundation. An EU–Russia Creative Industries Forum took place in 2014 in both Moscow and Brussels, as part of an EU–Russia Year of Science.[15] In the same year, an international conference was held in Lomonosov Moscow State University on the theme of *Creative Industries in the Reindustrialising World: Media Practices of the West and the East*. International speakers included Terry Flew from Australia, Francois Heinderyckx, outgoing President of the International Communication Association, from Belgium, and Xin Xin, from the University of Westminster's China Media Centre.[16]

In St Petersburg, a Centre for Development of Creative Industries was established by the end of 1990s. St Petersburg began to hold an annual International Cultural Forum in 2012. The forum is organised by the Government of the Russian Federation in collaboration with the Government of St Petersburg, aiming at protecting and promoting Russian culture, supporting cultural initiatives at regional and federal and international levels, as well as encouraging international collaborations.[17]

In September 2013, an audience of nearly 400 people gathered in the new contemporary art wing of the Hermitage museum in St Petersburg for the Calvert Forum, which marked the beginning of a new collaboration between St Petersburg State University's Smolny College and the Calvert 22 Foundation, a London-based gallery and arts organisation, aiming at raising the profile of Russia's creative sector.[18]

In Moscow, old industrial sites are said to be 'blossoming into creative centres of art and culture', taking over rundown factories in bleak urban areas in order to revive the beating heart of the city's cultural life and to develop a promising creative industry sector. Artplay, which is the first of its kind, occupies more than 74,000 square metres in a former manometre (pressure gauge) factory and is home to professionals in architecture, design, urban planning and interior design.[19] Winzavod, a contemporary art centre in the city's East Side, was born in the wake of the 2005 and 2009 Moscow Biennales of Contemporary Art, and is dedicated to visual arts by showcasing them in halls, private galleries and boutiques.[20] Garage, the contemporary culture centre, is one of Moscow's largest exhibition spaces and most fashionable patrons (Roman Abramovich's wife Dasha Zhukova is editor of the international *Garage* art/fashion magazine). The Fabrika Centre for Creative Industries is well known for its creations and exhibitions of cultural projects and work by well-known people.

Art Moscow was founded in 1996. The five-day fair takes place annually in the capital city. It includes seminars, talks, presentations, and an exclusive programme for international art collectors. In 2013 the 17th annual show coincided with the 5th Moscow Biennale of Contemporary Art.[21] A World Summit for Creative Industries was held in Moscow in 2014, as part of the Global Entrepreneurship Congress. Organised by the Moscow government and the Kauffman Fund, the Summit was designed to boost the importance of creative industries among the world business community. It would also promote Moscow as an international creative centre and develop an entrepreneurial ecosystem of creative industries going beyond territorial and industrial boundaries.[22]

Beyond the metropolitan centres of Moscow and St Petersburg, creative industries policies and initiatives have reached deep into Siberia, partly with the aid of international agencies such as the British Council. Krasnoyarsk in Central Siberia is famous as a city where aristocratic exiles were banished in Tsarist times, thereby establishing it as a centre for the intelligentsia. More recently it was the place of incarceration of Pussy Riot member Nadezhda Tolokonnikova.[23] In 2011, Krasnoyarsk was the first city in Russia to have its creative businesses 'mapped' by the Creative Industries agency and Siberian Federal University.[24] The Siberian Federal University, which is located in the city, maintains a chair in Creative Industries and is active in research.[25]

In addition, the development of the creative economy is supported by related educational initiatives, as the current education system in Russia, as in many other countries, cannot keep up with the demand for creative skills, or is not geared to teach them. The 'Strelka' Institute of Media, Architecture and Design in Moscow launched a higher education programme aimed at training a new generation of professionals. It also wanted to acquaint the wider public with contemporary creative projects, and to educate a market in order to create new demand for these products.[26]

Creative clusters are also actively involved in creative education. For instance, Artplay holds an annual Student Artfair, which showcases student work and attracts the interest of patrons, gatekeepers, and media as well as consumers. An Educational Program of the Moscow International Festival 'Circle of Lights' took place in October 2013 in the Digital October Centre at the Red October district. The aim of the programme was to expose the latest wave of accomplishments and trends noticeable on the multimedia/technology/light design scene.[27]

In 2012, Russia had the ninth largest international box office market, with ticket sales of $1.2 billion USD. In August 2013, the Russian government approved an anti-piracy law to support copyright protection. A Memorandum of Understanding was signed between rights-holders and several user-generated-content (UGC) websites in December 2013, to help both Russian and international film, television and internet companies to develop a growing legal online market. The move was spearheaded by the Federal Service for Supervision of Communications, Information Technology and Mass Media.[28]

India

India is the most populous (1.2 billion) democracy. It is the tenth largest economy, and one of the fastest growing countries in the world. It is where wealth and poverty, smartness and illiteracy, creativity and chaos collide.

Though 'creative industries' has appeared only occasionally in the policy documents of the Planning Commission of the Government of India from 2006, it has been related to cultural heritage and traditional cultural industries like crafts. Beyond that, the film industry undoubtedly takes pride of place in this field. 'Bollywood' produces over 800 films per year. The other outstanding sectors are architecture, design and digital content. According to the UK Trade and Industry department, who estimate the total market for these services at £41,109 million, digital content is dominant in this new group, valued at £25,613 million, i.e. 62 percent of the market, followed by architecture (£12,000 million, 30 percent). Though design took only 8 percent (£3,360m), the policy initiatives were much more evident here than in the other two sectors mentioned (UKTI, 2011).

In February 2007, India's first National Design Policy was approved by the Indian Cabinet, having been formulated by the Department of Industrial Policy and Promotion in the Ministry of Commerce and Industry. The policy highlighted the need for four new National Institutes of Design for educational purpose, the creation of an 'India Design Mark', that is, a symbol to recognise good design standards, and the establishment of a

Chartered Society for Designers, similar to one formed in the UK in 1930. In June 2009, the India Design Council was set up to implement the policy recommendations, with members from the fields of design, academia and industry organisations.[29] The objectives of the Council are to develop and promote design, and to stage India as a top design destination, as well as to manage the India Design Mark. The Council also established collaborative relationships with international design organisations such as Japan Institute of Design Promotion (JDP), to learn how the Good Design Award system has functioned in Japan since 1957.

The Ministry of Micro, Small and Medium Scale Enterprises (MSME) has also noticed the rise and the importance of design business. It launched a Design Clinic Scheme with the National Institute of Design under the National Manufacturing Competitiveness Programme (NMCP) in 2010 in New Delhi. The scheme proposes to benefit 200 industry clusters to create a dynamic platform for expert solutions, and to add value to existing products, such as agricultural products and bicycle components[30].

Certain forces are recognised as providing incentives for creativity and innovation in contemporary India.[31] First is the demographic structure. The heterogeneity and diversity of its population make India a fertile land for culture and creativity. Half of the 1.2 billion population is under 25, and these young people are increasingly empowered by social media technology. Second is technology. India ranks 23rd worldwide in terms of 'Technology' in Richard Florida's global ranking, according to which it is 'doing well'. The development of ICT industry in India is astonishing and is a major engine of the national economy. Furthermore, the mobile sector has grown from around 10 million subscribers in 2002 to pass the 900 million mark in early 2012.[32] In terms of the internet market, there was tremendous enthusiasm among dial-up users and an estimated 60 percent of internet users were still regularly accessing the internet via the country's more than 10,000 cybercafés. Nevertheless, the country has announced a National Broadband Plan, with which both fixed and wireless broadband are expected to grow rapidly.[33] Meanwhile, the creative economy in India is also characterised by informality and a focus on livelihoods. For instance, in crafts business, the informal network of apprenticeship is essential, but under-estimated in the national economy.

Some reports reached a similar conclusion that talent is in shortage in India's creative economy. In Florida's test, India ranked 44th on Talent, and with only 6 percent of its population holding a Bachelor's degree, universities are criticised as 'severely underperforming' in innovation.[34] This also indicates the severe social stratification and uneven development.

China

China is the second largest economy in the world. Three decades of economic reform and opening up have witnessed marked progress in hard power, but has China's image improved to the same extent?

In China, 'cultural industries' is the official term used since the adoption of the 10th Five Year Plan (2001–06), following the 16th Party Congress of 2000. Accordingly, provincial and local governments have been determined to find an appropriate 'cultural industries strategy' for the commercial exploitation of cultural resources (Keane, 2011). The 11th Five Year Plan (2006–10) categorised cultural industries into the following sectors:

- Film/TV production
- Publishing
- Distribution (*faxing ye*)
- Printing
- Advertising
- Performance
- Entertainment
- Cultural exhibition
- Digital content and animation

It advocated 'cultural innovation' in literature and arts, in media and digital content, and in the management of cultural enterprises. Furthermore, the Plan promised intellectual property reforms (State Council, PRC, 2006).

The terms 'creative industries' (*chuangyi chanye*) and 'cultural and creative industries' (*wenhua chuangyi chanye*, with a broader definition) were slow to be adopted, only to be found in the 2009 Chinese government's annual Government Work Report in the context of developing service industries.[35] According to Wang Yongzhang, former director of the Department of Cultural Industries in the Ministry of Culture, the content of Western 'creative industries' is similar to that of Chinese 'cultural industries', while 'cultural industries' is more suitable for China in strengthening 'independent innovation' (*zizhu chuangxin*) and building an innovative country (*chuangxinxing guojia*) (Wang, 2007). Furthermore, it ensures consistency in national policy. Favouring the term 'cultural industries' can also be attributed to the tradition of collective creativity (as opposed to individualism), the commitment to the appreciation, protection and promotion of

China's 'splendid civilisation over 5000 years', and the need to strengthen 'cultural power' and to ensure 'cultural security' as well as a solid and united ideology. In other words, there's a strong element of cultural nationalism involved. Nevertheless, it can be observed that a 'creative' tide is allowing the 'cultural industries' to be more innovative in China. Regardless of the term used, creativity, arts and culture, combined with digital technology, are becoming the new fuel of economic and social development (Li Wuwei, 2011).

In September 2009, a Cultural Industries Revitalisation (*zhenxing*) Plan was released by the Ministry of Culture in order to facilitate cultural development (*wenhua jianshe*) under the threat of the 2008 Global Financial Crisis. The theme of cultural innovation became a central element of policy statements. Numerous action plans and supporting regulations in funding and taxation etc. came out not only in major cities like Beijing, Shanghai, Guangzhou and Shenzhen, but also in second or even third tier cities like Hangzhou, Chengdu, Xi'an and Lanzhou.

Since 2012, a trend has emerged of embracing a 'convergence' development model, that is, 'culture + technology', 'culture + tourism' and 'culture + finance'. In May 2012, six national departments – the Publicity Department of CPC, the Ministries of Technology, Finance and Culture, the State Administrations of Radio, Film and Television (SARFT) and the General Administration of Press and Publication – had their first meeting on the convergence of culture and technology. They announced the first 16 national demonstration bases of cultural and technological convergence, respectively located in Beijing (*zhongguancun*), Shanghai (*zhangjiang*), Wuhan (East Lake), Shenyang, Hangzhou, Shenzhen, Chengdu, Changsha, Hefei, Xi'an, Tianjin, Chongqing, Qingdao, Harbin, Lanzhou and Changzhou. They released an *Outline of National Cultural and Technology Innovation Projects*, and the Ministry of Culture has released *The Twelfth Five Year Plan of Culture and Technology Development*. In January 2014, 18 more national demonstration bases were designated in cities, which enlarge the coverage of the policy still further.

In these initiatives it is evident that cultural industries precincts were regarded as the key structural elements of cultural development, following the success of 'science parks', while the central government initiated an 'innovative nation' strategy. Though many of the clusters are designed for cultural production purposes (e.g. animation), more and more creative places (especially the bottom-up ones) have changed the ideology of urban development (or redevelopment) and gradually reshaped the cultural landscape of cities. They follow a 'community-based' development process.

Nevertheless, expos, fairs, festivals and forums are also numerous. Many cities have their Cultural and Creative Industries Expo or Fair, and some (like Hangzhou and Xi'an) support annual animation festivals. In addition, companies like Tencent (China's largest and most used internet service portal),[36] Alibaba Group (which operates leading online and mobile marketplaces in consumer and business-to-business commerce, as well as cloud computing and other services),[37] and Huawei (a leading global ICT solution provider)[38] are becoming international competitors in the information age. The era of 'copycat' and 'catch-up' (Keane, 2007) is giving way to a new period in which Chinese brands operate globally under their own names, both corporately, as they are listed on Western stock exchanges, and in terms of consumer culture, where firms such as Huawei have found clever ways to translate their Chineseness (quoting the big smiles of Chinese artist Yue Minjun) into a Western pop culture idiom (see frontispiece).[39]

The 'creative heat' is on. In 2014, the State Council made 'promoting the integrated development of culture, creativity and design services with related industries' into official policy. The Ministry of Culture immediately responded to this with an Action Plan. It outlined key sectors:

- Creative design
- Animation and games
- Performance
- Entertainment
- Arts and crafts

It clarified the role of culture, creativity and design services in supporting equipment manufacturing, consumer goods industries and the residential environment. It also brought forward a strategy of integrated development between culture and technology, tourism, special agriculture and sports industries. At the same time the State Council released its *Suggestions on Promoting the Development of International Cultural Commerce*:

> ...supporting the integrated innovation of culture and technology ... increasing R&D investment in exported cultural products and services; developing key and core technologies with independent intellectual property; and supporting cultural enterprises to use international advanced technology, and to strengthen the capability of digesting, absorbing, and re-innovating. (State Council, PRC, 2014)

These documents reveal the importance of cross-boundary cooperation among government departments, between public and private institutions, and between cultural sectors and the rest of the economy. They also send a strong signal of long-standing support of cultural industries development.

There are, of course, obstacles in the way of a creative future for China. To name just two:

- *Intellectual property*: the tension between the protection of intellectual property rights (including those of international firms) and the open-source (and *shanzhai*) development model, which the country has relied on to date (Montgomery, 2010).
- *Education*: though most of the policy documents have a section on 'talent cultivation', the education system, especially schools that focus on achieving high scores for the National University Entrance Examination (*gaokao*), is criticised as detrimental to the development of imagination and creativity among young people. Even though university/industry links are emphasised and all sorts of training programmes for skilled or creative talent are offered by universities, enterprises or social education providers, the reform of the education Chinese children receive before taking the *gaokao* will be essential to the creative future of China.

South Africa

South Africa was among the first countries to announce an ambition to build a 'creative nation', with the purpose of developing its creative industries, following the British government's 1998 initiative (DCMS, 1998). In the same year, the South African Department of Arts, Culture, Science and Technology (DACST) appointed a Cultural Strategy Group – a multi-disciplinary consortium to draft and release *Creative South Africa: A strategy for realising the potential of the Cultural Industries*.[40] The report focused on four sectors, namely, music, film and TV, publishing, and craft. These were reckoned to be already evident in South Africa, and to have the potential to boost the economy and improve social welfare.

A series of Cultural Industries Growth Strategies was publicised for each of the key sectors. The content of this set of reports followed the DCMS's ideology and tried to apply it to the local setting. The policies covered hot issues in the specific dynamics of the creative industries, namely: tangibles versus intangibles; one off vs. mass production; convergence and interdisciplinary movement; and recognised problem areas such as training and skills development, technology, institutional structures, the spatial dimension, and copyright. Overall the creative sector was expected to benefit the economy, identity, image, innovation and creativity, tourism and social impact of the country.

In 2002, an Integrated Manufacturing Strategy (IMS) was issued by the Department of Trade and Industry (DTI), in which 'cultural industries' are recognised as one of South Africa's nine 'priority sectors'. In 2008, *The Creative Industries in South Africa: Sector Studies Research Project* was commissioned and released by the Department of Labour.[41] It is the second report on creative industries at national level with a focus on film, craft, music, performing arts, visual arts, and cross-cutting sectors.

The South African Department of Arts and Culture has played an important role in positioning the cultural and creative industries. From 2003, annual strategic plans were produced for the forthcoming three or five years on how the arts, culture and heritage sector would contribute to the national economy and employment. The Strategic Plan 2011–2016 and the Strategic Plan 2012–2013 share a quite similar structure – both of them consist of six programmes, which reflect local priorities:

- Administration
- Performing arts
- National language service
- Cultural development
- Heritage promotion
- National archives and library services

The *implementation* of creative industries initiatives is more evident at provincial or municipal level. According to *Gauteng's Creative Industries: An Analysis* (2008) released by The Gauteng Department of Sport, Arts, Culture and Recreation (GDSACR) and British Council, the total direct and indirect contribution of the 11,320 firms and organisations comprising the creative economy is 33.3bn Rand per annum in turnover, creating employment for over 182,000 people. The audio-visual and music sectors produced the most revenue per person employed. In terms of the number of firms and organisations active in the sector, design is the largest (25 percent), followed by craft (21 percent), audio-visual (11 percent), music (11 percent) and visual arts (10 percent). Just over half (54 percent) are members of industry and professional associations or lobby groups. In 2005, creative industries were recognised as an important element for the urban economy in the implementation of Joburg 2030, which is Johannesburg's blueprint for economic development over three decades. Cape Town is also considered a hub for the creative class and cultural tourism.

Developing countries face problems that would not occur to those who live in big cities or in high-investment environments. Thus, the South African film industry is impeded by leftover asymmetries in infrastructural investments, inherited from Apartheid days: the simple fact that townships and villages have no cinemas, and non-white communities have no tradition of cinema-going. Given the distance to city centres, transport and security problems, and the high cost of tickets, this doesn't seem likely to change. However, one entrepreneur has approached the issue from an unusual angle: if people can't go to the cinema, bring cinemas into the townships.

John Eschenburg is the driving force behind the *ReaGilè* (in Southern Sotho it means 'we have built') project, which aims to uplift communities through 'co-op cinemas' made from shipping containers (Tomaselli and Mboti, 2013). Eschenburg has been quoted as saying that this simple initiative has the potential to generate 37,000 jobs and re-invest potential profits of 350m Rand a year back into the local film industry. According to this report:

> These fully air-conditioned, prefabricated container-based miniplexes have a 60-seat capacity and are designed to bring cost-efficient and accessible film screenings to urban and rural townships on three-metre high-definition screens, with 9,2 channel surround sound. The complexes also contain a community police centre, a care centre, as well as a 30-seat computer centre, all situated on a 400 m² stand on a public open space or at a local school. Public viewing screens are erected on the complex exterior facing a specially constructed open-air amphitheatre. 'These screens can be used for sports and news channels,' says Eschenburg. 'The separate units are made from five shipping containers – they are made up in a factory – you connect up on site and within two days can be up and running.'[42]

According to Eschenburg, *ReaGilè* revolutionises the South African film-distribution landscape by tapping into a 40-million strong segment of the population that would not usually access films. Such is creative innovation – not devoted to using creative outputs to get 'bums on seats' in this instance, but in getting seats for them to sit on.

This chapter on the BRICS countries, along with the next on the MINT countries, demonstrates in detail that representative emergent economies, without exception, are characterised by creative, cultural and economic policies that bring together agencies and activists across the government, entrepreneurial and artistic sectors. It may be that there is still a gap between rhetoric and reality, policy and practice, real estate and 'scene', but this is another example of 'first approximation': what cannot be doubted is that the creative economy is 'everywhere', it is growing, and it is seen as an engine of cultural as well as economic development for societies with very different traditions and aspirations.

Notes

1. Jim O'Neill (September 2014) 'Give the BRICS more power: we need them on our side', *The Telegraph*. Available at: www.telegraph.co.uk/finance/economics/11078396/Give-the-BRICS-more-power-we-need-them-on-our-side.html.
2. For how such a juxtaposition may affect trade see, for example, www.smh.com.au/federal-politics/political-news/australia-to-question-brunei-over-stoning-laws-before-trade-talks-20140629-zsq1h.html.
3. See *Wall Street Journal*, 9 December 2013 at http://blogs.wsj.com/moneybeat/2013/12/09/oneill-man-who-coined-brics-still-likes-brics-but-likes-mints-too/.
4. See www.the-report.net/brazil/riodejaneiro-nov2012/211-branding-back-in-fashion.
5. Larry Rohter, 'A government gig for Brazilian Pop Star; Gilberto Gil becomes Culture Minister, but not everyone sings his praises', *The New York Times*, 31 December 2002. Available at: www.nytimes.com/2002/12/31/arts/government-gig-for-brazilian-pop-star-gilberto-gil-becomes-culture-minister-but.html.
6. Larry Rohter,'Brazilian Government invests in culture of hip-hop', *The New York Times*, 14 March 2007. Available at: www.nytimes.com/2007/03/14/arts/music/14gil.html?_r=0.
7. See www.globo.com/.
8. See www.forum-avignon.org/en/culture-and-creative-economy-riode-janeiro-challenges-changing-city.
9. See www.riocriativo.rj.gov.br/site/.
10. See http://www.latamtrainingcenter.com/?p=2829&lang=en.
11. See www.museudeartedorio.org.br/en/mar.
12. See www.forum-avignon.org/en/culture-and-creative-economy-rio-de-janeiro-challenges-changing-city.
13. See www.ied.edu/sao-paulo/home.
14. See https://en.wikipedia.org/wiki/Timur_Novikov; and for Olga Tobreluts see: http://au.phaidon.com/agenda/art/articles/2013/january/25/russian-digital-artist-olga-tobreluts-gets-huge-retrospective-at-moscow-museum-of-modern-art/.
15. See http://creativeconomy.britishcouncil.org/Policy_Development/news/russian-british-creative-economy-forum/.
16. See www.moscowreadings.com/.
17. See www.russkiymir.ru/russkiymir/en/news/common/news12048.html.
18. See www.theguardian.com/culture-professionals-network/culture-professionals-blog/2013/sep/25/russia-culture-st-petersburg-berlin.
19. See www.artplay.ru/.
20. See www.winzavod.ru/eng/.

21. See www.art-moscow.ru/en.
22. See www.summitofcreative.com/en/about/.
23. See www.theguardian.com/world/2013/dec/24/pussy-riot-members-reunited-release-russia.
24. See www.creativeindustries.ru/eng/news/260; results were published at http://cr-journal.ru/en/journals_en/99.html&j_id=7.
25. See https://www.youtube.com/watch?v=hVgc4PkOMB8.
26. See http://www.strelka.com/?lang=en.
27. See www.migz.ru/en.
28. See http://blog.mpaa.org/BlogOS/post/2013/12/18/Another-Important-Milestone-in-Russia-in-Building-an-Online-Creative-Marketplace.aspx.
29. See www.indiadesignmark.in/about/india-design-council.
30. See http://theinsidetrack.in/first-india-design-mark-awards-handed-out-at-nid/.
31. See www.eastasiaforum.org/2012/04/05/india-unleashing-potential-in-innovation-and-creativity/.
32. See www.internetworldstats.com/asia/in.htm.
33. See https://www.budde.com.au/Research/India-Broadband-Market-Internet-Services-and-Forecasts.html?r=51.
34. See www.eastasiaforum.org/2012/04/05/india-unleashing-potential-in-innovation-and-creativity/.
35. See www.china.com.cn/policy/txt/2009-03/14/content_17444081.htm.
36. See www.tencent.com/en-us/index.shtml.
37. See http://news.alibaba.com/specials/aboutalibaba/aligroup/index.html.
38. See www.huawei.com/en/.
39. See also www.shootgroup.com/2013/06/amit-naroop-capture-outstanding-features-for-huawei-g510-launch/.
40. See http://govza.gcis.gov.za/node/515418; and www.gov.za/documents/download.php?f=70493.
41. See www.labour.gov.za/DOL/downloads/documents/research-documents/Creative%20Industries_DoL_Report.pdf; and: https://www.thedti.gov.za/industrial_development/docs/eusatraefinalreportsummary.pdf.
42. 'Bringing the big screen to slums', *The Witness* 8 August 2013. Available at: www.witness.co.za/index.php?showcontent&global[_id]=104415.

11

GEOGRAPHY (2) – MINT, ETC.

MEXICO, INDONESIA, NIGERIA, TURKEY, JAPAN, KOREA AND INTERNATIONAL AGENCIES

The easy accusation against the MINT theory is that O'Neill overestimates the importance of individual capability and downplays the extent to which political violence, state repression and institutional corruption can hold back even the most enterprising person.

(New Statesman, 2014)[1]

The notion of the BRIC countries was coined in 2001 by Goldman Sachs economist Jim O'Neill.[2] Since then it has been extended to BRICS with the inclusion of South Africa, and in some versions (not authorised by O'Neill) it is given as BRICKS, with the addition of (South) Korea as well as South Africa. This uncertainty about which countries ought to be included is inevitable, since inclusion is based on 'good demographics' (large, youthful populations) and high rates of growth of GDP (Gross Domestic

Product) relative to advanced economies (typically the G7/G8). Such rates vary from year to year, and from country to country, and over time new players emerge as old ones falter.

Thus, more recently, O'Neill has coined another acronym to highlight a new set of high-growth developing economies with young populations. These are the MINT countries: Mexico, Indonesia, Nigeria and Turkey. O'Neill himself toyed with the idea of calling them the MIST countries, with 'S' standing for South Korea, but was convinced – apparently by the BBC – to include Nigeria (*New Statesman*, in the interview quoted above).

Bearing in mind, then, that these are sample countries, rather than a definitive list of picked winners, we move on now from BRICS to MINT, to illustrate the extent to which the issue of a creative economy and culture is ubiquitous, no matter what kind of country or economy is considered, and further to note that creativity is associated with economic growth and a future-facing population wherever you go. We have also included JK – Japan and Korea – as well as some international agencies, because of their global importance in design, style, creativity, pop culture, media and technology, and their status as highly developed countries, especially in digital connectivity.

Mexico

The creative economy is described as the 'new rice and beans' of Mexico, for which it has the resources, market and potential to grow.[3] According to UNCTAD/UNDP (2010: 180), Mexican creative industries account for 4.77 percent of GDP. ProMéxico, the government institution that is responsible for attracting foreign investment and for the export of goods and services, rated the creative industries as the fifth most important strategic industry for Mexico, after aerospace, agriculture, food and the automotive industries.[4] In the international market, Mexico is the leading Latin American country and ranked 18th in the world in terms of the export of creative goods. The export of creative services also rose from USD $62 billion in 2002 to $185 billion in 2008, with an average annual growth rate of 17 percent.

The Mexican government is devoted to developing its creative economy. In *Programa Nacional de Cultura 2007–2012,* a special chapter is dedicated to cultural industries. The government has launched a federal programme to provide funding and technical training for them. The programme is based on loans from the commercial banking system, granted on favourable terms, as a step towards initiating public/private cooperation in the sector. President Peña Nieto also established the *Instituto Nacional del Emprendedor* to coordinate and support policies for entrepreneurs and SMEs, to benefit start-ups in audiovisual design and production (Martinez, n.d.). In addition, successive governments have implemented a series of schemes to fund and promote creative businesses. Among the strongest are:

- *EFI Cine 226:* Provides a tax break for cinematographic producers;
- *FIDECINE:* An investment fund that finances the production, post-production and distribution of feature-length films;
- *TechBA (Technology Business Accelerator):* Provides a platform for technology-based local companies to facilitate their success in the international market;
- *ProSoft Mexico:* A development programme for technology and information-based services;
- *National Council of Science and Technology (CONACYT):* Provides government funding for private-sector research that can lead to commercial outcomes;
- *Pro-Audiovisual Fund (ProAv):* Government support for cinematography and audiovisual productions, with the aim of internationalisation.

The development of the Mexican creative economy takes a 'cluster' approach, with an emphasis on the digital sectors. The Federal Government has designated Guadalajara as the Digital Creative City, the most important place for digital media production enterprises, specifically in videogames, movies, multimedia and mobile applications.[5] Other industry clusters include (Martinez, n.d.):

- An interactive media and entertainment cluster in Monterrey;
- Creative industries cluster in Roma-Condesa;
- Interactive media and entertainment cluster in Nuevo Leon;
- InteQsoft in Querétaro.

Furthermore, Mexico is as enthusiastic for cultural events as are other Latin American countries. Expos, trade fairs, festivals, fashion weeks and conferences are held all year round. The Festival Internacional Cervantino in Guanajuato is one of the most important. It lasts 19 days and covers a wide spectrum of artistic disciplines including music, dance and theatre. In 2012 the festival hosted a total of 135 artistic groups from 26 countries and it received over half a million visitors.[6] Sectors also hold their own events. For instance, Mexico hosts as many as ten film festivals on a yearly basis, in Guadalajara, Guanajuato and elsewhere. International events are also featured. In 2013, MoMA (New York) dedicated its 'Destination:

Design' programme to Mexico, for which the work of over 60 designers was showcased and sold at MoMA Stores.[7] The 19th World Congress on Information Technology (WCIT 2014), claiming to be the 'Olympics of the ICT World', was held in Guadalajara in May 2014.

The cultural and technological infrastructure of Mexico are both well in place. Proximity to the world's strongest economy next door in the USA, and its own leading position in Latin America (for instance, in telecommunications), present great opportunities for the development of Mexico's creative economy. According to the ANUIES/IMD's *Competitiveness Yearbook 2012*, Mexico offers higher quality of human resources than the BRIC countries. Nevertheless, current training programmes are inadequate and business links are weak: these are the challenges that Mexico has to overcome.

Indonesia

According to World Economy Forum, in 2013 Indonesia ranked 38th out of 148 countries for global competitiveness. Its mobile users ranked at 6th and internet users 13th. Furthermore, it is the third largest Facebook user in the world. These rankings show that the social network market of Indonesia is large and growing. But challenges remain.

The uptake of creative industries in Indonesia can be traced back to the mapping documents published by the government in 2007, under the leadership of Trade Minister Mari Pangestu, followed by a research report in 2009 and vision plans to 2015 and 2025. The formulation and implementation of these plans involved 27 ministries or government units, which are designed to enhance the role of creative industries in the economy (Simatupang et al., 2012). After a Cabinet reshuffle, the new Ministry of Tourism and Creative Economy took over the 'creative industries' portfolio from Trade, with Mari Pangestu appointed as the new Minister in 2011,[8] with an emphasis on the correlations and convergence between tourism and the creative economy. This is not only reflected in President Yudhoyono's speech on the topic,[9] but also in the establishment of an Indonesia Creative Tourism Forum.[10] Given Indonesia's ethnic and cultural diversity, and the popularity of craft items such as batik and various 'maker'-style goods, ranging from houseware and furniture to musical instruments, it is no surprise to see creativity linked with tourism, such that traditional arts and crafts, heritage creative customs, forward-facing fashion and new media productions all go hand in hand.

Creative Industries are deemed to be viable avenues for job creation, poverty eradication, increasing national income, and nurturing national pride. The 14 focused sectors are:

1. Architecture
2. Design
3. Fashion
4. Movies, video and photography
5. Craft
6. Computer services and software
7. Music
8. Art market
9. Publishing and printing
10. Advertising
11. Interactive games
12. Research and development
13. Performing arts
14. Television and radio

In 2010, Minister Mari Pangestu said that the contribution of creative industries to Indonesia's exports (excluding gas and oil) reached around 7.5 percent – comparable with that of the UK and way ahead of 'advanced' neighbour Australia.

With the cooperation of international institutions like the British Council, cities such as Bandung and Jakarta are enhancing their image as creative cities. Bandung in particular is committed to creative branding. Like Indonesia as a whole, it is also a young city, with 60 percent of the population under 40 years old. The creative strategy has the support of the university sector in the city.[11]

Bali is the traditional capital of popular music of Indonesia (Baulch, 2007). Musicians are working with art communities as well as people from the fields of design, fashion, filmmaking, even urban farming. Small independent businesses started to flourish by 2008 and Bali Creative Communities was founded.[12]

In Jakarta, small creative businesses have emerged, set up by young people. The Old Town of Jakarta is being revitalised to become the creative playground of the city.[13] Creative hubs are emerging. A Creative Centre was established in Bandung by the Directorate of Cooperation and Facilitation in May 2012 as a gathering place for creatives in the digital economy, i.e. games developers, software application developers, etc.

Events like 'Creative Class, Unite (Welcoming Bali Creative Festival 2011)' and 'Creativities Unfold 2011: Building Business with the World's Creative Thinkers and Doers' are organised to assist the growth of the creative economy. An initiative called New Design Maker Indonesia aims to find and map potential design works and to select 50 designers to be awarded seed money, and offers mentoring and training programmes, business-matching, fieldwork trips, etc.[14]

Nigeria

Nigeria is now one of the most developed countries in Africa; set to overtake South Africa as that continent's leading economy. In 2014, the Nigerian National Bureau of Statistics announced that the country's GDP had reached $509.9 billion USD. A new calculation system included ten new categories, reflecting spending and income, as well as putting greater weight on fast growing sectors such as communications and entertainment. Recasting the statistical method reduced the share of mining and construction to 20 percent (from half, in previous accounts), and agriculture declined from over 30 percent to 20 percent. In contrast, the service sector doubled its share to account for 50 percent overall, and manufacturing increased from 2 percent to 7 percent. These figures show that Nigeria is moving away from an oil-oriented economy towards a modern service-based economy.[15]

However, except for raising international awareness of Nigeria, the new figures were received by some as 'an exercise in vanity' with little change observable on the ground.[16] According to the International Monetary Fund, while the GDP ranking has moved up 11 steps to become the world's 26th largest economy, the GDP per capita remained low, at 121st.[17] Poverty is still a severe problem. The Nigerian growth rate over the previous five years reached 7 percent, compared with South Africa's 3 percent, but the basic infrastructure in power, roads and communication did not compare with South Africa's. The mobile phone network and internet accessibility also leave much to be desired. In addition, South Africa still represents a responsible, developed and diversified economic system, which Nigeria has yet to achieve.

Agoralumiere International has conducted research on Nigeria's creative economy with the support of the Federal Ministry of Commerce and Industry (Kwanashie et al., 2009). The research drew samples from Abuja and Zaria. Via interviews with various actors and questionnaires to map the creative activities in the two cities, the research identified limited access to funds, a weak local market, poor training, etc. as obstacles to the development of the creative economy in Nigeria. It concluded with pertinent suggestions including the need to articulate creative assets embracing cultural, economic, social and technological aspects; the need to establish an action team across different ministries and sectors, to focus on the creative industries and assist production and export; the need to strengthen the competitiveness of Nigerian cultural goods and services within the framework of globalisation and liberalisation of the market; and the need to fight piracy.

In such apparently unpropitious circumstances, the rise of Nollywood has attracted the attention of the creative world (Lobato, 2010). With a production capacity of 50 full-length features per week, Nollywood has overtaken Hollywood as the second largest producers of film in the world (after Bollywood). The rise of this industry has shown the possibility of spontaneous growth of a sector and huge demand for entertainment. Film is now Africa's first medium, replacing music and dance. It profoundly shapes how Africans see their own continent, and it 'links distant societies, fosters the exchange of ideas and drives fashion trends'.[18]

Nollywood is based on informality in both production and distribution. The informality has largely eliminated the distance between the film and audience, given that most films are made into VCDs and consumed at home, not in cinemas. But shortcomings of this model are also apparent. Besides the question of quality, piracy is endemic. Storylines are not suited to the mainstream international market, although informal distribution of Nollywood DVDs is fully international. However, with the support of the Nigerian government, Nollywood could become better branded. Agoralumiere suggested that the government should promote Nollywood as an international platform by organising events like Cannes and Berlin Film Festivals.

In all, the creative economy of Nigeria has taken off, but is not fully fledged. Further steps are under way. In 2012, the federal government launched reforms of the copyright system, and a Nigerian Copyright Commission (NCC) was established in 2014.[19] The Bank of Industry (BOI), which manages the government's Entertainment Fund, restated the government's commitment to developing Nigeria's creative industry, so as to contribute to national economic growth. An initiative of BOI is to work with the All Africa Music Awards (AFRIMA) to find the talents scattered across the country. Another influential event is the annual Creative Industry Awards, inaugurated by the Creative Entrepreneurs Association.[20]

Turkey

Lacking official data, the creative economy of Turkey is mapped by international organisations such as UNCTAD and academics. The Creative Economy Report 2010 released by UNDP and UNCTAD has measured the import and export of creative goods and services of Turkey from 2002–2008. The areas covered include: art, crafts, audio-visuals, new media, performing arts, publishing, visual arts, advertising, architecture, R&D, and personal, cultural and recreational services. Data show the exports of Turkey's creative industries have increased from USD $4864 million to $6593 million with a growth rate of nearly 15 percent, while imports have increased from USD $1325 million to $3758 million, growing by over 25 percent. From 2002 to 2008, the main destination for Turkish exports was Europe (over 50 percent). Asia overtook America as the second major destination (increasing from 17 percent to 30 percent); while exports to the Americas fell (from 24 percent to 11 percent). Export to Africa also increased a little bit (from 3 percent to 5 percent) while that to Oceania decreased (from 1 percent to 0 percent).[21]

Lazzeretti and colleagues (2014) evaluated the cultural and creative industries of Turkey between 2008 and 2011. Their study uses DCMS's categories as a reference point in the hope of international comparison. Drawing on data from Turkish Statistical Yearbooks and other official sources, the study indicates that the number of employees in the Turkish creative industries is approximately 191,634 for 2011, an increase of 38 percent from 2008. The creative industries generated a 2 percent share of the total employment of Turkey by 2011.

The creative economy of Turkey is much more readily mapped at the city level. As the nineteenth-century French poet and statesman Alphonse de Lamartine put it: 'If one had but a single glance to give the world one should gaze on Istanbul'. Istanbul is undoubtedly leading Turkey's creative vibe. As an ancient city with a rich heritage from the Byzantine and Ottoman Empires, it also welcomes modern and contemporary art. Almost all of Turkey's major cultural and creative businesses have their headquarters in the city. Meanwhile, 49 percent of visits to museums and 30 percent of cultural performances in Turkey take place there.[22] Since its designation as European 'Capital of Culture' in 2010, it has become one of the centres for creative activities among European countries. Along with the capital city of Ankara, these two cities represent more than 64 percent of the total employment in Turkey.

Furthermore, some of the individual creative sectors are worth investigating. For instance, although Turkey is the leading exporter of furniture to Europe, the film industry is considered the most popular and outstanding creative sector in Turkey. The majority of film businesses are located in Istanbul, in particular in the district of Yesilcam; meanwhile, Antalya promises to be 'an emerging Eurasian film centre' as in 2006, Golden Orange Film Festival became a member of the International Eurasia Film Market, and started to host this market during the festival.[23] The development of the film industry is boosted by film festivals. While every year an average of 30 feature films is produced in Turkey, 35 film festivals are organised nationally or in collaboration with Germany, the Black Sea Region, and Far Eastern countries, etc.[24] Besides the Antalya Golden Orange Film Festival, which has been held annually since 1963, other major events include the International Istanbul Film Festival and Adana Golden Ball Film Festival.

The Ministry of Culture and Tourism sponsors a range of activities in cities in the field of theatre and film, as well as festivals, concerts, exhibitions, conferences and fairs.[25] At the same time, many of the non-profit organisations have played an important role. The İstanbul Foundation for Culture and Arts (İKSV) is one of the pioneers. Founded in 1973 by 17 businessmen and art enthusiasts, the original objective of İKSV was to organise an international arts festival in Istanbul. Now it hosts five signature biennales in the fields of film, theatre, music, jazz and design, as well as smaller events such as Filmekimi (a week of film screenings in October) and Phonem by Miller (alternative rock and electronic music performances in November). Moreover, it initiated an İstanbul Friends of Culture and Arts Tulip membership programme, which gathers art enthusiasts and provides members a variety of privileges during İKSV events.[26] Some other leading institutions include: The Association of Creative Industries Council (YEKON),[27] founded by 11 non-governmental organisations resulting from the disciplines of performing studies in the Turkish creative industries sector; and the Association for Intercultural Communication and Interdisciplinary Art.

Cultural spaces are also built in cities: for instance, the Vakko Fashion Center Nakkaştepe, which includes Turkey's first creative industries library – Vitali Hakko Creative Industries Library. It was inaugurated by Vakko, one of Turkey's leading fashion houses, in 2010.[28] In 2012, an Istanbul Centre for Creative Economy, Cultural Industries and Creative Cities was established at the Istanbul Commerce University, with the partnership of the Ministry of Trade and Customs, Metropolitan Municipality of Istanbul and Istanbul Chamber of Commerce. The aims of this Centre are to carry out policy-oriented research and to build global and local networks involving all related parties. UNCATD has supported the setting-up of this Centre, and was invited to join the advisory board with other international recognised experts. In 2014, UNCATD signed a Memorandum of Understanding to make its link with the Centre official. Its responsibility is to facilitate the development of creative industries networks in Istanbul.[29]

In all, the rich cultural heritage, the geographical bridge between Asia and Europe, and the open attitude to modern and diversified culture (albeit one that seems under attrition by an authoritarian central government), present great potential for Turkey to develop its creative economy. Furthermore, Turkey possesses a very promising talent pool and cultural market, as a country of young people (about 31 million of a total population of 71 million are under 25), and this young population is technologically connected and globally networked.[30] Nevertheless, in comparison to China, Riada Asimovic Akyol believes Turkey could boost its creative economy with 'improved education, closer ties to industry, greater incentives to innovate and better protection of intellectual property rights', as well as 'an environment that's open, stable and healthy to thrive', in order to secure and strengthen Turkish 'soft power'.[31]

Creative planet

The BRICS and MINT countries are among the fastest-growing economies in the world, while the BRICS are comparatively more developed than the MINT. These countries span Latin America (Brazil, Mexico), Asia (India, China, Indonesia), Africa (South Africa and Nigeria) with two that bestride Asia and Europe (Russia and Turkey). It is not necessary for the countries in the same region to share most commonalities; however, in some cases this is true.

The Latin American region is well known for its enthusiasm towards music, dancing, as well as carnivals/festivals. Along with the development of fashion and film, Brazil and Mexico are already 'creative'. The aim of promoting an official 'creative economy' is to translate cultural competitiveness into economic success by boosting the growth of creative enterprises. In the sense of hosting great cities and international festivals, Turkey can be a member of this group with its specific advantages in the talent pool and cultural market.

Many Asian countries are populous, and are going through an age of 'transformation'.[32] India has shown competitiveness in film and technological industries; China has been craving for innovation that has stronger economic significance. The theme of transformation indicates a new stage following the 'reform' period; that is, a shift from a low-cost manufacturing-based economy to a high-end knowledge-intensive economy, from copying to independent innovation and urbanisation, and from production-for-export to a fully mature domestic consumer market.

Meanwhile, Russia and China form an interesting pair: both of them are governed by 'strong governments' and have a history of 'the planned economy'. They are also both rich in culture (one in high culture and the other in traditional culture), but have experienced some trouble in innovating upon it. Nevertheless, the attitudes of entrepreneurs from the two countries towards their government are entirely different. According to O'Connor (2005), Russian entrepreneurs seem to be quite indifferent to official policy initiatives. In contrast, Chinese entrepreneurs are eager to follow the official policy line. Big construction groups (e.g. Zhongnan Group) invested heavily in animation; media groups initiated large-scale cultural projects. Whenever a national policy is released, the regions and cities followed, in their own way. For instance, every district of some cities built a cultural and creative industries office, which is responsible for promoting the creative economy, or more specifically, for building creative 'parks' and organising events in the areas under their jurisdiction. Nevertheless, many of these offices or district government were confused, at least at the beginning, about the 'creative industries'. Some of the parks survived and gradually they have more clearly positioned themselves, but many others have had trouble in running.

Some observers are of the opinion that China cannot be truly creative because resistance cannot go public; 'creative' only means creativity in economic terms. However, as our Chapter 7 ('everyone') has demonstrated, there is more way than one way to express dissent or difference, and creativity finds outlets other than the barricade or spray can in the street. Meanwhile, in Russia, artists find resistant culture attractive, but how that intersects with the public at large is not so clear, since it is not based in 'user' culture so much as in the intelligentsia, which is traditionally hostile to commercialisation. The question here is not about whether or not dissent or resistance is possible, but whether it is the best way to communicate with the population at large. For this, commercialisation can make ideological as well as economic sense.

South Africa and Nigeria are both 'brothers' and 'competitors'. The re-calibration of statistical systems and the growth rate of 7 percent caused Nigeria to surpass South Africa to become the largest economy in Africa. However, South Africa is still endowed with sufficient infrastructure and a mature environment for investment. Though poverty alleviation is still the primary task for the economy, Nigeria has developed an outstanding film industry and changed the cultural climate of Africa, with film overtaking dance and music as the leading edge of creative expression. South Africa seems to be ready for a creative economy, but the lack of an iconic industry may impede the confidence of the creative sectors. Nevertheless, the cultural spaces in Johannesburg and Cape Town are better developed, and the *ReaGilè* experimental township cinema project (see Chapter 10) shows how innovative solutions are being tried and tested to suit the local conditions.

Although South Korea and Japan are not in the BRICS or MINT (Korea is sometimes included by changing the formula to BRICKS), the two countries are essential to the creative landscape of Asia, and play a key role in the pop culture of the world. Japan and Korea have not only boosted their economy with creativity, but they have also become international cultural icons via such innovations as manga, 'cute culture' and the 'Korea Wave' (*hallyu*). The achievements of these creative economies are apparent and well documented in reports and in the scholarly literature: their experiences are much analysed, referenced and copied. We cannot analyse them here in the detail they deserve because of space constraints, but the example of Japan and Korea adds strongly to our argument that creative economy and culture is a globally networked phenomenon.

Japan

Japan has declared its pursuit of 'coolness', and the world seems to agree: a 2012 study by Adobe found that Japan is the most creative country and Tokyo is the most creative city.[33] The Japanese Agency of Cultural Affairs is dedicated to promoting art and culture by: (1) protecting cultural properties; and (2) initiating programmes of new cultural facilities, festivals and events, increasingly in contemporary arts, visual arts and music. In the late 1990s, the Ministry of Economy, Trade and Investment (METI) started to emphasise content industries – movies, music, games software and animation (Yoshimoto, 2003). These are considered as promising creative industries with great potential; subsequent promotion policies have been released, based on analysis and study, among which the most influential ones are the 'Cool Japan' initiatives.[34]

'Cool Japan' is an international branding strategy aimed at promoting the cultural and creative industries in Japan and abroad. It boosts the recognition of Japan's cultural influence, in J-pop, manga, anime, fashion, film, electronics, cuisine and the phenomena of 'cuteness' (*kawoi*) (McGray, 2002).[35] The METI has then announced that Japanese pop culture, including idols, anime and B Class Gourmet, are a key element for Cool Japan. In June 2010, the METI established a new Creative Industries Promotion Office to promote this as a strategic sector, again, 'under the single, long-term concept of "Cool Japan"', to incorporate the different government departments and to work with private sector partners.

Furthermore, a Creative Industries Internationalisation Committee was established with a specific focus on exploring overseas markets. According to an Interim Report from this agency, the GDP value of creative industries (though without a clear definition) has reached ¥64.4 trillion yen, and employment is estimated at 5.9 million people. These figures exceed those for the automobile industry. Even so, the worldwide popularity of Japanese culture is believed to be underperforming economically, because of 'piracy' (IP infringement by users-sharers) and insufficient distribution hubs. The sector's full potential is yet to be unleashed.

Hereby, facing a growing market for creative industries, which is estimated to increase overall from the current ¥463 trillion yen to more than ¥900 trillion yen in 2020, the Cool Japan Initiative 2014 has clearly stated three purposes: (1) to create a creative Japan boom; (2) to make profits from overseas markets; and (3) to attract inward investment in Japan and to promote tourism. A series of programmes has been developed to support the initiative. For instance, CoFesta (Japan International Contents Festival) is the largest comprehensive contents festival in Japan. Eighteen events involving games, animation, comics (*manga*), characters, broadcast, music and films, as well as content-related industrial events in fashion and design, are held in collaboration with each other. CoFesta 2014 attracted 1.8 million attendances and generated contracts worth $52 million in total. The Cool Japan Matching Grand Prix holds matching sessions to support collaboration with companies of different business categories; and a Cool Japan Fund has been launched to help the establishment and growth of creative businesses.

South Korea

Since the mid-1990s, the 'Korean Wave' (*Hallyu*) that features in TV drama, entertainment programmes, films, music, animation and games, has conquered the whole of East and Southeast Asia (Hui, 2007). Interestingly, it was considered as an unexpected outcome of media liberalisation – the need to remove controls over the distribution of dominant foreign audio-visual products (Choi, 2008). With a relatively small domestic market, the Wave also showed the Korean determination and endeavour to revitalise the national economy after the Asian Financial Crisis in 1997–1998 (Hui, 2007).

The development of Korean cultural and creative industries is very much related to its national policies and regulations. As early as 1972, the *Arts and Culture Promotion Act* was introduced to promote literature, fine arts, music, dance, theatre, film, entertainment, traditional music, photography, language and publishing. In 1994, to confront the domination of foreign cultural products in domestic markets, the Cultural Industry Bureau was established within the Ministry of Culture and Sports (which was renamed Ministry of Culture and Tourism in 1998), with six divisions, namely, cultural industry, publication and newspaper, broadcasting and advertising, film and video, interactive media, and cultural contents promotion. In 1999, the *Cultural Industry Promotion Law* was enacted together with a five-year plan for the *Development of the Cultural Content Industry*. In the following years, the *Content Korea Vision 21* was published in 2000 followed by the *Culture Contents Industry Vision 21* in 2002 (Hui, 2007).

It is not difficult to see that, entering the twenty-first century, the Korean government has further emphasised the importance of 'content' (Jin, 2012). The total amount of television programming increased from $US5.5 million in 1995 to $150.9 million – 27.4 times – in 2007. Korean cultural products were consumed mostly in Asia, with 57.4 percent in Japan, 18.4 percent in Taiwan, and 8.9 percent in China and Hong Kong. Among television programmes exported, drama comprised the largest share (87.8 percent) followed by entertainment (8.4 percent), while animation accounted for only 0.6 percent in 2007 (Jin, 2012).

Meanwhile, policies with an emphasis on building a knowledge-based information society have paid off. Korea is now the most wired country in the world. Its subscription rate of high-speed internet has in fact exceeded 100 percent, the smart-phone penetration is above 70 percent, and 4G is ubiquitous in public areas.[36]

Jin (2012) has identified a *Hallyu 2.0* or a 'Korean *digital* wave' (Goldsmith et al., 2011) as a new phase of Korea's creative industries development. *Hallyu 2.0* is boosted by social media technology and social network sites (SNSs) have become the main distribution channels of global cultural products. The Korean Wave is no longer limited to Asia, but also expands to other parts of the world. Psy's 'Gangnam Style' for example is the most viewed K-pop video on YouTube with a so far unbeatable record of 2.1 billion views (by Oct 2014).[37] In fact 'Gangnam Style' is not just the most-viewed K-pop video on YouTube – it's the most watched video, period. K-Pop and online games are drivers of the new phase or 'digital wave', with a growth rate of 159 percent from $US50.9 million in 2009 to $80.9 million in 2010; and to $177 million in 2011 with a 112 percent increase (Jin, 2012).

Digital content and the exploitation of overseas markets have presented new challenges to Intellectual Property Rights protection and 'actualisation' (Jin, 2012). In July 2011, the Korean government launched the *Fundamental Law for IPR*, and set up the National IPR Committee for copyright administration. It has also invested US$9 billion to build an 'overseas copyright information database' to promote cultural and copyright exchanges.[38]

With the inauguration of President Park Geun-Hye in February 2013, Korea has stepped into a new stage. In her inaugural speech, President Park put forward a vision of creating a 'Second Miracle on the Han River' by developing a creative *economy*. She defined the term 'creative economy' as 'the convergence of science and technology with industry, the fusion of culture and industry, and the blossoming of creativity in the very borders that were once permeated by barriers.'[39] In June of the same year, the Korean government introduced its Creative Economy Action Plan. It followed the essence of the President's speech, i.e. a focus on innovation by building an ecosystem for a creative economy, and democratising it. Facing an economic structure where the sales of the top 30 conglomerates (or *chaebol*) took up 82 percent of GDP in 2012,[40] as well as an aging society, *entrepreneurship* is seen as the redeeming lifeblood of the new economy. The creative economy initiative is carried out by a series of programmes that encourages the establishment of venture capital, start-ups and education reform, for a more tolerant society.

International agencies

UN

International organisations play an important role in sharing the experiences and helping towards the localisation of creative approaches. The United Nations (UN) is the intergovernmental organisation with the largest number of members in the world. The specialised agencies and programmes of the UN that are involved with the creative economy include: The United Nations Educational, Scientific and Cultural Organisation (UNESCO), World Intellectual Property Organisation (WIPO), United Nations Development Programme (UNDP), and the United Nations Conference on Trade and Development (UNCTAD). On some occasions, the World Bank and the International Monetary Fund (IMF) (which are not UN agencies) have also conducted studies and released data on the creative economy.

UNESCO has initiated a variety of activity or research programmes to support cultural development in many countries. The most well known programme in relation to creative economy is UNESCO's Creative Cities Network. It connects the cities all over the world with extraordinary performance in seven categories, namely, literature, film, music, crafts and folk arts, design, media arts, and gastronomy. So far there are around 40 cities in the network. It aims to share the experiences of creative urban development and strengthen cultural identities of the member-cities through events and exchange programmes. Furthermore, a Culture and Creative Industries Knowledge Bank has provided access to over 500 studies, reports, surveys and mapping documents relating to the cultural and creative industries around the world.[41]

Because of the kinship between creative industries and intellectual property, WIPO – the World Intellectual Property Organisation – is also considered as a key organisation of the creative economy. In recent years, WIPO has prepared or commissioned a number of studies mapping different limitations and exceptions in many different countries in terms of cultural and creative industries.[42]

The UNDP and UNCTAD also initiated research projects on the creative economy. Their *Creative Economy Report* of 2008, 2010 and the 2013 (special edition) are now handbooks for knowing the global cultural landscape. Their statistical methodology is not universally accepted, however.

EU

The European Union (EU) is probably the second most powerful intergovernment alliance in the world. With the European Commission (EC) as its executive body, the EU, now comprising 27 countries, represents an increasing (but contested) political integration among European countries that were previously in conflict. It works primarily through economic policies and social affairs, as well as cultural affairs.

The European Capital of Culture project is a leading project for supporting the cultural and creative industries in Europe. Unlike cities that win lifetime membership when joining the UNESCO Creative Cities Network, the city that wins the title of 'European Capital of Culture' has one calendar year to organise cultural events under this title. Since 1984, over 50 European cities have held or are going to take over the torch. In addition, the project has a strong European flavour – it is designed to highlight the richness and diversity of cultures of Europe, and it aims to unite the European people on a common cultural base.

Furthermore, the European Commission has initiated a series of actions and programmes, including the Creative Europe Programme. Activities have included: a pilot project on the economy of cultural diversity; the publication of a green paper on the potential of cultural and creative industries;[43] and a workshop on 'The Future of ICT for Creativity and Creative Industries', etc.[44] Through the European Science Foundation, the EU also funds pan-European research into the creative industries, for instance through HERA (Humanities in the European Research Area), which has invested over €16.5m Euros in creative industries and cultural dynamics research (2009–11) and a further €18.5m for research into 'cultural encounters' (2012–14).[45]

UK

As 'first mover' in naming the creative industries, the UK has been the benchmark nation for this discourse. The British Council has been the leading institution in cultural exchanges, cannily combining the arts, education and business promotion. Founded in 1934, the British Council has expanded to over 200 offices in over 100 countries in the world. Each office serves as a power station for its own initiatives, and promotes connections between headquarters and the local culture. The British Council also focuses on a few priority countries in a more in-depth way. In 2014, these were Brazil, Russia, Vietnam, Indonesia, Nigeria, South Africa and Portugal. Tailored projects were co-developed to support local culture and talent, and to strengthen long-term links with the UK.

The activities of the British Council include internationalising British cultural events (e.g. Future Everything Moscow), R&D projects (e.g. Cultural Shift), professional development and skills (e.g. Nesta's Creative Enterprise Toolkit), industry exchanges (e.g. Creative Hubs Exchange) and policy investigations. Among these the Cultural Shift programme and the Young Creative Entrepreneur (YCE) programme have generated great interest for young people. The Cultural Shift programme calls up hackers to work in teams for 48 hours in order to pitch a finished prototype to a panel of judges. In two years the programme travelled to Kenya, Zimbabwe, Nigeria, Lagos, Brazil, Egypt and Russia.[46] It can be seen as part of the Maker Movement described in Chapter 8. The YCE programme aims to identify new leaders of global creative businesses, and bring them together to promote international collaboration. The YCE Awards have been held in 54 countries in ten years, and have connected 500 young entrepreneurs, which inspires start-up businesses globally.

UK Trade and Investment (UKTI) also pays great attention to the creative economy. In 2013, it set up a Creative Sector Taskforce which includes some top companies and aims to help creative businesses to win £500 million-worth of overseas contracts over the following three years. In June 2014, along with the Creative Industries Sector Advisory Group, it published a research report named *UK Creative Industries: International Strategy* to help increase exports and inward investment.

Tomorrow, the world...

Besides international organisations from developed economies, alliances of developing countries also participate in creative economy development. For instance, The Dakar Plan of Action on Cultural Industries was adopted in 1992 by the Organisation of African Union (OAU) Heads of State and Government, in recognition of the potential role of cultural industries in driving economic and social development. However, necessary action has not been taken to put the creative economy at the forefront of development in member countries. In October 2008, in Algiers, African Union Ministers of Culture further articulated a Plan of Action for Cultural and Creative Industries, recognising the importance of creativity outside the cultural sector.

In all, scholars, consultants and international organisations from developed economies are eager to offer toolkits to developing countries. Many countries follow the '3T' model proposed by Richard Florida (2002), that is, to enhance a city's strength in 'technology' and 'talent', as well as to create a more 'tolerant' atmosphere, in the hope of moving forward in competitive rankings. They also build cultural quarters, renovate creative clusters, and organise events to create scenes, expecting cultural, economic and urban development to follow. Governments try to identify those key sectors that are already growing or have that potential, and to articulate policies in finance, law, etc. to boost the growth of these sectors. As well, countries have developed their own distinctive versions of a creative economy. Some are more fashionable, some are craving for innovation, and some are characterised by frugal innovation through the informal economy. 'Catching up with the West' or 'finding a new path' is not just a question facing Russia and China, but one that also faces other developing countries and emerging economies. The evidence suggests that these countries are not just following developed creative economies, or even following 'the market'; they are growing in their own way, everywhere.

Notes

1. *New Statesman*, interview with Jim O'Neill, by Sophie McBain, 23 January 2014. Available at: www.newstatesman.com/2014/01/after-brics-mints-austerity-britain-and-big-c.
2. Original paper at www.goldmansachs.com/our-thinking/archive/archive-pdfs/build-better-brics.pdf.
3. Andrés Reyes, CEO of BOXEL STUDIOS cited in Martinez (n.d.): 10.
4. See http://negocios.promexico.gob.mx/english/06-2011/businessTips/index.html.
5. See www.mexico.doingbusinessguide.co.uk/opportunities/creative-and-media/ (Powered by International Market Adviser, in association with UKTI).
6. See http://eleconomista.com.mx/entretenimiento/2012/10/21/festival-internacionalcervantino-rompe-record.
7. See http://negocios.promexico.gob.mx/english/08-2012/lifestyleFigures/art01.html.
8. See http://indonesia.travel/en/news/detail/517/minister-mari-elka-pangestu-leads-ministry-for-tourism-and-creative-economy.
9. See http://gov.indonesiakreatif.net/en/sentra-kreatif-rakyat/.
10. See www.thejakartapost.com/bali-daily/2013-06-01/creative-tourism-new-mantra.html.
11. See www.britishcouncil.org/indonesia-creativity-creative-cities-bandung.htm.
12. See www.thejakartapost.com/news/2012/10/12/after-bombs-bali-youth-drives-creative-industry.html.
13. See www.britishcouncil.org/indonesia-common-creativecitites-jakartacity.htm.
14. See http://indonesia.travel/en/news/detail/517/minister-mari-elka-pangestu-leads-ministry-for-tourism-and-creative-economy.
15. See www.tradingeconomics.com/nigeria/gdp-growth.

16. See www.aljazeera.com/news/africa/2014/04/nigeria-becomes-africa-largest-economy-20144618190520102.html.
17. See http://newspaper.jfdaily.com/isdb/html/2014-04/08/content_1156802.htm.
18. See http://www.economist.com/node/17723124.
19. *Osun Defender* at www.osundefender.org/?p=59776.
20. See www.thisdaylive.com/articles/boi-partners-afrima-to-boost-nigerias-creative-industry/176704/.
21. See UNDP & UNCTAD, Creative Economy Report 2010.
22. http://www.worldcitiescultureforum.com/cities/istanbul.
23. Durmaz, Bahar, Yigitcanlar, Tan and Velibeyoglu, Koray (2008) 'Creative cities and the film industry: Antalya's transition to a Eurasian film centre', *The Open Urban Studies Journal*, 1: 1–10.
24. A. Kamera, available from: http://www.kameraarkasi.org/festivaller.html.
25. http://www.worldcitiescultureforum.com/cities/istanbul.
26. See www.iksv.org/en/aboutus/history.
27. See www.yekon.org/.
28. See www.labkultur.tv/en/blog/vitali-hakko-creative-industries-library-turkeys-first-creative-industries-library.
29. See http://unctad.org/en/pages/newsdetails.aspx?OriginalVersionID=772&Sitemap_x0020_Taxonomy=Creative%20Economy_Programme.
30. See www.publications.parliament.uk/pa/cm201012/cmselect/cmfaff/1567/1567we24.htm.
31. See www.todayszaman.com/news-315211-what-about-creative-economy-in-turkey.html.
32. See 'Asian Creative Transformations' at www.creativetransformations.asia/.
33. The study interviewed 5000 adults across the US, UK, Germany, France and Japan. See www.adobe.com/aboutadobe/pressroom/pressreleases/201204/042312AdobeGlobalCreativityStudy.html.
34. Available at www.meti.go.jp/english/policy/mono_info_service/creative_industries/creative_industries.html.
35. Douglas McGray, 'Japan's gross national cool, foreign policy', available at http://www.foreignpolicy.com/articles/2002/05/01/japans_gross_national_cool.
36. 'Venture capitalists' insights on South Korea's creative economy and the role of startups', Retrieved from www.forbes.com/sites/meehyoekoo/2014/03/03/venture-capitalists-insights-on-south-koreas-creative-economy-and-the-role-of-startups/2/.
37. See www.timesofisrael.com/israeli-site-pioneers-do-it-yourself-tv-productions/.
38. 'How Korean wave trends the world?', available at http://english.sipo.gov.cn/news/iprspecial/201403/t20140320_919866.html.
39. 'President Park pledges new era of hope, happiness', available at http://www.korea.net/NewsFocus/Policies/view?articleId=105860.

40. 'South Korea can't just order up creative economy', available at www.bloombergview.com/articles/2013-05-30/south-korea-can-t-just-order-up-creative-economy.
41. See www.unesco.org/new/en/culture/themes/cultural-diversity/diversity-of-cultural-expressions/tools/ci-mapping/.
42. See www.wipo.int/ip-development/en/agenda/flexibilities/resources/studies.html.
43. See http://ec.europa.eu/culture/policy/cultural-creative-industries/index_en.htm.
44. See http://ec.europa.eu/digital-agenda/en/news/future-ict-creativity-and-creative-industries.
45. See www.esf.org/hosting-experts/scientific-review-groups/humanities-hum/hera-network/hera-joint-research-programme-2009.html.
46. See http://creativeconomy.britishcouncil.org/projects/culture-shift/.

PART III

FUTURE-FORMING (WITH THREE BUTS)

SCEPTICISM

12

'CECI TUERA CELA'

In Hugo's Hunchback of Notre Dame, Frollo, comparing a book with his old cathedral, says: 'Ceci tuera cela' (The book will kill the cathedral, the alphabet will kill images). McLuhan, comparing a Manhattan discotheque to the Gutenberg Galaxy, said 'Ceci tuera cela.' One of the main concerns of this symposium has certainly been that ceci (the computer) tuera cela (the book).

(Umberto Eco)[1]

'Ceci tuera cela' [This will kill that]

One of the hardest things to do when looking at future-forming possibilities is to see beyond the fears, fantasies and fights of the present (often presented as facts) and to identify what will emerge to replace them, for good or ill. A classic statement of this sensation is Victor Hugo's *Notre Dame de Paris* (1831) – better known as *The Hunchback of Notre Dame*. It is set in 1482, in the decades immediately following the invention of printing. At a crucial moment, Hugo has the antagonist Claude Frollo utter a memorable phrase: 'Ceci tuera cela' – 'This will kill that' (Book V, Ch. 1). 'This' is the printed book; 'that' is the medieval cathedral – and the whole world it stands for (see Figure 12.1). Democratic, secular print culture will supersede the authority of the church and the system of beliefs and images embodied in the great edifice in which the action is set. Readers of Hugo's Gothic masterpiece are left in no doubt as to the significance of this utterance (he devotes two chapters to discussing it: Book V, Ch. 2 and Book VI, Ch. 1). But the companions who witness it are not so sure. One of them responds: 'Hé! But what is there so alarming in this?' The other (who happens to be the King of France in disguise) agrees: 'He is mad!' After all, it's just a book!

We mention this story because the phrase 'Ceci tuera cela' – 'This will kill that' – regularly returns when new technologies of communication emerge, looking insignificant or contemptible to incumbent stakeholders but revolutionary or portentous to others. The death of the printed book in its turn has been predicted at the hands of cinema and broadcasting (Marshall McLuhan), the computer (Umberto Eco), videogames, e-books, the internet and 'the cloud'.[3] Despite scholarly scepticism about 'technological determinism',[4] it is clear (with the hindsight of centuries) that changes in communications technologies, once taken up and generalised across a society, do indeed bring down the curtain on previously dominant forms (Ong, 2012). However, they are never quite so obvious at the time. Transformations in how we organise our knowledge systems tend to be greeted at first with scepticism, dismissal and a hostile question: 'But surely…?'

Scepticism is certainly warranted where 'hype' is concerned, but at the same time the fears, fantasies and fights of the present will fade, and new systems emerge. This book proposes that we are in such a phase of transformation – to a creative economy and culture – a contention that is routinely greeted with dubious 'but surely' objections in the scholarly literature. This chapter and the next one consider three of them.

FIGURE 12.1 'Ceci tuera cela': illustration for Hugo's *Notre Dame de Paris*, by Aimé de Lemud (1889)[2]

The 'Three Buts' (Chapter 13) are: (1) **Control** (freedom); (2) **Sustainability** (comfort); and (3) **Divides** (knowledge). Consideration of each in turn makes for a long chapter, but Chapter 13 is really three chapters in one, while this one is an introduction that seeks to situate scepticism itself into a 'regime of knowledge', and to argue for an approach that values future-facing collaborative dialogue over disciplinary purity, if that is achieved only at the cost of defeating adversaries, and thereby collapsing diversity of thought into a 'party line'. The present chapter also introduces a general or systems model of the difference between control and chaos, to set the scene for the 'three buts' to follow.

But surely…?

An early study of news discourse, *Understanding News* (Hartley, 1982: 113–4), includes a section on how TV news programmes use the format of interviews to stage conflict – not only to report on it but also to dramatise the news narrative *as* conflict. Hartley identifies three forms of questioning routinely asked by interviewers. They are:

1. *How does it feel…?* You're not an expert but you're one of us: please provide emotion but no information.
2. *Isn't it…?* You are an expert, and what's more you're *our* expert: please tell us more.
3. *But surely…?* You're not one of us. What you want to say is not as important as our hostility towards you, which is what this station will communicate.

Type 1 is the *soft question* form, used for 'vox pops' and human interest, feel-good and sports stories. Type 2 is the *leading question*, used to coax information out of interviewees in line with the angle of the story adopted by the news organisation or journalist. These first two types effectively make the interviewee into a protagonist in the drama/conflict of the story. Type 3 is the classic *tough question*, used to exclude the interviewee from the 'we'-community represented by the interviewer; effectively making them and their knowledge 'our' antagonists.

It's a familiar set-up to this day. Typically, 'but surely' questions go to those who pose some sort of threat to a supposed equilibrium: strikers and demonstrators, people with radical or minority views, foreigners whose countries are different from or in dispute with 'ours', and others.

Universal-adversarial knowledge

This is how 'universal-adversarialism' works in the domain of journalism, which itself is a prime means of disseminating new information in mediated cultures. The news does not treat information as an inert information input. Instead the news brand, be that a show (Ten Eyewitness News, SBS World News, etc.), a station or a corporation (CBS, CNN, BBC, etc.), takes on the role of an actor in a drama it stages between differently weighted and moralised types of information, by using its own institutional voice to speak *as* the community it addresses, as in 'we Americans' (G. Baym, 2000). That tactic *universalises* the 'we' identity and its knowledge, but simultaneously excludes outsiders (however defined) and their information, as *adversaries*, actual or potential. In the process, mainstream news lumps all kinds of 'other' together, making little distinction, in terms of their discursive positioning, among enemies, terrorists, dissidents, deviants, people with 'foreign' ideas (culture, religion, ideology), oppositional groups or organisations, minorities, or youth. All of 'these people' (or their advocates) tend to get 'but surely' questions. Thus we are left with a view of the world where 'we' can know anything and everything using our own resources, language, nation and actions (universal), which means that what 'they' know must be misconceived, malicious or misleading, a potential threat to truth and ultimately to 'us' (adversarial). Our 'information' about the world is pre-sorted to represent ourselves, not the world (Luhmann, 2012).

Whether the newsworthy interviewee is an anti-social citizen or political potentate, the journalistic thrill is in the chase, not directly in the truth. The news stages social problems and political conflict as adversarial sporting events, sport being our culture's preferred form of 'live drama'. TV commentators favour competitors from 'our' country (however poorly they perform), even as they revel in the 'world stage' afforded by international games and championships. This is a very obvious example of what evolutionary bioscientist Mark Pagel (2012b) calls 'aggressive parochialism'.[5] It seems to be a general characteristic of cultures (demic groups) seeking to defend themselves from internal and external threats, including theft or subversion of knowledge. The pattern is to characterise knowledge itself as partisan, and to treat 'knowledge agents' who bring new information into the group as trustworthy only if we already know what they will say! On the model of Olympic sport commentating, 'our' defeated hero is worth more than 'their' victorious one – trust is more valuable than truth.

If Pagel is right, this is not an example of bad faith in the media, but of something more fundamental: it's an example of how *culture* works across many (perhaps any) boundaries – between groups, languages, nations, and domains of knowledge (Hartley and Potts, 2014). Certainly, we find that the supposedly truth-seeking and dispassionate world of scholarship is not exempt from the universal–adversarial tendency. Definite strategies can be observed in much writing about the creative industries, for example, which seek to enlist readers into a partisan cause (we *versus* they). The study of culture involves self-expression, values and judgement as well as description and argumentation, and it has become highly politicised, staged as a struggle between 'critical' and 'neoliberal' ideologies, or between 'realist' and 'postmodern' theory, or between 'art' and 'commerce'. This being the case, it is not surprising to find strategies of foe-creation, adversarial exclusions and attempts to police the boundaries of a 'we' community, in order to impose limits to the sayable or thinkable in relation to scholarly treatments of the creative industries domain. In short, academic discourse is 'universalist' in its attempt to explain all phenomena, but at the same time it is adversarial – tribal, or at least demic – in putting boundaries around what 'we' know, thereby characterising 'their' knowledge as duplicitous or threatening. Thus, universal-adversarial rhetoric has emerged, and communication *between* 'opposing camps' is strained or brought to a halt.

The world of scholarship in the study of culture, commerce, communication and creativity is characterised by cultural rather than scientific knowledge-strategies that have become automatic, carried on through the logics of a certain mode of colloquy. Instead of seeking the truth whether palatable or not, the field has become a rhetorical proxy for academic politics (for instance, see Breen, 1998; Miller, 2004; Kenway et al., 2006; Ross, 2007; Cooke and Lazzeretti, 2008; O'Connor, 2010; McGuigan, 2010). The 'but surely' approach predominates, making value judgements, political affiliations, and demic boundary-policing more important than expertise or knowledge. This is a pity, because it impoverishes the necessary work of argumentation (in the Popperian sense) to establish the grounds of inquiry (to a first approximation), on which further exploration and evidence gathering can be anchored, thereby advancing knowledge.

Consilience – constitution in dialogue

We want to address some of the problems associated with the creative industries and with creative industries research. However, 'but surely' questions (or 'critical approaches') of the generalised type will not work. Twentieth-century political (adversarial) categories of 'left' (progressive, libertarian) and 'right' (conservative, authoritarian) no longer hold. Which 'side' of an argument is future-facing and which is anchored in the past cannot be decided at the general (tribal) level, but only on a case by case basis. Instead of adversarialism on behalf of a pre-chosen 'we' community, in this book we argue for a conciliatory path, where the boundary between 'we' and 'they' is not determined in advance (like a barricade) but is recognised as a zone of interchange and translation among different domains (like a trading post), producing new information more intensely *because* of the clash of difference. 'Consilience' (Wilson, 1998) of this type does not mean agreeing 'uncritically' with everything 'we' do while disagreeing 'critically' with everything 'they' say; instead, it means working across boundaries of difference to understand what is at stake in an argument.

In the case of a creative economy, which we have posited in this book to be a general characteristic of the contemporary period, not just a sector of the 'capitalist' or 'neoliberal' economy, it is important to make this move, because the engine of innovation – new knowledge applied to new circumstances – is generated along these boundaries in the clash of difference. Creativity itself is a product of myriad different instances and styles of 'we'/'they' interaction and clash. The habit of 'aggressive parochialism' may have deep roots in cultural evolution as well as political argumentation, but as knowledge globalises and human groups expand to the scale of the species it is not an adequate strategy for explaining how new knowledge may be gained, except at a higher level of abstraction and integration where the clash of competition between antagonistic forces produces newness (rather than a 'winner'). In fact, the expansion of human groups, cultures, demes, and networks up to global scale causes new problems of its own, which a universal–adversarial approach can't even see, much less solve.

The first priority is to isolate difficulties that need attention, and for that, a multivalent community of argumentation is preferable to sectarian stand-off. The task of improving knowledge about the creative economy, thence to improve performance, whether in access and use or efficiency and quality, needs a conceptual community of those who care enough to argue about the best approach. Such a community is not restricted to those who already agree with each other ('isn't it?'), but is most vibrant when riven with 'robust' disagreement and disputation ('but surely') – while still recognising the disputatious parties on 'both sides' of the argument as creative members of the same community.

The trick is to *link*, not to separate, different approaches, ideologies, values and political affiliations in a larger-scale 'discourse public', a community of readers, doers, and thinkers which works socially as a form of 'poetic world-making' (Warner, 2002: 422–4) to create future possibilities using new knowledge gained from different sources and agents. As Russell Prince (2010: 136) puts it, it is 'the ongoing dialogue and connections across space that give the idea [of the creative industries] vitality'. The creative economy is not independent of its own conceptualisation, but is *constituted in dialogue* by a globally dispersed conceptual and policy community (or semiosphere), made up of very disparate people, from practitioners to theorists, marketeers to ministers. Creating 'insiders' and 'outsiders' is not only premature but risks dissolution of the creative economy idea altogether. We do not wish to propose definitions that are designed primarily to gain control of the debate. Rather, we seek to isolate the most important issues that need debating. Without divergent views, the very concept of the creative economy will fade away from public attention.

Economics or politics?

It is in that spirit – seeking to enhance the vitality of a concept by paying serious attention to its shortcomings – that we turn to 'the Three Buts'. Certain fundamental issues regularly come up when the creative industries (and their study) are discussed, although they are by no means confined to the creative sector as conventionally conceived. Nevertheless, if we are to approach the creative industries in terms of 'the Three Bigs' – across the planet, among everyone, and throughout the extended-economy – in other words as a *general capability* or 'social technology' for innovating knowledge, then it is only to be expected that such a capacious idea will be especially vulnerable to criticisms that also apply generally to modern productive life, everyday culture, and geopolitical competition. In short, if there are 'Three Bigs' that contribute to creative innovation and the growth of newness and knowledge, then there are at least *three big buts* that question whether any such claim can be made in light of opposing tendencies.

This is a common experience in modernity, where 'progress' in knowledge, freedom and comfort for some (Hartley, 1996) seems so often to precipitate – or even to be a product of – its hideous 'other' for others: war, colonialism, slavery and economic exploitation; sexual and other forms of personal oppression; holocaust and genocide; climate-change, environmental degradation and extinction of other species; resurgent religiosity and ideological intolerance. It should be quite easy to counter any claim of improvement in conditions for the human population at large with a quite justified 'but surely…?' question.

It is important to remain open to such questions, including in their more mundane, less apocalyptic guise, where relative gains *here* (profits for company *x*) are offset by relative losses *there* (sweatshops for developing country *y*), where freedom for some entails servitude for others, or the growth of knowledge is hijacked by elites leaving majorities in ignorance. Is this the fate that awaits the creative economy and digital networks (Zittrain, 2008)?

But equally, paying attention to longer term trends, it is important to remain open to the possibility that today's low-wage and exploited population, with limited access to clean air and nutrition, let alone education, welfare and political representation, may be evidence not of a system of rigid power-differentials between the 'haves' and the 'have-nots', but of the 'growing pains' of an emergent system that will – in time, and taken at population level – improve everyone's circumstances.

Such was the case in nineteenth-century London and Glasgow; such is the case in contemporary urban China. No-one would argue that the great American cities – New York, Chicago – were built without corruption, racketeering and gangsterism; but built they nevertheless were, to become the latest wonders of the world: this took capital *and* labour; not one or the other (Cowen, 2013). Again, the same can be argued in the case of emergent economies – check out contemporary Shanghai or Shenzhen. The acid test for future-facing as opposed to repressive/regressive 'regimes' in both cases is whether the engine for growth – the growth of knowledge – is still running in favour of general improvements, taking large populations out of poverty, and the activism of representative associations through which citizens can advocate and agitate for their own interests.

Control – a *system* concept

There are three types of control that have attracted critical attention: technical, political and commercial. We will discuss each of these in the next chapter. But first we need to lay out some general principles. The situation is not one of simple opposition, or binary choice between two alternatives: *either* you have control, *or* there will be chaos; *either* you have freedom, *or* there will be tyranny. Instead, there is an entropy gradient from order to disorder (as shown in Figure 12.2 below), with an optimum state of 'poise' somewhere between total control (impotence) and chaos (entropy), where the system works best (resilience, adaptability, efficiency) because it has enough flexibility to change and enough structure to remain stable.

```
                   Entropy gradient
ORDER→                                          ←CHAOS
                          ──╫──
                      |←'Poise'→|
```

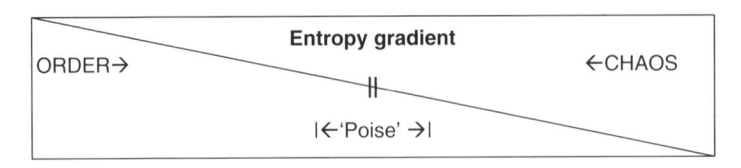

FIGURE 12.2 Control: not the opposite of chaos but a position of 'liquidity' or 'antichaos' in a 'poised system' (Kauffman, 1991)

This zone of poise is not predefined, but must be found by trial and error, a process that is inherent in a complex adaptive system itself, as part of what is known as 'autopoiesis' or 'self-creation', because complex systems with resilience enough to survive are *self-organising* (Luhmann, 2012), whether they are biological, technological or social systems.

In that context, 'control' as such is neither positive nor negative: it is endogenous to a complex system. However, human agents, especially leaders and control-elites, tend to think that control needs to be *imposed* exogenously, from the outside, and the more the better. Thus, in practice, policy activity tends to veer towards deciding not how much control the *system* wants, but how much control the *leadership* wants. As a result, policy settings tend to require more 'order' than 'chaos' – more control is imposed than is needed to keep a complex system in poise, be that system an organised population (nation, city, market) or an 'engine' of productivity (firm, institutional bureaucracy, technical network). Policymakers fear that just as an engine needs a governor to regulate speed (rotational speed of the driveshaft or road speed of the vehicle), so governors and regulators are needed to stabilise forward motion (into the future) of complex social systems. Unlike centrifugal or fly-ball governors, however, social governors and regulators have minds of their own, and are not always proportional in their action. Almost invariably, the control setting is too high, leading to inefficiency (lack of flexibility; slow speed) in the self-organising running of the system, producing friction in the form of resentment and dissatisfaction among those whose sociality is thus controlled.

Most critical attention is paid to political and commercial control, which is exerted through direct coercion, government regulation or market power. The extremes are unviable. Total control is rigidity and impotence; total openness is chaos and disorganisation. Some degree of organisation is required; but some degree of unpredictable chance is also necessary for the system to thrive. An open market, open competition, and personal freedom still require regulation, both formal via rule of law, and social via informal sanctions, to keep the playing field level for cooperating players, to discourage free-riders, to assist disadvantaged or developing groups, and to train new entrants into the system. But over-regulation, prohibitions, private deals (corruption) and the arbitrary or capricious exercise of power, all damage the workings of the system as a whole.

Productivity requires some balance among alternative and often contending pressures. Different systems, phases, and regimes may experience (or be subject to) different settings at the same time: as for example in some countries where markets are opening up, family relations (private life – gender roles, etc.) remain rigidly controlled (i.e. where inequality is social rather than economic); or in others where a tendency towards centralising control (including bureaucracy), or government intervention and prohibition, go beyond any real risks to stability, imposing a rigidity that, far from protecting the system, eventually causes it to disrupt and re-form. Dictatorships are the common example of this, but the tendency remains in democratic forms, which are also commonly subject to authoritarian impulses from ideologically motivated parties or personalities.

Stuart Kauffman has explained the general principle of tension between order and chaos in complex, self-organising networks, using Boolean mathematics to show that computer systems and biological systems (organisms) display the same behaviour. He suggests that order is analogous to 'solid' inflexibility; chaos to 'gaseous' disorder; and the transition phase or adaptation space between the two states is 'liquid'. In any complex network – and we suggest that this applies to social systems like politics and commerce as much as it does to technological or biological systems (because all such systems are based on communication and knowledge) – there is a 'poised' zone of 'liquid transition between ordered and chaotic organisations'. This 'liquid' state is crucial for the survival of systems, because it is where dynamic change or *evolution* can be observed, and successful networks 'converge toward the boundary between order and chaos':

> Networks on the boundary between order and chaos may have the flexibility to adapt rapidly and successfully through the accumulation of useful variations. ... Poised systems will ... typically adapt to a changing environment gradually, but if necessary, they can occasionally change rapidly. These properties are observed in organisms. (Kauffman, 1991: 82)

Kauffman's characterisation of the optimum balance or poise of evolving systems can be laid out as a diagram (see Figure 12.3). On the left extreme is

Centralised control		Self-organising system		Uncoordinated entropy
Order ('solid')		Poise ('liquid')	‖	Chaos ('gaseous')
Technical/matter Order→	o	Organic	‖	←Chaos
Political/social Order→	o	Freedom	‖	←Disorder
Commercial/network Order→	o	Open market	‖	←unorganised
Actual situation =	o	poised system =	‖	
		|------------policy gap------|	

The tension between order and chaos in complex, self-organising networks. The figure shows that a 'poised system' (‖) may not coincide with the actual situation (o), resulting in instability and unsustainability where there is too much or (more rarely) too little control. The purpose of policy here is simply to narrow the gap between the actual situation and the poised state for each system (technological, political, commercial, etc.). Good policy is not to *impose* control but to *find*, by trial and error, the 'liquid' state where systems can both adapt and sustain themselves.

FIGURE 12.3 Order, chaos, poise and policy

order: frozen, inflexible, unalterable, impotent; on the right is chaos, disorder, disorganisation, entropy; and somewhere between is a 'liquid' or poised state of (adaptive and productive) tension between chaos and what Kauffman calls 'antichaos' (1991: 78), where dynamic systems 'crystallise' into a high degree of order (shown in Figure 12.3 as position | |).

However, as Figure 12.3 also shows, most real social systems, such as political and commercial systems, are not left alone to find their own poise. On the contrary, they are subject to control, imposed externally by agencies such as governments and firms, as well as being built into technologies and matter itself in order to channel users to proprietary solutions. These points (shown in Figure 12.3 as **o**) tend systematically towards the pole of control. Political and commercial discourses routinely cite fear of disorder or chaos to justify authoritarian control, but that 'solution' (command and control) is just as dangerous. Political disputation is properly about whether more control or more openness is required in any given setting. The trick for policymakers is to find the optimum point of poise (which is self-finding in natural systems), without knowing it in advance, and then to keep the actual situation for any given example as close to that point as possible. The trick for analysts is not to argue for one extreme or the other, but to gather and sift evidence that will locate the auto-correcting 'liquid' state, and to argue for moving technical, political and commercial control practices nearer to it.

Notes

1. Thus, Umberto Eco is quoting Marshall McLuhan quoting Victor Hugo quoting Plato. 'This symposium' refers to a colloquium on the future of the book, at the Program in History & Philosophy of Science, Stanford University, September 1997. Available at: www.stanford.edu/dept/HPS/HistoryWired/Eco/EcoAfterword.html.
2. Source: University of Zurich, available at www.mediality.ch/galerie.php?id=26.
3. Here are two examples: http://insolublepancake.blogspot.com.au/2013/03/tuera-cela-on-books.html (Kindle); and http://futurebook.mit.edu/2012/05/ceci-tuera-cela/ (videogames).
4. See David Chandler's helpful account at www.aber.ac.uk/media/Documents/tecdet/tecdet.html.
5. Pagel (2012b) argues: 'The fact that cultural allegiance is most vividly expressed not in ethical behaviour but aggressive parochialism suggests it has been instrumental in protecting human beings throughout their evolution'.

13

THE THREE BUTS

De omnibus dubitandum – doubt everything.

(Karl Marx's motto, 1865)[1]

One of the purposes of this book is to demonstrate that a good deal of what is now regarded as 'exogenous' to economics – lying outside or external to the economic model in widest use – ought to be counted as 'endogenous', i.e. generated within the model. The cluster of factors that we call culture certainly generates what economists call 'exogenous shocks' – unexpected or unpredictable events that change an economy, but which can't be explained by the model. In this chapter we return to this theme, working through some of the forces that shape both cultural and economic creativity 'from without', in the sense that these pressures are exerted by agencies that are not directly involved in the creative process, but which are endemic to any cultural or communication system.

They are what we call – in true 'but surely…?' style (see previous chapter) – the 'Three Buts': (1) Control; (2) Sustainability; and (3) Divides.

Each is a good example of how 'exogenous' forces (from the point of view of individual decision-making) are also 'endogenous' (from the point of view of the system). In economics, such considerations are often discounted as being beyond the scope of the discipline. In the study of culture and creativity they are often at the centre of attention, as proxies for values that are understood as fundamental but threatened. In the way of things, where difficult things are routinely named after their opposites (thus, ministries of 'defence' are for war; ministries of 'health' are for sickness and death), the 'three buts' are most readily recognised through what they negate. Thus, *control* is seen as the threat to *freedom*; *sustainability* is the problem brought about by its opposite – unsustainability – which is a threat to *comfort* (material wellbeing) (Hartley, 1996); and *divides* means the problem of inequality between groups, and the treatment of segments of society as 'they' groups, which threatens *knowledge*. Thus, what look like 'exogenous shocks' – the exercise of power, ecological damage and social inequality – are also 'endogenous', because they determine what kinds of freedom, comfort and knowledge are available to a group or deme, whether they can be sustained, and how they may be able to grow and renew themselves.

(1) Control (freedom)

- Technical control
- Political control
- Commercial control

Technical control: the internet

In the context of technological networks, of which the most elaborate and important example is the internet, the problem of control can be illustrated quite simply by noting that *both* extremes – extreme control versus extreme openness – lie at its physical heart, from its earliest inception.

The computing, connectivity and content-sharing inventions that led to the internet and the World Wide Web were accelerated by World War 2 and during the Cold War. Computer science was given a decisive boost through the military code-breaking work of Alan Turing, first theorist of computing and of algorithms, and others in the 1940s, when national survival was at stake for countries across Europe and Asia, from Britain to China.

The internet itself was pioneered in the 1960s, during the most aggressive and paranoid phase of the Cold War, when the space race, U-2 spy-plane crisis, Berlin Wall, Cuban Missile Crisis, Sino-Indian War – and *Dr Strangelove* – made the doctrine of East/West conflict and 'Mutually Assured Destruction' seem normal. At that time, US military communications were conducted through telephone lines (as well as by radio). The telecommunication system was both highly centralised and vulnerable to attack. In the event of a nuclear strike on the USA, the destruction of the centralised command and control function would leave no means for a Presidential order to be communicated to US forces. The ability to send a simple 'Go' or 'No-Go' message would be wiped out in the first strike and, along with it, the political stance of nuclear deterrence or 'Mutually Assured Destruction' on which Western security policy rested. The geopolitical strategic balance of the world, and with it the lives of millions, hung from the thin thread of a telephone wire.

This problem was solved in principle by an electrical engineer, Paul Baran:

> It was necessary to have a strategic system that could withstand a first attack and then be able to return the favor in kind. The problem was that we didn't have a survivable communications system, and so Soviet missiles aimed at U.S. missiles would take out the entire telephone-communication system. ... that was highly centralized. Well, then, let's not make it centralized. Let's spread it out so that we can have other paths to get around the damage. (Paul Baran)[2]

Baran proposed shifting from a centralised to a *distributed* system, using a simple (and now iconic) diagram to visualise how a *distributed system* can survive substantial damage. If information is reticulated through the system in small 'packages' – a term coined by the Welsh computer scientist Donald Davies[3] – it can find its way through whichever links and nodes are still active, rather than relying on a single line of communication. The system as a whole is more robust, being able to sustain substantial losses without collapsing as a system. Grimly, Baran's solution would work: the retaliatory order: 'Go!' (i.e. deliver nuclear annihilation to an adversary's cities and citizens) could still get through.

In the event, neither the military authorities nor the incumbent telco (AT&T) adopted Baran's model when it was offered to them in the 1960s. It was declassified, thus coming to the attention of internet pioneers such as Lawrence Roberts, who liked the robust network and 'packet switching' model rather than circuit-switching (or direct line) connections.[4]

Baran's distributed mesh of links and nodes, then, was the first 'diagram' of the internet (Figure 13.1), even though it wasn't designed for that application.

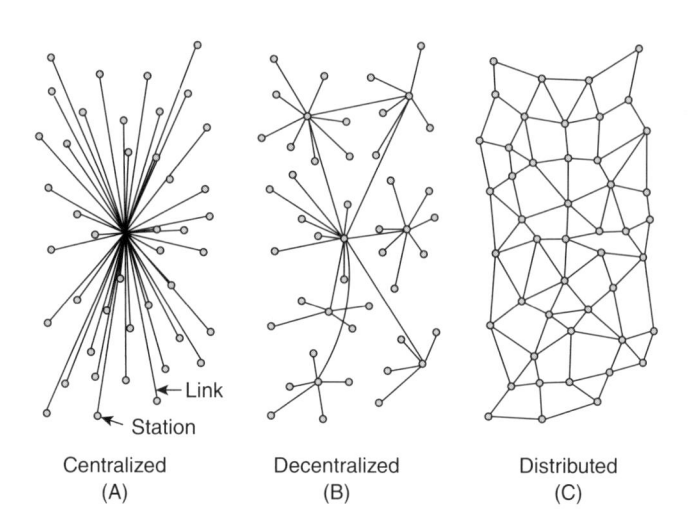

FIGURE 13.1   Paul Baran's 1964 diagram
(*www.cybertelecom.org/notes/baran.htm*)

It was important, however, because it 'dethroned' command-and-control hierarchy, and made 'control' disappear as a separate function, distributing it locally, handing it over to the user. Such a system would still enable doomsday 'Go/No Go' decisions to be transmitted by commanders, but in order for that to be possible the technology had to permit any node in the system to originate messages as well as to relay or receive them, i.e. *not* to be under the direct control of commanders.

Here, the 'poised position', which is connected openness, comes into focus. Many technical pioneers of the internet and World Wide Web were minded towards libertarian rather than authoritarian values, and wanted the system to be as open, universal and self-organising as possible. They wanted human systems (government, corporations) to shift further along the 'control/freedom' gradient towards the 'open' side, following the logic of technological systems. That open vision has remained strongly associated with internet activism, both corporate and individual (Benkler, 2006; Zittrain, 2008). It is well summed up in the work of the Internet Society, founded in 1992 by pioneers Vint Cerf, Bob Kahn and others. The Society represents over 130 organisations, collectively responsible for standards, policy and education. It is also the parent for the Public Interest Registry, which is responsible for the dot-org domain. At the outset the Internet Society was largely focused on engineering and technical standards related to Internet Protocols, but it has more recently taken on a wider educative and advocacy role, for instance by establishing the Internet Hall of Fame. Its mission statement could hardly be more 'open' in aspiration:

> *The Internet Society is a leading advocate for a free and open Internet, promoting the open development, evolution and use of the Internet for the benefit of all people throughout the world.*[5]

On behalf of its many corporate and individual members, the Internet Society promotes an open-access, affordable and reliable system that is controlled by its users, not by Network owners or governments. It favours transparent processes and consensus-based decision-making:

> *The Internet Society helps to make sure the beliefs at the core of the Internet's success remain with people that use it. Policies will shape if it stays that way or if control shifts away from the user and more towards Network owners. We envision a future in which people around the world can use the Internet to improve their quality of life. Standards, technologies, business practices, and government policies can sustain an open and universally accessible platform for innovation, creativity, and economic opportunity. Our vision of an Internet that is truly for everyone gives us our strength, motivation, and energy.*[6]

Its vision of the future is explicitly oriented towards an internet that is 'truly' for '*everyone*'. In recognising that technology, firms and governments '*can* sustain' an open-access, universal system, it recognises implicitly that these are the culprits when 'control shifts away from the user'.

Thus, technical control inevitably becomes entangled with political and commercial control; and technical capabilities do not determine actual situations, which are an outcome of pressures from different directions: the technological architecture; users (whether organised into advocacy associations or simply acting for themselves in social networks); firms; and government agencies. Technological control itself shifts 'down the line', as for instance where corporations require users to purchase specific formats or equipment (e.g. Mac or PC), favouring proprietary rather than generic parts and systems, which reduces interoperability; or where content-providers require you to purchase a bundle of services (pay-TV channels) if you want to access just one show (*Game of Thrones*);[7] or where governmental or other regulatory agencies block access to certain types of site, content, or user, for moral–political reasons. This is where popular dissatisfaction with the internet originates – not at the level of its fundamental architecture but via the impediments put in the way of open access and user-control by regulatory agencies or rent-seeking enterprises. The 'but surely' question is perhaps better addressed to them.

Political control

'The internet' can mean many things. Among them is 'Western threat to our country's national security'. High profile government interventions are newsworthy, for example when the government of Turkey moved to ban Facebook and Twitter after comments critical of the Prime Minister were widely circulated in 2014.[8] The best-known country in relation to imposing political control on the internet is China. Not only does the central government routinely regulate its own domestic users' access and restrict online activities, but it also opposes internet openness as part of its foreign policy, using diplomacy to build a coalition of countries opposed to internet freedom. Such a stance sees no difference between 'criticism' and 'overthrowing the government', and incidentally casts internal dissidents as adversarial outsiders, as is evident from this 2014 news story in the *New York Times:*

> Guo Shengkun, China's minister of public security, said at a six-nation security conference in Tajikistan that Russia and Central Asian countries must strictly control the Internet and prevent 'external forces' from trying to overthrow governments and 'provoke a new wave of color

> revolutions.' ... 'This is a serious threat to the sovereignty and security of countries in the region and is a shared concern of the S.C.O. [Shanghai Cooperation Organisation] member states,' Mr. Guo said ... 'external forces are using the social-economic contradictions and problems' to try 'to overthrow the authorities.'[9]

'The authorities' in this case are not about to let the system self-organise to find its own 'poised' position. There is no doubt that authoritarian (centralised command-and-control) governments tend to mark the line closer to the 'control' end of the spectrum compared with Western democracies. However, few of the latter practise what they preach. In 2013, the year of Edward Snowden's revelations, the USA, Australia and UK ranked fourth, fifth and tenth on a list of 60 countries surveyed for internet freedom:

> In fact, global internet freedom has been in decline for the three consecutive years tracked by this project, and the threats are becoming more widespread. Of particular concern are the proliferation of laws, regulations, and directives to restrict online speech; a dramatic increase in arrests of individuals for something they posted online; legal cases and intimidation against social-media users; and a rise in surveillance. (Kelly, 2013: 1)

The Freedom House Index measures three categories:

> A. **Obstacles to Access**: *assesses infrastructural and economic barriers to access; governmental efforts to block specific applications or technologies; and legal, regulatory, and ownership control over internet and mobile phone access providers.*
>
> B. **Limits on Content**: *examines filtering and blocking of websites; other forms of censorship and self-censorship; manipulation of content; the diversity of online news media; and usage of digital media for social and political activism.*
>
> C. **Violations of User Rights**: *measures legal protections and restrictions on online activity; surveillance; privacy; and repercussions for online activity, such as legal prosecution, imprisonment, physical attacks, or other forms of harassment. (Kelly et al., 2013)*[10]

Internet freedom seems to be most jealously guarded in Nordic countries (Iceland; Estonia) and most strictly controlled in Ethiopia, Syria, China, Cuba and Iran.

Political control follows technological change as well as precipitating it, so of course 'the government' has followed everyone else into the internet. The latter's reticulated mesh of interconnections and searchable data have allowed an extension of surveillance over the user-populace at a scale unparalleled in history, across all spheres of life. As Julian Assange (WikiLeaks) and Edward Snowden – among many others – have demonstrated, Western governments are addicted to snooping on their own citizens and spying on everyone else, just as much as are the authoritarian states. Here, the politics of technical control are most keenly contested (Andrejevic, 2007; Best, 2010; Morozov, 2011; Bennett and Segerberg, 2012).

Beyond direct government control, political control takes other forms, including influence by wealthy elites and lobbyists, or ideological path-dependency that favours existing meanings over new ones (hegemony). The democracies are not exempt from this mode of control. A recent US study tested whether 'economic elites', 'average citizens' or 'organised interest groups' influenced US policy decisions (Gilens, 2013; Gilens and Page, 2014). It found that 'economic elites and organised groups representing business interests have substantial independent impacts on U.S. government policy, while average citizens and mass based interest groups have little or no independent influence'. The authors conclude:

> In the United States, our findings indicate, the majority does not rule – at least not in the causal sense of actually determining policy outcomes. When a majority of citizens disagrees with economic elites and/or with organized interests, they generally lose. Moreover, because of the strong status quo bias built into the U.S. political system, even when fairly large majorities of Americans favor policy change, they generally do not get it.
> (Gilens and Page, 2014: 22–3)

This study was widely publicised under the heading 'America no longer a democracy'. Here is where the politics – of campaign funding by economic elites, the power of lobby groups, and the influence of corporate interests over elected officials – takes over from the economics. While the 'big end of town' seeks to extend its control over uncertainty by bending governments and legislatures to its will, the real game may be going on elsewhere.

Commercial control

It is easy to see that big business and economic elites can exert political control, often through proxies, out of all proportion to their demographic size. And there does seem to be an inexorable law that the rich get richer (Piketty, 2014). 'The rich', however, are not a stable group: individuals come and go;

firms rise and fall; countries change competitive position. What drives this dynamism is not under the control of rich people as individuals. Instead, they benefit from system-wide dynamics, which, because we are in the realms of uncertainty, conform to probabilistic variation and chance, not to linear predictability. The distribution of reward, celebrity and wealth follows a power law curve, where the 'winner takes all' in the sense that those (very few) at the 'head' are exponentially better off than those (very many) along the tail. However, as noted, positions change; and perhaps more important, as the system evolves, all of the agents gain the absolute benefits of growth, no matter what their relative position on the scale: *everyone* achieves more knowledge, social connectivity, semiotic and economic affluence. Thus, control may not be the first requirement for success in enterprise. It may even be that corporations struggling hardest for control – instead of striving for, say, cooperation and connectivity, newness and innovation, carving out a new niche or interacting with a new kind of audience/user – are dinosaurs, belonging to the industrial–mechanical Cold War era rather than to the creative–digital era.

'Commercial control' does not apply to all things commercial or even corporate. It is important to resist too expansive or abstract a definition of 'the' market as if everything in it and all market forms are the same. Where 'commercial control' is worthy of comment is when it interferes with self-organising mobility and entrepreneurial exercise: when it crosses the line into rent-seeking, oligarchy, monopoly or restrictive practises, and when its strategy is to confine people to the role of consumer, rather than the more creative and productive roles of user and producer. For it remains the case that *some* firms and some industry sectors crave control, not only of their own operations but also, to reduce uncertainty and minimise risk, control of markets, technologies, people's minds, and government support, even if – at the system level – such self-interested tactics are counterproductive. Even 'digitally native' tech giants seem to get hooked on control once they achieve a dominant position; or, which may amount to the same thing, everyone worries that they do.

Copyright

One important issue in the question of commercial control that affects the creative economy is that of Intellectual Property (Hargreaves, 2011), especially copyright (rather than patents, which are more important in the realm of inventions and material products). There was a time when copyright, which has its origin in the imposition of property rights on authorship and artistry (Hartley, 2013), was an arcane concept, largely confined to business-to-business transactions, for instance the use of published material by another publisher, or the protection of literary and artistic works in the international marketplace (Bern Convention). However, perhaps counter-intuitively, copyright has extended deep into everyday life and now, following the evolution of digital media and information-based networks, attends individual micro-actions by consumers (computer clicks).

In the digital environment, however, copying is fundamental, not fraudulent, and can be done an infinite number of times without degrading an image or text. This compromises the very notion of an 'original' and a 'copy', as it had applied to analogue processes (from print or film or videotape, for instance), where successive generations of copies would lose progressively more information. Against this, the revolutionary implications of digital copying – infinitely replicable perfect versions – impacted first on the recorded music industry, whose long run of prosperity began with the invention of the vinyl LP or long-playing record in 1948, which led to the ascendancy of recorded music sales over sheet music sales. Record labels' dominance over the distribution of popular music came to an end once users and their service-providers could copy audio/video files freely online, without compromising sound or picture quality.

The response of the music industry was to use copyright forcefully to maintain their analogue position in the digital era. Copyright enforcement was pursued aggressively by corporate lawyers, extending in scope along the way, from action to protect valuable properties such as master copies of commercial movies, to action against private citizens who shared or downloaded audio and video files as part of their domestic consumption and social communication routines. Perhaps for the first time in history, an entire commercial sector sought to preserve its business plan and ensure its survival by making criminals and pirates out of its own customers. As a result of the legal success of – and legislative support for – the incumbent corporations, the digital era has not seen the collapse of copyright, but its aggressive extension, for instance the term (from 50 to 70 or 100 years from the death of the author), the definition of an 'artistic' work (to industrial products, blank forms), or enlarging infringement to include private users. As a result, everyone online is confronted by decisions that may result in breaches of the law on a daily basis. Reform of the law has been slow or stymied by the copyright lobby. There is a fundamental tussle between 'producers' of content (more accurately, their publishers and legal enforcement agents) and 'consumers', just at the very time when that invidious distinction is being eroded by interactive media and social networks, where the communication of meaningfulness requires all agents to be producers.

The over-controlling demands of copyright enforcement extend even to public education, where the focus on introducing new users to the literacy and to the body of work associated with digital media and expression is hindered by a tangle of rules and costs associated with getting permission to show material to students. Instead, education authorities and universities pay out significant sums to corporate copyright-holders for the privilege of stimulating demand in the next generation of user-consumers. Copyright and public-library lending rights make no distinction between commercial authors and academic ones, so the odd situation has arisen where the public education system pays private publishers (especially journal publishers like Elsevier) for the use of knowledge that has been generated by taxpayer-funded scholars, who themselves may benefit from royalties or public-lending rights when their own students buy or borrow their books from the library. Such a system is clearly not dedicated to the open spread of knowledge, or to the improvement of the intellectual stock of a country's future 'human resource'. It is therefore not surprising to find that many in the education field, including research funding bodies as well as individuals, favour some version of open access and open publishing, where publicly funded research is available free of copyright (as it has been for many years by NASA, for instance).[11]

In this they are moving closer to the position that China (notoriously) occupied during the period of post-1978 'opening up' under Deng Xiaoping, where copyright enforcement was weak while economic growth was strong. The 'copyright industries' such as music, film and publishing, prospered – to the consternation of Western firms – without copyright control (Montgomery, 2010). In this, China's creative economy was structured more like the fashion industry, where copying is endemic (although, influenced by the rhetoric of the intellectual property lobby, the Western fashion industry has – ill-advisedly – begun to flirt with copyright protection). Since joining the World Trade Organisation in 2001, China has moved slowly towards an enforcement regime that resembles that of the West, although variably enforced in practice. This is occurring just as Western-based internet activists and some educational agencies are pressing for reform to ensure that the spread of (digital) knowledge – especially taxpayer-funded research findings – should be given the same legislative and legal protection as corporate property rights. Thus, a continuing tussle between increased control (the copyright industries and their legislative allies, along with international agencies such as WIPO) and increased openness (China, fashion, internet libertarians) characterises the creative economy. One side seeks too much control, the other wants less: the 'poise position' is yet to be found.

The example of copyright is just one where the technological and political 'affordances' of the digital era are prevented from being developed by commercial control strategies that are fundamentally 'rent-seeking' rather than risk-taking or innovative enterprise. The problem is not whether rent-seeking agencies are entitled to enforce their rights, or even whether those rights should be amended or limited by legislative reform. The problem is that the commercial control system and its legislative allies are interested in property not in communication, and in protecting past knowledge (that's what copyright does) not stimulating newness.

There are many other forms of corporate and commercial control; and many critical studies drawing attention to it, some scholarly, some partisan or activist, many both (see, for instance, Jones, 1998; Vaidhyanathan, 2005; Benkler, 2006; Chadwick and Howard, 2008; Zittrain, 2008). Large companies buy out small ones (often with the minnow's enthusiastic approval) and then shut them down to protect their own lines from competition. This can be a way of controlling markets, rather than enlarging or modernising them. Corporate marketing and behind-the-scenes influence (lobbying; influence of wealth: Gilens, 2013) promote 'consumerism' as a social or cultural value, binding whole populations to the business of making big firms more prosperous. Corporate control *versus* creative openness is a general and ongoing tension in the creative economy. Policy needs to be directed towards maintaining not a 'free' market but a 'poised' one, where large-scale organisation, coordination, and production is held in tension with population-wide sharing or spreadability of knowledge (Jenkins et al., 2013), such that there is flexibility and openness to change, adaptation, nudging and thus innovation from as wide a range of cultural sources as possible, rather than only from strictly controlled corporate actors.

(2) Sustainability (comfort)

- Wasted planet
- Wasted words
- Wasted people

Wasted planet

It is routinely claimed that 'we' – humans within the globalised economic trading system: i.e. everyone, everywhere, across all of the economy – produce unsustainable quantities of waste, beyond the carrying capacity of land and sea. While technological growth has been exponential and economic growth not far behind, we are said to live on a 'finite planet', a fixed resource that cannot sustain indefinite growth without 'threatening' the environment (Sachs, 2014).[12] We are also said to be a species that is addicted to wastefulness, which – so the story goes – characterises many of our cultural–economic practices, from conspicuous consumption

(Veblen, 1899) or 'affluenza' (de Graaf et al., 2001), to a throwaway society encouraged by businesses that have built 'planned obsolescence' into their products and marketing-driven desire into their customers, such that 'we' (Americans, in this case) have become 'more wasteful, imprudent, and carefree in our consuming habits' (Packard, 1960) since the invention of the consumer economy in the 1950s. Thereby, so the argument goes, we are not only destroying the planet, but also 'amusing ourselves to death' (Postman, 1985). Thus, the global economy, based on domestic consumerism, has changed from being about 'goods' to being about 'bads', inaugurating the 'risk society' (Beck, 1992).

Commonly listed planet killers are, in order:

1. Overpopulation
2. Global warming
3. Deforestation
4. Unstable agriculture
5. Cars
6. Accidents (e.g. Exxon Valdez; BP Deepwater Horizon)
7. Coalmining
8. Invasive species
9. Overfishing
10. Dams (Discovery TV)[13]

To a sceptical observer, the doomsday scenario may itself appear to be a symptom of affluence, since the 'sustainable development' discourse and associated activism are concentrated in the West, conveniently growing in amplitude just after advanced economies have begun to reduce their own pollution and clean up their own cities. Observers from emergent economies may be forgiven for wondering whether this is fair. Just as the rest of the world is catching up, it turns out that the planet can't bear any more affluence.

Such a cynical riposte is not justified, however, simply because (as the song has it) 'we're all in this together'. There's only one planet, and garbage is global. Furthermore, citizens in Beijing are likely to be more worried about pollution than citizens of Calgary, because there's more to worry about.[14] Thus, this is a 'one planet' issue. London faced death-dealing smog and a lifeless river as recently as the 1950s, just as Beijing does now. 'As goes London, so goes Beijing,' as one commentary put it:

> *The final defense against the smog is to leave. Just as wealthy Londoners escaped the choking peasoupers by going to their homes in the countryside, more and more wealthy Chinese and expatriates simply leave Beijing. ... The tale of polluted London has been a very long one, spanning well over a century. Beijing cannot take that long; it would be a catastrophe for China and indeed for the whole planet. But rather than chastise Beijing with a Western holier-than-thou air, we all need to cooperate in recognizing that economic development desperately needs to be decoupled from environmental damage and destruction and taking appropriate steps.*[15]

Although the most polluted cities in the world are currently in India and Pakistan, and 'No Chinese cities ranked in the top 20 most polluted cities' (CNN, 2014),[16] nevertheless, China is often cited as the most polluted region of the world, doubtless because of its fast rate of economic growth compared with others; or, alternatively, because an American-driven online opinion environment is pursuing geopolitical great-power rivalry with China not India. Either way, China has the reputation for hosting the 'world capital' of electronic waste or e-waste: Guiyu in Guangdong Province. This region was brought to world attention in 2002 by Western environmental campaigners (the Basel Action Network and Greenpeace: Puckett et al., 2002), since when both central and local government authorities in China have sought to clean it up (CNN, 2013).[17] Even so, the scale of the operation is impressive:

> *With a population of 150,000, including 100,000 migrants, Guiyu is home to more than 300 companies and 3,000 individual workshops that are engaged in e-waste recycling. Of Guiyu's 28 villages, 20 are engaged in e-waste recycling. Most of the recycling labourers are rural migrants from outlying agrarian regions such as Hunan and Anhui who take the menial jobs of dismantling and processing e-waste informally for an average wage equivalent to USD 1.5 per day. Many of these workers are women and children. (Wang et al., 2013: 22)*

According to Wang and colleagues (2013: 4): 'in 2011, an estimated 1.2 million tonnes of televisions, 0.44 million tonnes of refrigerators, 0.32 million tonnes of washing machines, 0.99 million tonnes of air conditioners and 0.67 million tonnes of computers were discarded' within China, to add to unknown quantities of containers full of e-waste imported from Japan, Korea, Vietnam and further afield. The same study also lists the number of electronic gadgets in use in China in 2011 (see Figure 13.2).

The authors comment: 'Eventually, when these products reach the ends of their life cycles, they will become obsolete and pose a significant challenge

APPLIANCE	QUANTITY
Mobile phone	796,600,000
Colour TV	519,700,000
Washing machine	338,900,000
Refrigerator	338,900,000
Telephone	240,000,000
Computer	227,300,000
Camera	114,700,000

FIGURE 13.2 Total household stocks of home appliances and electronics in China, 2011 (figures from Wang et al., 2013: 12)

to China's waste management system.' That 'significant challenge' is not just internal to China. The 'three bigs' clearly apply in this context. Environmental risk impacts 'everywhere', applies to 'everyone' and involves the whole economy; 'everything'. So the question is not whether emergent economies should bear the heaviest burden to 'save the planet'; the trick is to find solutions that benefit 'everyone, everywhere, and everything'. Already, the *problem* is global, although solutions, where found, tend to be applied in national or sectoral isolation, despite NGO and UN efforts to stimulate coherent global action.[18] Anxiety about wastefulness grows concomitantly with economic growth. The extension of mass affluence to previously poor countries has drawn attention to the globalisation of pollution. The 'economic miracle' *is* the 'environmental nightmare'. Just follow the dirt.

Wasted words

Sustainability is associated with environmental and climate changes, arising largely from industrial pollution and domestic waste, i.e. 'matter out of place', or 'dirt', as Mary Douglas put it in a classic study (1966: 36). She continued: 'where there is dirt there is system'; specifically, the rhetorical and cultural system we use to sort 'matter' into categories. Thus, 'matter out of place' is primarily an anthropological phenomenon: 'dirt' doesn't exist in nature; it is what we say it is, how we react to it, and how we treat it. In deciding what is 'clean' and what is 'dirty' – thereby organising or systematising our culture's sense of its own sustainability – we are guided not by nature but by human bodily functions. As Douglas observed, our *cultural* sense of order is bound up in our *corporeal* materiality, which means that we treat the boundary of the social in a similar way to the boundary of the body.

Matter that transgresses that boundary – bodily fluids, whether sexual (power) or excremental (danger) – are accorded special treatment. They are subject to taboo, which involves simultaneously overvaluing and undervaluing matter that crosses a border, or mixes two bodies. It seems that humans are apt to transfer to the natural environment the system by which they police bodily boundaries and thereby produce the category of 'dirt'. Thus some products of the social or economic body are regarded as powerful or sexual (products of newness, like a new car or consumer desirable); some are regarded as dangerous or excremental – and this includes 'waste' from factories (effluent; CO_2), households (landfill), farms (e.g. fertiliser run-off) and more recently electronic waste (e-waste), i.e. computer and mobile-device parts.

As Maxwell and Miller (2012: 165) put it, 'Media technologies generate meaning, but also detritus and disease'. Their point is to draw scholarly attention back from content of media messages and towards the materiality of media equipment, which remains strangely *immaterial* in media-studies discourse (given that media scholars are typically more interested in TV content than the factories that make TVs). Maxwell and Miller want to arm-wrestle scholars out of 'the rather musty corridors of academic labor and media critique', and haul them into the grim reality of 'the polluted corridors of material production and death that derive from a risk society' (p. 19). Their rhetorical ploy – to link 'detritus' with 'disease' and 'material production' with 'death' – renders media production as a whole (the labour process as well as discarded products) as excremental *'dirt'*; something to be ashamed of, especially among those of us who pay heed to words in preference to things.

However, it is words that are doing much of the work here. Maxwell and Miller don't like 'cybertarians' who treat new media as if they are powerful (sexual); instead they want to take them round the back – to the 'Global South' (Ch. 4) in effect – to discover that the materiality of media is shameful (excrement). Well, rubbing our noses in it may be salutary, but it won't fix the problem. For that, Maxwell and Miller turn to 'green citizenship', imagining a workers' collective forged among all those who make media (apart from users or audiences): an alliance of 'computer scientists, engineers, designers, market researchers, miners, mineral brokers, refiners, chemists, factory laborers, server-warehouse employees, telecommunications workers, truck drivers, salespeople, office clerks, and above- and below-the-line media-production workers' (2012: 150) – the last category designating those more familiar as writers, producers, directors and actors (above-the-line) and production crews (below-the-line).

Maxwell and Miller's rhetorical strategy is to play down the *semiotic reality* of media in favour of 'material production', although they certainly recognise the meaningfulness of semiotic activism, e.g. Greenpeace painting Hewlett Packard's factory roof with the giant legend 'HAZARDOUS PRODUCTS' (Maxwell and Miller 2011: 150–1). Thus, it isn't as if these are different kinds of reality. Instead, as Maxwell and Miller concede, a 'model for analysis and activism alike' is to *combine* material and semiotic aspects of the 'commodity sign' by attending to its 'design, manufacture, electricity, use, disposal and recycling' (2011: 151), not just to one of these.

But two things can be lost in the type of account that reduces signs to commodities in the pursuit of a critical account of capitalist commercial markets. First, they may downplay the self-correcting capabilities of the productive system itself. For instance, given external prompts and internal discoveries, including observation of the unforeseen outcomes of large-scale industrial activity, remedial action is already evident, even in apparently (i.e. rhetorically) blighted areas like Guiyu, and China more generally. A combination of government regulation, citizen-activism, and entrepreneurs in the recycling industry are finding ways to improve the material circumstances of e-waste (Minter, 2013), even as it is being paraded as an example of market failure.

Second, they may downplay the importance of creativity itself, as if production and policy are causal (the 'economic base', in the Marxist jargon), while signs, symbols and meanings – and their communication across groups and networks – are secondary (or 'superstructure'). Such a distinction misses another form of waste, which may affect millions more than e-waste, and that is wasted meanings. Living as humans do in a semiotically saturated environment, where 'talk is cheap' and anyone connected to any kind of media encounters more words per day than at any time in history, 'waste' nevertheless extends to words, most of which, uttered by most people, go unheard and unheeded (Hartley and Potts, 2014: Ch. 8). So a counter-'but surely' question arises: Does a focus on industrial production rather than cultural development come at the expense of countenancing another kind of waste – that of human creative and communicative potential?

Wasted people (human resources)

Wastefulness applies not directly to matter (which is indifferent to such categorisation), but to human productivity. The real 'but surely' question for 'sustainable development' concerns the capability of a creative – and green – economy to harness, benefit from and reward the creative potential of the whole population – to extend the 'good life' to everyone capable of enjoying it, even while 'treading lightly' on the planet. Many countries are grappling with aspects of this problem, seeking to boost productivity while extending creative engagement by addressing youth unemployment, long-term and intergenerational welfare-dependency, and extending working life beyond the retirement age, recalibrating the concept of a working life from an agricultural–industrial to a knowledge–creative society. At the same time, the demographic profile of the global workforce has changed radically since

World War 2, with many more women and part-time workers than in the industrial era, and fewer children, although child labour continues in less developed countries and rural economies.

One unforeseen consequence of these changes is that the status of work, leisure, and idleness has changed, almost inverted, over the past century. Idleness was honorific:

> Back in 1899 Thorstein Veblen ... argued that leisure was a 'badge of honour'. Rich people could get others to do the dirty, repetitive work—what Veblen called 'industry'. Yet Veblen's leisure class was not idle. Rather they engaged in 'exploit': challenging and creative activities such as writing, philanthropy and debating.[19]

So says *The Economist*, noting an important class distinction of the modern era between 'industry' (labour) for the industrious classes and 'exploit' (bold or daring feats) for the 'leisure class' (Veblen, 1899). The 'idle rich' were no such thing, but they were not tied to *work* in the way that industrial workers were. Their 'labour' involved pursuits that constituted an elaborate form of 'costly signalling' – a family could advertise its wealth if the head of household did not engage in breadwinning or industry, but spent their time doing laborious but useless tasks – learning Latin and needlework are mentioned by Veblen, in addition to *The Economist*'s literary, political and volunteer work. In short, there was a structural difference between 'honorific' and 'utilitarian' work (Sahlins, 1976: 179–204); one that also distinguishes what we would now recognise as creative enterprise – literary, artistic and entrepreneurial – from 'repetitive' labour.

The distinction between leisured affluence, albeit busy, and the working poor goes back much further than Veblen.[20] But it became a cultural cliché of industrial times: the good life could be measured by leisure – putting your feet up. However, times have changed, according to *The Economist*:

> Veblen's theory needs updating.... Work in advanced economies has become more knowledge-intensive and intellectual. There are fewer really dull jobs, like lift-operating, and more glamorous ones, like fashion design. That means more people than ever can enjoy 'exploit' at the office. Work has come to offer the sort of pleasures that rich people used to seek in their time off. On the flip side, leisure is no longer a sign of social power. Instead it symbolises uselessness and unemployment.

This change involves two aspects. First, the 'knowledge-intensive' creative economy now *encompasses* the type of creative, intellectual and bold or daring work that was once the preserve of the leisure class. Second, affluent people are now routinely overworked and time-poor. Conversely, the poor are now characterised not by repetitive work but by its absence or prevention, resulting in *enforced unproductivity*: the unemployed; migrants (especially those whose visas forbid them to work); people living with disabilities; children and seniors are all bearers of idleness as a badge of uselessness at best and at worst, shame.

In such a world, the onus is on activists and policymakers, entrepreneurs and welfare agencies to look for ways to extend further through the social strata of the creative era the once-aristocratic skills of 'exploit' and the arts. Here is where 'the good life' may involve working insanely hard, but in a community, for a cause (Leadbeater, 2014). As democratisation of communication extends further than ever before owing to digital media, so the opportunities for new styles of work confront the wastefulness of industrial employment with a viable alternative. If it's good enough for aristocrats, it's good enough for everyone, everywhere.[21]

(3) Divides (knowledge)

- Economic divides
- Political divides
- Cultural divides
- Creativity divides

Economic divides

There is widespread concern about income inequality, as the gap between the wealthiest and the poorest grows, in both affluent and emerging economies. Inherited wealth pays ample returns, bankers earn jaw-dropping bonuses, and CEOs out-earn their shareholders, while unemployment grows among unskilled workers, under-employed women, and young people. Global popular unrest, associated with the 'Occupy' and 'We are the 99%' movement, and with various democratic 'Springs' or 'Colour' revolutions, is often explained by reference to income inequality: people are said to reject *government* (especially supra-national forms like the EU)[22] on the basis of *wealth*.

But the mere presence of very rich people, even in less affluent countries, does not necessarily signify that something is radically amiss, except in kleptocracies. The main thing is whether the system is geared to deliver general improvement, as in China, Vietnam, and post-authoritarian Indonesia, and thus that billionaires can emerge from enterprise and markets; or whether wealth comes from political control of national assets, and thus theft (Suharto's Indonesia, Marcos'

Philippines, Mobutu's Congo/Zaire, etc.). Among economists, at any rate, a distinction is maintained between, on the one hand, active entrepreneurs like Bill Gates, Microsoft co-founder, or the Chinese paper-recycling mogul and one-time world's richest self-made woman Zhang Yin (Cheung Yan)[23] and, on the other hand, passive owners of inherited wealth, e.g. all 20 of Bloomberg's top 20 female billionaires in May 2014, who inherited their wealth from fathers or husbands, although some play an active role in the business.[24] The difference is that entrepreneurs and self-made billionaires are said to have earned their fortune by innovation and enterprise that create wealth or opportunity that benefits everyone; whereas simply living off earnings per share or rents does little to keep economic activity dynamic and future-oriented.

Anxiety about income inequality and the sources or uses of billionaires' wealth (and thence political influence) has resulted in widespread discussion centred on a recent study by French economist Thomas Piketty (2014). He has suggested that general improvements have stagnated while the wealth of the already very wealthy has accelerated. Here, it is not the difference between rich and poor that should worry observers, but something that seems at first sight to be a more arcane economic formula:

$$r > g$$

This translates as: r (rate of return on wealth) > (is greater than) g (growth rate of the economy, or GDP). Piketty's analysis claims that 'wealth' – i.e. investments, including inherited shares and property – has grown at a greater rate than GDP: in other words, over the long term, the rich are getting richer, and the difference between the top 0.1 percentile (the super-rich) and everyone else is increasing.

Piketty's work caused quite a stir in the forums of public thought: his book launch in New York was supported by no less than two Nobel Laureates – Paul Krugman and Joseph Stiglitz.[25] Krugman summarised what he liked about Piketty's argument in his own long-running *New York Times* blog. First, extreme inequality has been rising. Second, inequality divides the population between 'the one percent and within that the 0.1 percent' on the one hand, and everyone else on the other, including educated elites and middle-class earners. Third, the power law, winner-takes-all argument (i.e. that the most enterprising reach the top) does not hold: it is not active entrepreneurs who comprise the richest 0.1 percent, but inheritors. Krugman concludes:

> *We may face a political-economy spiral of inequality, in which great wealth brings great power, which is used to reinforce the concentration of wealth. ... We're talking about creating an environment favorable to "patrimonial capitalism", of sustained dominance by family dynasties.*[26]

Political divides

'Political divides' refers most readily to ideological difference between parties (Red vs. Blue States; Left vs. Right; Green vs. both), right up to state-sponsored aggression against internal populations (surveillance and policing) or external 'threats' (sanctions, war). Where citizen-associations are strong, then institutional political opposition can 'represent' political divides, converting them to discourse and thence remedial action over time. Where ruling elites are radically divided from their populations, state authoritarianism is opposed by citizen-activism, from 'peaceful protest', via phenomena like Anonymous, WikiLeaks and the Edward Snowden leaks, all the way up to insurrectionary 'Springs' (Arab and other), and various Squares across countries and generations: Grosvenor, Tiananmen, Taksim Tahrir, etc. Alternatively, there are various models of politics where divides are expressed by refusal of mainstream values (e.g. the Occupy movement) or by disengagement (runaway experiments, from the Pilgrim Fathers to hippy communes).

Cultural divides

'Cultural divides' refers to religion, racism, utopianism, the politics of the personal, or 'community' tensions, sometimes flaring into violence; often keeping neighbouring demes in adversarial contact over very long stretches of time. In a more mundane context, cultural disaffection may take the form of withdrawal: refusal to buy certain products (associated with a group across the political divide); 'tribal' taste preferences (restricted to certain types of music, movies, entertainment); disengagement from civic participation; 'cults'.

The lesson of this analysis of 'divides' may not be economic (e.g., impose a global wealth tax) but political, fuelling popular disaffection, direct action and voting shifts towards the extremes. Even *The Economist*, standard-bearer for free-market opinion, spelt out why this is an argument about fairness and living standards (via its 'Free Exchange' economics blog):

> Mr Piketty's ... argument is that the living standards of many people around the rich world are now unnecessarily low, because of the nonchalance with which elites have approached distributional issues over the past generation, and that continued heedlessness of this sort will ultimately undermine the growth-boosting institutions of capitalism. His argument is that economic growth that concentrates benefits on a small group of people will probably not be tolerated as fair, even if living standards among the masses are not completely stagnant.[27]

Whether or not inequality, political division and community or cultural tensions will cause a popular backlash or find a way to mutual accommodation is decided case by case. However, the conduct of this debate holds some immediate lessons for those who are interested in a creative economy. First, there is a league table of debating forums. The attention received by any new idea depends on whether or not its proponent can gain exposure in the most prestigious or influential outlets. The intense publicity and attention surrounding Piketty's work in national and international newspapers, political weeklies and media commentary on both sides of the Atlantic – and thence, beyond – has not been matched in the context of the creative economy (the closest contender would be Richard Florida's work on the 'creative class' in the mid-2000s). The high-level transatlantic 'commentariat', including all the major newspapers, political weeklies, celebrity bloggers and a significant sprinkling of Nobel prize-winners, seems not to have been as stirred up by the vicissitudes of creative emancipation as they were by Piketty's take on the inequality of wealth. They simply haven't given it the same level of attention (column inches).

Second, and not unrelated, there does not seem (from that perspective) to be so much at stake in the creativity domain: after all, the creative industries comprise a small percentage of the economy, and the politics of culture is not a high priority. Compared to inequality, the *general failure* to promote *general improvements* in population-wide, economy-wide and planet-wide creative enterprise is hardly noticed. It is not seen as a scandal of intellectual failure, but as a sideshow.

Creativity divides

Thus, for instance, when a new Secretary of State (cabinet minister) was appointed to the UK's Department of Culture, Media and Sport in April 2014, prominent commentator Peter Preston (former Editor of *The Guardian*) wondered why it mattered at all:

> The DCMS isn't much of a department. Basically, it takes money ... and distributes it to dozens of quangoid organisations who reach their own conclusions about how to spend it ... There have been 12 cabinet culture supremos in 22 years, a shuffling, shifting trickle of talent passing through. There's no day-to-day function they perform that couldn't be farmed out ...[28]

If political opinion leaders can't see the point of representing creativity and culture at the highest level of government, then that is at least partly because the case for why it matters has not cut through. In other words, the 'conceptual community' (Prince, 2010) or 'discursive public sphere' (Warner, 2002) that is debating matters of creativity has not succeeded in reaching platforms that command general rather than specialised or academic attention. If anything, general interest is fading. This is because the creative sector looks to observers like special-interest groups fighting among themselves for inconsequential ideological difference, small-beer ideas and table-scrap economics: not an edifying sight. Compared with this, the reception given to Piketty's book is remarkable. The question is not whether he is right or wrong (opinion is divided), but that he has got everyone talking. He 'meets a need', as Clive Crook (former Editor of *The Economist*) put it.[29]

People in the domain of 'public thought' don't want to talk about creativity; they want to talk about inequality.[30] Economically speaking, rather than politically, this may be a big mistake. It may be that Piketty and his Nobel-laureate supporters are asking the wrong question. *Is it* indeed inequality that drives the growth system? Or is it capitalism's Schumpeterian restlessness (Metcalfe, 2008), and thus *mobility* — of resources, people and knowledge? Does 'growth' (Piketty's measure) matter as much as 'evolution'? If the latter, then the implications for growth policy are different. As Stan Metcalfe argues, such policies:

> ... depend on a bottom-up rather than an aggregate economy-down perspective ... they depend on the stimulation of enterprise and entrepreneurship; and ... they depend upon the open, unbiased operation of market institutions. They are properly described as policies for an experimental economy and the problem for the policy makers is that they must accommodate the waste and narrowly conceived inefficiency which is essential to all evolutionary processes. (Metcalfe, n.d.: 47)

A bottom-up, experimental, entrepreneurial, open market set-up that is tolerant of short-run 'waste and inefficiency' is constantly in a process of creation — that's what a creative economy is. But its importance may not be visible from within the walled-garden debating ground of the US-dominated blogosphere. From that (relatively affluent) perspective, since inequality is self-evidently unequal, it is easy to take the further (moral) step to conclude that it is unfair and the most important policy problem is to stop it.

However, the most important policy problem is to understand what drives growth, which is newness; and how the affluence arising from growth may be generalised. Newness is to be found at the margins of the existing arrangements — where new players emerge from the 'bottom' of the old economies (e.g. start-ups, exploiting new inventions and new knowledge), and among new or 'emergent' economies in countries like China, Brazil, Indonesia, Nigeria. Disaffection may well characterise the already affluent in the old economies, as it has in parts of the EU and in the radical Occupy movement internationally, but that may not halt the entrepreneurial seizure of new opportunities elsewhere. Dislike of the very wealthy may be *understandable* (the things they do and say!), but it may not be the best policy for *understanding* how whole populations may improve their self-directing circumstances. Visceral hostility to demonised personalities (Rupert Murdoch; Gina Rinehart) doesn't stand in for working out how everyone, everywhere, across the economy, might do better for themselves.

The fact that policymakers can't 'see' why creativity is just as important as inequality does not mean that it isn't. Our argument is that when reconceptualised along the lines of the 'Three Bigs', the creative–digital economy – integrating the microproductivity of user-created knowledge into production of newness – is becoming the chief means for addressing the kind of inequality that leaves 'the poor' as a kind of timeless residue at the bottom of rigid hierarchies. In other words, the means to redress inequality is to understand what drives economic growth in the future, and to put that knowledge in the hands of those who may benefit from it, rather than seeking to iron the wrinkles out of the residue of past growth. Many commentators continue to rely on a base/superstructure model, even those who have no interest in a Marxist approach. They see economic inequality (often reduced to wages, without reference to welfare, superannuation and education 'savings' held by the state on behalf of citizens) as a cause of change, for which there is not that much empirical evidence (Americans aren't all that passionate about equality; activists aren't all that economically literate). At the same time they neglect or downplay *cultural and knowledge inequality*, for which there is hardly a lexicon, never mind a coherent advocacy group or policy strategy.

Thus, there seems to be little political 'demand' for equality of access to, understanding and creation of culture and knowledge, beyond libertarian, whistleblowing and anti-censorship advocates like the Pirate Party, WikiLeaks, or Index on Censorship. This is what really needs to change.

A new set of critical priorities is needed, devoted to promoting the democratisation of creativity and knowledge. We have seen pointers in this book – the maker movement, DIY citizenship, user co-creation. There's still a long way to go, however, before the knowledge commons is open to all and creativity brings the 'good life' to everyone:

> As we crossed the Malakand Pass I saw a young girl selling oranges. She was scratching marks on a piece of paper with a pencil to account for the oranges she had sold as she could not read or write. I took a

photo of her and vowed I would do everything in my power to help educate girls just like her. This was the war I was going to fight. (Yousafzai, 2013: 182)

With the ever-present possibility that it may turn out the other way round, a possibility embodied by Malala Yousafzai herself, the question should be: Will 'this' (education for cultural and economic emancipation) kill 'that' (wasted lives)?

Notes

1. This motto is in Karl Marx's 'Confession' (a Victorian parlour game), recorded by his daughter Jenny (1865). Available at: http://www.marxists.org/archive/marx/works/1865/04/01.htm.
2. Paul Baran, interviewed for *Vanity Fair*, K. Mayo and P. Newcomb (July 2008), 'How the web was won', available at www.vanityfair.com/culture/features/2008/07/internet200807.
3. See http://internethalloffame.org/inductees/donald-davies.
4. For the story (and further references), see www.cybertelecom.org/notes/baran.htm.
5. See more at http://internethalloffame.org/inductees/donald-davies#sthash.R3Wud7Mx.dpuf.
6. Internet Society: 'What we do; why it matters', available at www.internet-society.org/what-we-do/why-internet-matters.
7. As in Australia – see www.businessspectator.com.au/article/2014/4/7/technology/will-foxtel-reap-its-game-thrones-bounty.
8. See, for example, www.neurope.eu/article/turkey-ban-twitter-and-facebook.
9. *New York Times*, 'China: allies urged to control internet', by E. Wong, 19 April 2014: A7. Available at: www.nytimes.com/2014/04/19/world/asia/chinese-official-urges-russia-and-central-asian-allies-to-control-internet.html?partner=rss&emc=rss&_r=0. Other member countries of SCO are Ukraine, Georgia, Kazakhstan, Kyrgyzstan, Tajikistan and Uzbekistan, although only four were reported as present at this meeting. 'External forces' referred to Western countries.
10. See http://freedomhouse.org/report/freedom-net-2013-global-scores#.U1Spwcc08b0. Freedom House is a 'watchdog' organisation based in New York that is supported by the US and Dutch governments, philanthropic foundations (e.g. MacArthur) and Google, among others: http://freedomhouse.org/donate/our-supporters#.U1SsFcc08b0.
11. 'NASA still images; audio files; video; and computer files used in the rendition of 3-dimensional models, such as texture maps and polygon data in any format, generally are not copyrighted. You may use NASA imagery,

video, audio, and data files used for the rendition of 3-dimensional models for educational or informational purposes, including photo collections, textbooks, public exhibits, computer graphical simulations and Internet Web pages. This general permission extends to personal Web pages': www.nasa.gov/multimedia/guidelines/index.html#.U3gYrC-1ldg.
12. Inaugural Curtin Sustainability Lecture and Showcase, with Jeffrey Sachs (Director of Earth Institute, Columbia University) at http://new.livestream.com/Balconi/Curtin-Sustainability-Lecture. The Sachs presentation begins at 29 minutes in; the 'finite planet' section begins 52 minutes in.
13. Discovery TV (2011) 'Top 10 ways man is destroying the environment', by Matt Schwarzfeld (4 November). Available at: www.discovery.com/tv-shows/curiosity/topics/10-ways-man-destroying-environment.htm.
14. Calgary won the 'world's cleanest city' accolade. See www.huffingtonpost.ca/2013/05/18/calgary-worlds-cleanest-city_n_3299545.html.
15. Heidi Strebel and Jean-Pierre Lehmann: 'London and Beijing: a polluted tale of two cities: how Beijing's tale proceeds from here will determine what kind of planet we leave behind', *The Globalist*, 12 November 2013. Available at: www.theglobalist.com/london-beijing-polluted-tale-two-cities/.
16. 'Top 20 most polluted cities in the world', by Madison Park, CNN, 8 May 2014. Available at: http://edition.cnn.com/2014/05/08/world/asia/india-pollution-who/index.html?iref=obinsite, citing the World Health Organisation's Ambient Air Pollution Database 2014.
17. 'Despite the environmental degradation and toxic fumes permeating the air, many in Guiyu said that conditions have improved dramatically over the years', quoted in 'China: the electronic wastebasket of the world', by Ivan Watson, CNN, 31 May 2013. Available at: http://edition.cnn.com/2013/05/30/world/asia/china-electronic-waste-e-waste/.
18. See http://sustainabledevelopment.un.org/.
19. 'Nice work if you can get out: why the rich now have less leisure than the poor', *The Economist*, 19 April 2014. Available at: www.economist.com/news/finance-and-economics/21600989-why-rich-now-have-less-leisure-poor-nice-work-if-you-can-get-out?fsrc=nlw|hig|4-16-2014|8329786|39493970|AP.
20. Thomas Hobbes, in *Leviathan*, backdated leisured affluence to Classical Athens, where it gave rise to an unexpected novelty: philosophy – '*Leasure* is the mother of *Philosophy* ... they that had no employment, neither at home, nor abroad, had little else to employ themselves in, but either in telling or hearing news, or in discoursing of Philosophy publiquely to the youth of the City' (1651: 683–5).
21. The Lascelles family, earls of Harewood, exemplify a traditional, leisure-class aristocratic family whose scions were productive and widely admired for their lifelong engagement with the creative economy. George Lascelles, the seventh earl, was a champion of English opera; the eighth is a television producer. Of the seventh earl, Queen Elizabeth II – his cousin – remarked,

'Funny thing about George. You know, in most respects he's perfectly normal' (www.theguardian.com/music/2011/jul/11/the-earl-of-harewood). David Lascelles (eighth earl) was a producer for Welsh independent filmmaker Chris Monger and went on to work for Zenith Productions, producing *Inspector Morse*, *Wide-Eyed & Legless*, *Moll Flanders* and films such as *Richard III* (one of his ancestors) and *The Wisdom of Crocodiles*. As Earl he produced *Carnival Messiah* at Harewood House to celebrate the bicentenary of the abolition of slavery, and brought Bhutanese craftsmen there to erect a Buddhist stupa (www.jamyangleeds.co.uk/component/content/article/53-from-the-archive-/90-david-lascelles). Thus may 'leisure-class' exploits contribute materially to creative innovation.

22. In the EU Parliament Elections of 2014, a curious outcome was that in the more affluent countries like the UK, France and Denmark, right-wing anti-EU parties did well, while in economically struggling countries like Greece, Spain and Portugal, left-wing anti-EU parties did well. Either way, the prospects for the EU seem bumpy.
23. Details at http://genevalunch.com/2010/10/12/worlds-3-richest-women-chinese-but-not-fashion-moguls/.
24. Bloomberg Billionaires Index, accessed 28 May 2014 at www.bloomberg.com/billionaires/2014-05-28/cya/aqaaa.
25. See www.newrepublic.com/article/117407/thomas-piketty-speech-economics-sensation-visits-new-york.
26. Paul Krugman's *New York Times* blog for 16 April 2014 at http://krugman.blogs.nytimes.com/2014/04/16/piketty-day-notes/.
27. '"Capital" and its discontents', by R.A. at www.economist.com/blogs/freeexchange/2014/04/inequality.
28. Peter Preston, 'Maria Miller: just another departure through the revolving door at DCMS: The furore over resignations and appointments is concealing the unhappy truth that culture isn't much of a department'. *The Observer*, 13 April 2014. Available at: www.theguardian.com/politics/2014/apr/13/maria-miller-dcms-revolving-door-culture?INTCMP=ILCNETTXT3487#start-of-comments.
29. See www.bloombergview.com/articles/2014-04-20/the-most-important-book-ever-is-all-wrong.
30. The opponents of Piketty's position have plenty to say about why he's wrong, but not this. See for instance, www.forbes.com/sites/kotlikoff/2014/05/15/will-the-rich-always-get-richer/.

OPTIMISM

14

FUTURE-FORMING

The generalization has often been surmised, and has been more and more firmly established by biographical research ... that the roots of important original achievements can almost always be found in the third decade in the lives of scholars, that sacred decade of fertility.

(Joseph Schumpeter, in Allen, 1991: 51)

Summary of the argument of the book

The story so far

In this book we have tried to develop some simple models for the analysis of creativity in the context of contemporary global markets and digital mediated culture.

- We see creativity as a *systems* phenomenon. The system that generates creativity is *culture*, not individual behaviour.

- Culture and knowledge should be understood first as part of *communication* (i.e. as social, not behavioural).

- Culture should be seen in a new way, not as high-art or heritage, nor as habituated custom and practices, but as the group-forming imperative of humans.

- *Culture makes groups*. Cultural groups are always 'we' groups or *demes*, and they are always (explicitly or implicitly) set against 'they' groups. 'We' are bonded in language and semiotic webs of meaningfulness; demes make individuals, not the other way round.

- *Demes make knowledge*. It follows that knowledge is both *universal* ('our' knowledge adequately explains the world and is binding on all) and *adversarial* ('their' knowledge is false, duplicitous, or threatening).

- Groups learn and change in competition and conflict with other groups. That learning process is social not psychological – knowledge accrues in institutions not just in individual brains. It is sometimes cooperative, often not.

- We call the process of social learning *creativity* or *innovation*. It is generated most intensively along the *boundaries* between groups.

- When a group or deme extends its boundaries to incorporate the knowledge of another group, that process can often be disruptive, painful or even lethal – it can be experienced as conquest or colonisation, piracy or plagiarism, the 'end of the world as *we* know it'. It doesn't *feel* like cooperation, and it doesn't conform to standard senses of the word 'creative'. But, looked at from the system perspective, the net gain in knowledge, its new utility for the members of the 'take' group, and its new potential for novel combinations with other knowledge and uses, accrues new advantages to the system as a whole, even to the 'give' deme or group, and tends to the *growth of knowledge* and its overall coordination.

If culture makes groups and groups make knowledge, *new* knowledge is essential for survival under *uncertainty*: uncertainty of time (unpredictable change) and of place (niche and environment). This is why creativity and innovation are important. They are the grit that provokes the cultural organism to generate a pearl, allowing the organism to survive by generating new value where there was danger. There can be nothing more important for the survival of groups than creativity/innovation, even though much of their conscious investment of time and energy is in keeping things the same.

Because groups or demes are made by culture in a process of adaptation to circumstances and environments, it is impossible to define a group in advance, beyond the basic requirement that it comprises numbers of *non-kin* humans bonded/bounded by communication and knowledge, from which identity, sociality, meaningfulness and a sense of bounded externality are derived. Indeed, groups are scale free – cultural demes may be as small as a hunting party or as large as a nation, even a species. Demes may be 'real' (tribes) or 'virtual' (fans); they may be concrete (all speakers of a given language) or abstract ('citizens', 'audiences', 'the public', 'consumers'). Demes or groups are not only organised in shifting *opposition* to other groups, but also in overlapping *complexity*, such that individuals belong to multiple demes, simultaneously or successively.

In such a scenario, who we are, what we know, and how we relate to various 'theys', are all far from determined in advance. On the contrary, such knowledge is radically uncertain. Certainty about identity is a delusion.

The *less* that any group or person is aware of inter-demic complexity, the more 'certain' (and deluded) their knowledge systems are likely to be, based on what Thorstein Veblen (1898) called 'animistic thought' (anthropomorphism as cause) not 'materialism' (matter-energy as cause). Animistic knowledge-systems (from cosmology to family roles) will impute demic identity to the world ('we' were put here by divine will; 'we' have always been here, known these things, opposed those others).

Conversely, the *more* that people and groups are conscious of this uncertain but elaborate complexity of relations and differences, the more reflexive culture becomes. It needs to create knowledge about itself, rather than projecting a fantasy self onto the world. Culture makes groups, groups make knowledge, but knowledge of the complexity of that arrangement makes for doubt, scepticism, relativism, multiple or ambiguous identities, and the need to be able to deal with difference and indeterminacy. Human knowledge of causation evolves from a 'mechanical' relationship with reality to a 'quantum' one, where *probabilities* and *relationships* among forces replace certainties and 'objective' essence (of self, thing, other).

Doubtless some individuals – in pre-modernity, priestly castes and ruling families; in modernity, certain scientific groups – achieve such 'probabilistic' consciousness earlier than most, but the remarkable thing about the era of the internet, accompanied as it is by global mediation and exchange (via the *semiosphere*), is that that reflexive awareness of the elaborate complexity of multiple and competing meaning-systems and demic groups is necessarily widespread among whole *populations*. It is also *mediated*: communicated in the weekly drama serial, the nightly news, minute-by-minute status update, and via the multiple 'selves' that each person creates, communicates or publishes, and simultaneously 'consumes', as they connect, browse and interact with multiple 'we' groups and multiple 'they' groups – online, in the city, or in media. In short, multi-demic belonging and inter-demic encounters proliferate, for each individual and across an unprecedentedly large proportion of the population.

The traditional 'uses' of culture and knowledge – to confirm identity, place and meaningfulness in a slow-changing and relatively isolated smallworld – give way to new uses of culture and knowledge. Now the imperative is *reflexivity under uncertainty*: learning to process difference (*translate*) and to navigate change (*trajectory*) across multiple cultural/knowledge boundaries, differences, conflicts and clashes. The opportunity for creativity and innovation at these boundaries is radically increased, because 'everyone', 'everywhere' is a potential source of new ideas, which may then be tested through social networks. This is an *evolutionary* view, because it posits random variation (new *ideas* from whole populations), but selected adoption (via meso-level *institutions*), and *cultural* replication – it is the culture/knowledge 'organism' that survives, not the individual (Pagel, 2012a, 2012b).

The take-out lesson to be drawn from this logic is that if you are interested in creativity and innovation (a preoccupation of both cultural critics and economists), then you need to take account of the extension of the potential for creativity and innovation across whole populations, and you need to note that more people are more reflexively linked to multiple, multivalent demes and groups than ever before. In such a situation, where we're dealing with *complex systems*, interacting and shifting in relation to one another at planetary (semiospheric) scale, the *policy settings* devoted to promoting creativity and innovation will look pretty paltry if they don't take account of a reflexive, productive population that is continuously creating groups (*autopoiesis*), and in the (often disruptive) interactions generated by these processes, creating newness and knowledge that may prove 'useful' much more widely. Hence, policy needs to move from a *'mechanical'* approach (engineered innovation in professional labs) to a *'probabilistic'* approach (population-wide random variation, speeded up by institutionalised 'search' functions across demes and knowledge domains), in which *everyone, everywhere, across all of the economy and culture*, is a participant, part of the overall productivity of the system. Policy settings need to shift from central control, 'picking winners' and high investment in firms, to distributed control (self-organising systems), trial and error and experimentation, and investment in populations (education, connectivity, nurturing associations).

A new analytic lens

When confronted by something new, our *demic* habit is to reject it as 'they' knowledge. This is pretty much what happens at the scholarly or analytic level, not just in vernacular thinking, with a new conceptualisation of culture and creativity. It is much easier to incorporate a familiar concept of culture into a known set of economic players and problems (this is what 'cultural economics' does). It is much harder even to 'see' culture as the group-making mechanism that generates knowledge and thus newness in conditions of uncertainty among competing groups, both actual and mediated.

How, then, to reduce this seething sun-surface of complex energy-matter to something that can be *studied*? How to reduce the glare of the newly-observed object, such that a cooler understanding of its properties, forces and interrelations can be discerned? We use a series of lenses, each of which has three components (for heuristic reasons).

First, the *levels of complexity* can be understood more easily using Dopfer and colleagues' (2004) tripartite structure of **'micro–meso–macro'** (MMM), where:

- *Micro* – refers to the level of individual agents. For this purpose, an 'agent' can be a single person, like a user, or a micro-enterprise, like sole trader;
- *Meso* – refers to an intermediate level where institutions are found: institutions are defined in the abstract as 'populations of rules'; in more concrete terms an institution is any cluster of agents acting in concert – a deme or group; an organisation; or a 'social institution' where patterned behaviours are shared for certain purposes or actions;
- *Macro* – is the system level – the level of populations, the semiosphere, of culture and knowledge, as well as that of 'macroeconomics'.

In economics, there's a well-established distinction between microeconomics (individual decision-making), where supply and demand are found, and macroeconomics (total economic activity) where large-scale and abstract patterns are found, such as growth, inflation and employment rates. The MMM system does not map neatly into this schema. The intermediate meso-level is where dynamism, evolution and change are found. An evolutionary approach to culture, creativity and knowledge needs to shift analytic attention from the micro-level (individuals; behaviour) to the meso level (groups; institutions; rules) and to explain both by reference to macro-systems (populations; demes), in order to understand how creativity works as part of (produced by) *complex systems*.

To make a start towards such an approach in relation to the creative industries and creative economy, we have identified what we call the 'Three Bigs':

- *Everyone* – a population approach, not a behavioural one. The latter always reduces the scope of the study to some kind of elite: either trained artists and 'creatives' in expert situations; or creative firms, which are said to create value by producing property (intellectual property) that expresses the individual creativity of an artist or other talent. 'Everyone' challenges this approach by locating creativity at population level, where it is produced (by everyone) in their meso-level group interactions and knowledge-creating communication. Thus 'property' is not the basis of value-creation, but something more like a 'commons' (Ostrom) or a 'club' (Buchanan).
- *'Everything'* – not just extension of creativity from a specialised creative industries sector to 'all of *the* economy', but also an extension of 'the' economy to encompass all of the productivity of the cultural-knowledge creative systems and their interactions.

- *Everywhere* – a planetary approach, based on the notion of the semiosphere (itself differentiated from the biosphere and geosphere, thus connecting the domain of knowledge and culture to material processes and interactions). It's no more helpful to say that creative industries are a 'first-world' phenomenon or confined to advanced economies or the Anglosphere than it is to make the same claims about some new infection like SARS. Sooner or later it'll get out, and eventually it'll get everywhere. Thus, the creative industries are most intensively *studied* in the Anglosphere and in the EU, but they are *practised* across the globe in a coherent system of interconnected domains, often in competition with each other, such that emergent or developing economies (e.g. Indonesia) may display more sophisticated creative economy policies than advanced ones (e.g. the USA). Watch out America!

Of course nothing goes according to plan. SNAFUs are normal. In recognition of this, we have identified 'Three Buts' that cross and clash with the 'Three Bigs' to uncertain effect. They are:

- *Control (everyone)* – people are organised into 'we' communities which are systematically adversarial in relation to 'they' groups. In other words, groups contend, compete, clash and cooperate, with agents and meso-level institutions vying for control within groups, and groups vying for control over each other. Control can be subdivided into three types:
    - Technical control
    - Political control
    - Commercial control

    These three overlap at every point: political and commercial control can be exercised by controlling technology. Opening up new opportunities results in new opportunities for control. Extension of systems to populations results not only in more participation but also in more surveillance (Andrejevic, 2007).

- *Sustainability (everything)* – sustainability as a 'bad' is the problem of waste. There are three types of waste:
    - Wasted planet
    - Wasted words
    - Wasted people

    'Wasted planet' refers to pollution and environmental unsustainability, typically resulting from industrialisation and large-scale production techniques. 'Wasted words' refers to the common prejudice of academics, policymakers and critics against *semiosis* – the systematic preference for 'material' 'reality' over talk (talk is cheap – as if that's a bad thing!), media (media are immaterial, illusory, duplicitous, etc.) and style (apparently no match for substance). We beg to differ: the creation of meaningfulness is radically undervalued in current social and economic theory. Most words are wasted: what most people say most of the time doesn't 'count', isn't heard, cannot be valued. We need to find a better way to establish value in semiosis. 'Wasted people' refers to the underdevelopment of 'human resources' around the world, not only in developing countries, where the effect is most spectacular, but also among unfavoured demographics in any society: 'they' groups including refugees and migrants; children; women in some circumstances; ethnic 'others' and minority identities. Universal education for girls is the first priority.

- *Divides (everywhere)* – gaps between haves and have-nots. Three of these are (see Chapter 11):
  - Economic divides
  - Political divides
  - Cultural divides

  At stake in all such divides is (a) inequality – asymmetry of knowledge or access to it for different groups; and (b) perceived victimhood of a 'we' group or deme in relation to some other 'they' group, and thus an urge or desire for restitution, retribution or revenge. This kind of thing can persist long after its original cause (when 'community tension' persists among people of different ethnic origins for centuries), and sometimes deme-based governments feel justified in taking repressive actions against perceived adversaries among their population long after their own group's previously subjugated position has been reversed. Thus 'divides' are readily understood in negative terms, but that's not the whole story. In our systems approach, 'divides' are of course also 'boundaries' – zones of intense meaning-creation and exchange, margins where new knowledge (and, thus, creativity and innovation) are to be looked for. Victim-thinking is merely 'animistic' here.

We have argued in addition that the 'Three Buts' are named after the values they negate – freedom (control), comfort (waste) and knowledge (divides).

Complexity and conflict

Complexity and the market

Complexity theory favours *open* systems, which self-create, self-organise and self-correct, in order to adapt to change, both in their own internal elaboration and in the environment surrounding them. Is this in fact where advanced knowledge economies and creative societies are heading? Can we look forward to Kauffman's 'poised system' in market relations (see Chapter 12), or is inherent instability and complicatedness (i.e. *disordered* chaos) going to be met by defensive, 'command and control' responses where order is *imposed* by external (exogenous) organisations and agencies that can get away with 'the brute force of monopoly', at least for a while?

In other words, can 'market forces' really work to maximise and to harness the creativity of the whole population? Or, is the future the one that the critics and pessimists have warned us against? Here, 'market forces' lead to monopoly, cartels, corruption and self-interest among corporations, while consumers are deprived of self-directing agency in the systems they use, and are reduced to behavioural responses that can be manipulated by marketing strategies. Is 'the citizen' an outmoded concept in a system where whatever 'we' do can be tracked and put under surveillance, providing more 'big data' for corporations to 'mine' and exploit?

Given that we're talking about future scenarios here, such a possibility has to be admitted, and it is certainly frequently imagined. We are living in a world system of political controls that do not match the world systems of economic enterprise, mediated communication or cultural experience (Lee, 2010). One response has been that states themselves have become entrepreneurial. This can be seen in developing countries, where low economic freedom and an authoritarian state can coincide with high or ultra-high growth, and with governments at central or provincial level who are richer than most private investors. But it is also a feature of the mature democracies, where, as Mariana Mazzucato (2013) argues, the private sector tends to invest only after an entrepreneurial state has made the high-risk investments. She cites examples from the green revolution to biotech and from pharmaceuticals to Silicon Valley. She argues that this amounts to a way of privatising the rewards of public risk. That argument carries over insistently to our own sphere of scholarship itself, where publicly funded research is reported via privately owned journals, which then charge publicly funded universities for access to the knowledge they've created! Small wonder that demand for Open Access publishing is increasing, not least because government funding agencies are beginning to require that the results of research they have funded must be published via Open Access.

Meanwhile, states seem to be playing catch-up with markets – bailing them out in times of crisis, or setting up their own enterprises to compete on the 'if you can't beat them join them' principle.

'Critical' approaches to the market are quick to imagine worst-case outcomes, and sometimes they're proved right. One very obvious example is the apparently inexorable trend towards corporate appropriation of the internet. Once a haven for freethinking libertarian experiments and hopes, the internet that most people know has rapidly transformed into a series of 'gated communities' of branded private property. The 'information superhighway' is patrolled by policing agencies looking for terrorists, perverts, hackers and pirates, corporate lawyers looking for copyright infringement, whistleblowers and leaks, and service-providers willing to compromise (do what lobbyists ask) for the sake of market stability. Thereby, the potential use of the Web for copying (one of its most novel attributes: the ability of digital technologies to make infinite copies without degradation), filesharing, torrenting, etc. is eroded, along with 'open' identity, anonymity and multiple IDs for users. What was once the attraction of online interaction becomes marginal, deviant and suspect. Security is maintained by big business and their legislative allies, who are willing to make criminals out of their own consumers in order to abolish the 'commons' aspect of the Web, and to impose external control over users' ability to make infinite, perfect copies of materials that they might want to share.

Meanwhile, users themselves are being conditioned by all available means to resume their industrial role of low-waged labour (the 'precariat' of freelance, part-time, 'intern' and voluntary workers) and high-demand consumers. Their 'privacy' is an illusion – corporate knowledge of individual 'consumer behaviour' has never been greater, while what consumers can do to protect their identity is under steady attrition. In its pioneer days the internet *was* an 'open system' of almost miraculous potential; it is becoming – isn't it? – a high-street mall, patrolled by unsympathetic security guards, hedged about by official rules and regulations, pushed around by corporate self-interest, and 'used' by an untutored populace that is kept in disorganised ignorance, such that the cynical observer might ask 'What's new?' – this is (big) 'business as usual!' (Zittrain, 2008).

Another future scenario might say that paranoia about market forces is itself based on an outmoded binarism between 'we' and 'they' classes; one that focuses on adversarialism rather than on the growth of knowledge from which all classes benefit. This perspective recognises that the disruptions and inequalities associated with the Industrial Revolution, and many economic innovations thereafter, nevertheless produced more affluence, more quickly, for a greater proportion of humanity than ever before, in just two or three generations (McCloskey, 2010). From such a perspective, we might point to the development and growth of the internet as a unique experiment in the history of knowledge technologies – it's the first 'mass medium' to be developed by private enterprise, and took a mere 30 years – one generation – to span the planet in a web of signification and significance. Naturally there will be glitches, setbacks and 'bad neighbours', but that does not detract from what the internet and mobile telecommunications have already afforded to untold millions of citizens around the world, with access to sources and resources, advice and apps, informal tuition and formal learning, of such breadth and scale that persons can only 'sample' it via search functions whose potentiality we've barely begun to explore.

It's not just a case of seeing the glass as half-full rather than half-empty, it is more a case of observing an Alice-in-Wonderland glass that can inflate to giant scale and keep filling, seemingly endlessly, before our very eyes. That's the Web. Of course, there's the Queen of Hearts bustling everywhere (cunningly disguised as corporate lawyers and state enforcement agents), shouting 'Off with their heads!', but that is neither the direction of the narrative nor the moral of the story. Indeed, a future scenario should not worry so much about the bad behaviour of incumbent players, as history tells us that they come and go, but focus more on the opportunities for *new* players to make new things and meanings for themselves, and for all of this to be possible on a previously unimagined scale.

This is the scenario offered herein, that looks towards a situation where the whole population is active and engaged in DIY culture, making and connecting both online and off. There's no guarantee that such a future will eventuate, at all or for everyone. The idea instead is to see that a commitment to openness, to a 'commons' approach to knowledge, and to inter-group interactions and exchanges, are what is needed to sustain the growth of knowledge in the 'creative economy'. To observe that this 'open future' cannot be discerned in present arrangements is merely to set a policy objective: what should be done about it? How can population-wide, planetary-scale, cultural-economic microproductivity be enabled, educated and encouraged to make new enterprise, new knowledge?

Conflict and the user-citizen

One of the themes of this book is that 'Doing It Yourself' is an emergent reality for 'the people formerly known as the audience' (in journalism-commentator Jay Rosen's famous phrase). Where tomorrow may differ from today is in the extent to which this shift from 'passive' consumption to DIY culture is taken up. On the one hand, it is quite clear that citizens are willing to take action from time to time, whether this takes the form of spectacular and theatrical street-interventions like the Occupy movement, graffiti, protests and demonstrations, or in more 'civil' actions at town meetings, planning hearings, etc. Citizens banding together to make things – from community gardens to an electoral dance-off competition[1] – are bringing new talents, new ideas and new solutions to public attention, using 'real' space as well as 'cyberspace'. As we have discussed in earlier chapters, DIY or user-created media online are matched by the maker movement and 'scenes' offline.

This is all evidence of 'bottom-up' activism, and of the desire of the 'people formerly known as the audience' to take control of what they can, when they can. As Jay Rosen cautioned, this doesn't mean that 'big media' or corporate shenanigans will collapse or go away. It's a trend, not an achievement:

> I'm not claiming that the power shift is total, or even decisive. Only that it's significant, and changes the equation. Exclusive influence, monopoly position, the right to dictate terms, dynastic continuity, priestly authority, guild conditions for limiting competition — these have been lost, not the entrenched media's social and market power, which as you say remain considerable.[2]

The idea of the media thinking for us (as a new priesthood) has been defeated; but the media are still socially and commercially powerful – television is still more influential than online self-representation. Furthermore, commercial pressures are systematically skewed towards turning you from a citizen into a consumer. If you want to be a citizen, you *must* 'do it yourself' (or 'do it with others') – the 'representative' media can't and won't do it for you (as often as not their 'news' stories about digital or DIY culture will pursue vested interests – their own or their business allies).

This is why direct citizen 'resistance' is important. The extent to which populations are taking responsibility for their own representation (often showing high-risk bravery to do it) is a barometer of change. The popular 'response' to authoritarian (state or commercial) control is to find as many ways to achieve and exercise autonomy as possible: sometimes on the street; sometimes in the spoof; sometimes in the choices and identities people craft for themselves in private (Baym, 2010; Papacharissi, 2010; Gauntlett, 2011). The future seems to promise more of the same: a continuing 'low intensity conflict' between control-addicted state and commercial organisational forces, and autonomy-desiring citizens of almost infinite variety, distributed across many different platforms and domains.

We can predict the probabilities readily enough: there will be complexity, crisis and conflict; it will involve markets, states and citizens; and it will be about openness and autonomy trying to establish itself at every level, against the inertia and habit of imposed control. The question we can't answer is how long it will take networked DIY creativity to emerge as a dominant force in the dynamics of change, what role will be played by which new institutions, or whether it will all be stymied by conspiracies of 'organised minorities' who will continue to defeat 'disorganised majorities'. The answer is up to you. No, us!

The stakes are high. As Charles Leadbeater (2014) has wisely put it: 'The basic unit of sustained innovation is a creative community with a cause'. Not only will a 'community with a cause' advance their cause, but also, oftentimes they prove to be the 'source of newness' for the system more generally – the 'unit' of sustained innovation.

Knowing and doing

The last chapter of a book such as this often turns from the internal arguments of the case being presented towards a kind of 'What is to be done?' format. What suggestions do we have for further study and research? What unresolved problems remain? What difference would it make if the field devoted itself wholeheartedly to solving those problems?

DIY disciplines

Such questions take a time-honoured form, but what they point to is a very real opportunity for some DIY work at the *disciplinary* coalface. We have presented the case for a systems approach to the creative economy, and we've outlined some of the concepts, claims and scenarios deployed in that approach. But there are definite shortcomings.

One is that there's very little existing work from this perspective to which we can point, to give examples of it in action and concrete analyses of creative industries. One of the few exceptions is Jason Potts' work (see references), especially his 2011 book *Creative Industries and Economic Evolution*; and for basic conceptual ground-clearing see Hartley and Potts (2014). We would draw your attention also to the magisterial work of Carsten Herrmann-Pillath (2010, 2013), and point out also that many authors have provided clues, concepts and case studies of the sort of work that is required. It's just that not much of it is applied directly to the cultural and creative industries and the creative economy. The best of such work is by David Throsby (2010), Ruth Towse (2014) and Terry Flew (2012, 2013), and of that work, very little takes a 'cultural science' approach.

Another shortcoming is that the present authors are not trained as systems scientists. We are trained in media, communications, culture and management. In order to take our approach much further, an interdisciplinary team is needed to carry out field studies of 'everyone', 'everything', 'everywhere' in action, and to analyse the relative impact of the 'three buts' and 'future scenarios' on these 'three bigs'. An example can be found in Hartley et al. (2012), who applied a cultural science or systems approach to the construction of a comprehensive 'Creative City Index'. But to make further progress we need more cultural scientists. We really need help with this! *You* can help.

Theory and practice

There are two ways to help: through 'theory' or knowing and 'practice' or doing. You can join the creative industries in practice; or you can research the creative industries. The inherited expectation (amounting almost to an industry myth) is that you must choose between them, typically by studying first (or not at all), then practising, which is the real goal. This prejudice extends to belittling knowledge itself (as in the infamous put-down, 'those who can, do; those who can't, teach'). Strangely, the idea that theory and practice are chalk and cheese is reinforced by universities, because they perpetuate a strong distinction between practice-based and theory-based courses. The best students in practice-based courses (such as a BFA or MFA) are expected and encouraged to leave for the industry, never to return (even without graduating, if their talent is scouted in the meantime). In the best theory-based programmes, on the other hand, the best students may aspire to further training in the knowledge domain itself, via doctoral study followed by a teaching and research career. These divergent pathways are accepted as different specialisations.

But that divergence causes real pain and difficulty for *practice*-trained individuals who want to turn to *knowledge* creation. Typically, they don't hold a PhD, so they need to retrain as an academic, a process in which the friction between the informal know-how of the creative workplace and the formal disciplines of academic fields of research is intense but unresolved: people are hired because they have industry experience but then they need to demonstrate academic credentials to practise as teachers, and even more so as researchers. The outcome of this tension is that individuals tend to grab ad hoc theories to manage their own needs (they want to talk about their art but end up rehearsing social and textual theory imported from the meta-discourses of the day). There's also a culture of mutual resentment: artists resent deans because they feel under-valued; but deans resent artists because of their unearned sense of entitlement. The development of a coherent mode of study for researching the creative industries, one that includes both practice and theory appropriate to the object of study, is much rarer than you might think, because formal institutional cultures, procedures and organisational structures keep them apart.

Divergence between practice and theory is exacerbated further by social and cultural distinctions that operate in the world beyond education. One is the difference made by attending prestige institutions, such as Oxford or Harvard, whose graduates may find an entry-point into the industry more readily than the graduate of a less well branded alma mater, even when the Ivy-leaguer has studied something unrelated to the creative industries or to the job description they seek to fill.

Another distinction is the one between 'creatives' and 'suits', where the latter are graduates in economics with an MBA, or lawyers with an LLB, rather than graduates with a Bachelor of Creative Industries in the creative arts and design, performance, media production, creative writing or journalism. MBAs and LLBs are the ones who aspire to managing or owning the industry, as opposed to producing artisanal 'content'. In contrast to those who teach in the 'studies' side of creative disciplines, there is no shame attached to the fact that *these* graduates can't make a movie, a dress, an image, sound or story: their function is to create wealth. Here too – in Business Schools – is where *research* in the creative industries finds its most congenial home, in the form of industry analysis, using tried and trusted economic methods and measures, keeping production (understood as an industrial process) apart from consumption (understood via marketing), and both of them well clear of creativity, which is seen as a scarce resource (intellectual property).

The 'swimming lesson'

There still is no accepted, well-distributed model of how 'knowing' and 'doing' can be brought together in formal educational settings. As a result, the convergence between the two is informal. In the era of mass higher education, unpaid internships, freelance (casual) work and multiple careers, the convergence of knowing and doing itself is experienced without being theorised. You can study – a term that includes learning and teaching, researching and publishing – and practise at the same time. Thus, students work in or close to the business while taking classes at other times of the day or week; teachers freelance as practitioners; firms undertake their own research. Various branches of the creative industries have moved more or less completely to graduate-entry (e.g. journalism), requiring acquaintance with a formal knowledge domain prior to entry. There are of course still pockets where graduates are rare (e.g. fashion modelling), or where the best chances go to those who attend specialist academies or conservatoires (e.g. performing arts – music, dance, acting).

Convergence works at the micro, DIY level, rather than at the meso, institutional level. Individual students find work (often via unpaid internships) in the industry. Individual observers find ways to explain it. There is some cross-fertilisation (you may find a PhD in the studio or an artist in the academy), but wastefulness is considerable, because such 'knowledge out of place' rarely 'counts' (commands esteem or a pay-rise) in the new environment. Further, the cost of formal education is accelerating, so the more qualifications you have, the more you have to earn to break even.

Small wonder that the convergence between knowing and doing, theory and practice, thinking and making, is more evident within the creative industries than in their formal study. Here, perhaps, one of the most important sources of knowledge about the industry (it would not 'count' as research in the traditional sense) is the production and circulation of discourses *about* the industry, *for* the industry, *by* the industry. The most important of these may be the least discussed, because it operates at the macro, *system* level, which few observers attempt to encompass. Professor of Communication Vicki Mayer (2014) has commented on the extent to which the creative industries as a whole – as a 'sector' of the economy – are complicit in a kind of fictionalisation of their own role, claiming socio-centrality for creative media and cultural expression, and thereby claiming an exceptionalist status for their own labour practices:

> Creative industries have succeeded in promoting their own aura, connecting their goods to modernity and putting their executives at the centers of their own narratives of the good life. ... Media and cultural industries have cultivated their own importance as the bards of social meanings and values. Who would not be willing to accept poor pay, seasonal gigs and even the humiliation of failure, if it meant becoming part of society's power and prestige center? (Mayer, 2014: 59-61)

Evidently, Mayer herself is sceptical about their 'importance as the bards of social meanings and values' (although we would argue that this conceptualisation can be defended).[3] She retains an *industrial* view of the creative industries: as she pithily puts it, 'creative work is still work', with attendant problems of poor pay (or none), short-term contracts and the 'humiliation of failure'. In this view, the creative industries are guilty of a kind of group-think that is also a contemporary version of what used to be known as 'false consciousness', when they promote their own socio-centrality while using that as a cover for exploitative labour practices, 'creating' the so-called precariat.

We doubt that the reality is as conscious, coherent or conspiratorial as that. There is no necessary connection between the authors of 'myths' (if that's what they are) about the industry and those who benefit from hiring cheap labour. Indeed, many of those who extol the virtues of creative work are themselves struggling to make ends meet. They are not doing it to pull the wool over the eyes of innocent newcomers; rather, they are part of a system in which this presumption is widely shared, among both insiders and the audiences and consumers for whom celebrity, showbiz, media and cultural industries are indeed a source of 'meanings and values'. It would take more than a critical sociologist to undo that value-system.

The reality is that gaining secure employment is always going to be risky in a chaotic marketplace that seeks to invent *future* meaningfulness, and *values* work not on the basis of institutional position or training but on that of 'newness', which is judged by individual reputation, industry esteem, audience attention, and that most insecure of notions, 'demand' (which cannot be known in advance of supply).

The way the production of meaningful newness has been 'managed' (again, informally, without anyone 'taking charge') is by what can be described as 'the swimming lesson': that period, typically the first five years out of school or university, when an individual 'sinks or swims'. Many move on to other careers (or fail to find one); some find a way to align their talents, ambitions and opportunities with the openings and requirements of the industry, gaining know-how by means of proximity, imitation, endless repetitious rehearsal and knock-backs, a willingness to learn and to work in teams, such that in the end an individual aspiration is honed into what is in many respects its own opposite – an ability to work effectively and consequentially in a *system*. It may seem even more wasteful than formal education, and people trying to join it are vulnerable to both economic and creative exploitation. But that's not what the system is *for*. What the system is doing with all these potential recruits is *future-forming* – searching among likely candidates for those who can face the future and produce the most valuable but most elusive 'commodity' of the creative industries, which is *newness*.

'Newness is quiche!'

This may be why there is so much talk in the industry about the industry, and so many minutes of media attention or column inches of magazine and press coverage go to talking about media attention, magazines and press coverage. It's partly self-regarding, of course ('look at *me!*'), but it is also *searching*; an anxious, reflexive discourse about what the creative system needs to stay in front, which is something that can't be known in advance.

Small wonder that insider advice abounds on how to get into the industry. It's worth looking at an example to show how such advice deals with the tensions between knowing and doing; learning and leading; being a know-nothing but at the same time being the hope for the future. A relevant example comes from the UK-based *i-D Magazine*, a successful, high-end, trend-setting and directional magazine with an international readership, devoted (as its masthead puts it) to 'ideas, fashion, music, people'. In 2014 it ran an issue devoted to the theme of 'Newness'.

The opening editorial spread set the tone: 'We called on nine budding young photographers and nine sparkling new stylists, teamed them up and invited them to shoot one image defining what "newness" means to them' (*i-D* 331, 2014: 25). What it means is then illustrated over these captions:

- *Opportunity*: 'Those who criticise our generation forget who raised it'
- *Fearless*: 'Youthful and raw'
- *Inspiration*: 'Everything new is old'
- *Purity*: 'It's the new age of innocence'
- *Fresh*: 'You've got to see things with fresh eyes'
- *Witty*: 'Newness is quiche!
- *Truth*: 'Newness comes from looking internally and thinking about what would be the most creative. … we really wanted to show true character'
- *Visionary*: 'Newness is individuality and sexuality, people who refuse to live by the modern world's standard of living'
- *Change*: 'Reinvention and an opportunity for innovative change'

Or, as Editor in Chief Holly Shackleton put it: 'The world needs new ideas, and we want to hear yours! So let's get out there and do something new' (*i-D* 331, 2014: 20-41).

No matter what the 'handpicked selection' of 'new generation' contributors said, or how they pictured 'newness', the emphasis was on *teamwork*, a theme that was taken up in the 'text' part of the editorial, written by freelancer Tish Weinstock. She opens with a well-worn line: 'Breaking into the creative industries is difficult, expensive, and takes a hell of a long time. But don't give up hope just yet!' Her full-page column details just how difficult it can be for interns and newbies. In the end she recommends teamwork, noting that *i-D Magazine* itself started that way:

> After all i-D begun [sic.] as a fanzine in 1980, when Terry and Tricia Jones took a risk and put straight up pictures of punks on the pages of a homemade fanzine. This endeavour wasn't about making money: it was about cataloguing the DIY aesthetic of punk that was spilling and spewing all over the streets, which commercial magazines refused to acknowledge. Just like Terry and Tricia did in the 1980s, it is by pushing the boundaries of creativity, working alongside new talent, and trying to

produce something new, something different, that will not only grab the attention of the creative industries, but will get the creative industries flocking to you.[4]

Tish Weinstock is a practitioner of what she preaches, having defended unpaid internships in *The Huffington Post*, presumably on the basis of personal experience.[5] Her website introduces her as one who took up freelance writing after leaving Oxford University with a degree in History of Art, going on to contribute to magazines such as *Lula*, *The Tatler*, *Garage* and *Vanity Fair* as well as *i-D*. There seems to be no substitute for practice; which means getting noticed by the incumbents, or going it alone with a team – or, preferably, both, combining a DIY team with getting noticed by the incumbents.

Convergence?

As for 'theory', or knowledge, that is incorporated into practice. Because creative practitioners want to put their knowledge into what they're making, how they do that might be a trade secret. Standing back and working out larger patterns – as we have tried to do in this book – probably needs to be done at arm's length from making and creating, not to mention trying to get and keep work, or relating to an audience.

Currently, the skills needed to create 'content' *in* the creative industries are not the same as those needed to create knowledge *about* those industries. As things stand, gaining such knowledge remains a matter of lengthy training in an institutional setting that is about as far removed from creative practice as can be imagined, whether you're in the Business Faculty or the Creative Industries Faculty. However, the two worlds are not separate: the creative industries are peppered with individuals and organisations devoted to creating knowledge about themselves, either on an 'insider' basis, where market trends and business opportunities are identified from analytic sources, or on a storytelling basis, where it is possible to make a career in the creative industries by understanding and communicating about them – as a columnist in fashion and style magazines, for instance.

Someone who personifies that kind of DIY knowledge is the (then) teenage blogger, publisher, actor and public speaker Tavi Gevinson (see Figure 14.1). She is interviewed in the same issue of *i-D* mentioned above, as a 'poster girl' for the fashion blogging 'movement'. According to *i-D*, 'Truth be told, Tavi opened the floodgates for a new generation of talented and opinionated young stars. The dusty walls of the fashion establishment crumbled, cliquey catwalk shows suddenly became more democratic, and young voices mattered more than they ever have before'.[6] She started her

FIGURE 14.1 Tavi Gevinson at *Makers: Women Who Make America*, New York (February 2013)[7]

fashion blog *thestylerookie.com* when she was 11, moving on in her mid-teens to found *Rookie Mag*.

i-D interviewed Gevinson for her 18th birthday:

> *i-D: Tavi, you and your friends have been used to doing it for yourselves since your early teens, carving out your own career paths...*
>
> *Tavi: ... I don't think our culture is completely without hierarchy yet. I think it's time for cultural gatekeepers to give up these illusions of who 'deserves' to be famous, be heard or have influence, based on old-fashioned ideas about success. Literally none of it matters. ... So I hope this glorification of old institutions and prestigious publications can be balanced with consideration for what audiences are actually responding to. (p. 97)*

Gevinson's online magazine (*Rookie Mag*) and printed yearbooks are an experiment in finding new ways to work with what 'audiences are actually responding to', combining a team of like-minded staff with new ways of interacting with the readers, who are not only consumers but also contributors. More pertinently, *Rookie Mag* is not devoted to creating a niche in the desirable teen-girl market; it works as part of that culture. Gevinson herself belongs to it, and she wants her demographic to *know itself* better. She points out that what she pioneered — which prestigious incumbent institutions are now 'scrambling' to copy — is 'to use the internet in a way that's ... genuinely effective and exciting to people'.

The audience response is not desired for its own sake only, but for the sake of forging that 'unit of sustained innovation' imagined by Leadbeater (2014) — a 'creative community with a cause' — among teenage girls. Says Gevinson: 'With *Rookie*, a lot of it is about using online to get people to do stuff offline, so we have a lot of DIYs and really try and inspire our readers'. She characterises the staff writers as people with a cause:

> Me and many of our staffers are feminists and that informs how I approach everything. ... Girls my age are used to being fed a lot of girl power rhetoric, so I wanted to do something that would be more in-depth, something that isn't intimidating to girls who were not spoon-fed this stuff [feminist theory] from a young age. (i-D, 331, 2014: 98)

What is being described here are *relations of knowledge*: Gevinson and team know their audience; the audience knows them and uses that connection to improve their own knowledge — in ways that are both practical ('a lot of DIYs') and theoretical (feminism for girls), achieved through mutual contact via the magazine, which is not only a producer/consumer *business* but also an addresser/addressee *culture*.

'Beyoncé theory'

This is closer to a 'crowd-sourcing' model for the growth of knowledge than a 'training' model, although both sides, the production team and the audiences, are 'learning by doing'. Cultural science, the approach we are advocating, which seeks to apply systems thinking to understand creativity (the creative industries, creative economy, the cultural industries — by whatever name!), needs to learn from this scenario.

The first lesson is that *working in teams* is essential, both to *intensify* like-mindedness (a community with a cause) and to *combine* different skill-sets and knowledge domains, e.g. combining all of the following:

- Humanities-based analysis of meaningfulness;
- Social-scientific approaches to structures, relations and agency;
- Business or economics-based approaches to industry;
- Computer-science models of networks dynamics;
- Statistical approaches to scale and probabilities.

A second lesson is that the creation of new knowledge along these lines will proceed more successfully if it takes seriously the potentialities of the system it seeks to understand: you can connect 'everyone', 'everywhere' with 'everything' if you adopt *crowd-sourcing* solutions: internet-based, interdisciplinary, dispersed and often informal, immersed in both practice and theory, bringing to bear formal disciplinary approaches where they are useful.

Tavi Gevinson signed off her (now 'mostly defunct') blog *thestylerookie.com* by explaining how 'documenting' her teenage life and living it – *knowing and doing* – are the same thing. She calls the period between 13 and 17 years old '*forever*', a period 'in which one feels both eternally invincible and permanently trapped'. She writes:

> Reflecting and archiving is not the same as dwelling in the past. It is not anti-living, but a part of life, even a crucial one. We do this to highlight one thing above others, so that a special moment can take up more space in our brains than an inconsequential one; so that, by plain math, our personal worlds contain more good things and fewer bad ones. Or more interesting things and fewer blah ones, since you have to record the bad, too.[8]

Over at *i-D*, Gevinson shares how she's going to tackle university study now that she's 18: 'I'm hoping to design my own major. … It may be obvious from *Rookie*, but I'm very interested in the intersections of society with pop culture, so I'll probably be taking Beyoncé theory, or whatever!' (*i-D*, 331, 2014: 98).

Bravo! When we read this we thought that perhaps we should change the title of our book to *Beyoncé Theory*, but in truth such a book is yet to be written. Can any university in the current set of arrangements even imagine that subject? What would *Beyoncé theory* look like? We think that it would include an attempt to understand the micro–meso–macro system in which the sign 'Beyoncé' gains meaning, value, agency and global communicative power, and how this demonstrates the intersections of society and (pop) culture as both systematic and future-forming, such that it would be to the advantage of everyone, everywhere, across 'everything', to understand how that works.

Notes

1. See https://www.youtube.com/watch?v=wzyT9-9lUyE.
2. Jay Rosen (June 2006) 'The people formerly known as the audience'. Available at: http://archive.pressthink.org/2006/06/27/ppl_frmr.html.
3. One of us has written about the 'bardic function' of contemporary popular media: see Fiske and Hartley, 2003; Hartley and McWilliam, 2009.

4. 'How to make it in the industry', by Tish Weinstock, *i-D Magazine*, 331, Summer 2014: 26. Available at: www.tishweinstock.com/#!how-to-make-it-in-the-industry/crak.
5. See www.tishweinstock.com/#!im-an-intern-not-an-idiot/cfua.
6. 'All you need is a little faith, trust and pixie dust', *i-D*, 331, Summer 2014: 91–9. See also this profile from the *New York Times* available at http://tmagazine.blogs.nytimes.com/2014/06/06/tavi-gevinson-on-rookie-magazine-and-growing-up/.
7. Picture courtesy of Wikimedia: Creative Commons License (https://commons.wikimedia.org/wiki/File:MAKERS_event_New_York_Feb_7,_2013.jpg). Original image by The Jauretsi at http://flickr.com/photos/11901158@N00/8453062878. Full-sized image at https://upload.wikimedia.org/wikipedia/commons/archive/e/ed/20130208095037!MAKERS_event_New_York_Feb_7%2C_2013.jpg/.
8. See www.thestylerookie.com/ (3 December 2013). See also www.rookiemag.com/2013/12/editors-letter-26/ December 2013).

ACKNOWLEDGEMENTS

We would like to acknowledge the Australian Research Council, which supported much of the research on which this book is based, especially:

- John Hartley received an **Australian Research Council Federation Fellowship**, The Uses of Multimedia: Citizen Consumers, Creative Participation and Innovation in Australian Digital Content (FF0561981), 2005-10.
- Part of the research was conducted at the **Australian Research Council Centre of Excellence for Creative Industries and Innovation** (SR0590002), 2005-13 (Cultural Science programme).

The views expressed herein are those of the authors and not necessarily those of the Australian Research Council.

Wen Wen and Henry Siling Li would like to acknowledge the China Scholarship Council, which supported their doctoral research, upon which some of the materials in Chapters 7-11 is based.

We are grateful to the Faculty of Humanities at Curtin University, which supported Wen Wen to make an extended visit to Western Australia in order to facilitate the preparation of this book. Similarly, we are grateful to the Institute for Cultural Industries (SICI), Shenzen University and especially to Professor Li Fengliang, for supporting John Hartley and Henry Siling Li to visit Shenzhen. Curtin University Centre for Culture and Technology (CCAT) supported Hartley and Li during the course of the research on which the book is based, and enabled us to get on with writing it up.

We are grateful to our colleagues at SAGE Publications, especially Chris Rojek, who commissioned the title, Gemma Shields and Delayna Spencer, our editors, and Katherine Haw, our production editor.

Parts of Chapters 4 and 5 are adapted and updated from John Hartley's introduction to Lucy Montgomery (2010), *China's Creative Industries: Copyright, Social Network Markets and the Business of Culture in a Digital Age*. Cheltenham: Edward Elgar. The idea of 'urban semiosis' was trialled in Hartley's 'Urban Semiosis: Creative Industries and the Clash of Systems',

International Journal of Cultural Studies, 18(1), 2015. Parts of Chapter 7 are adapted from Li, Henry Siling (2012) *Seriously playful: The uses of networked spoof videos in China*, PhD thesis, Queensland University of Technology. Parts of Chapters 8 and 9 are adapted from Wen, Wen (2012) *Scenes, quarters and clusters: New experiments in the formation and governance of creative places in China*, PhD thesis, Queensland University of Technology.

REFERENCES

Albrechtslund, A-M. (2010) 'Gamers telling stories: understanding narrative practices in an online community', *Convergence*, 16(1): 112–24.

Allen, R. (1991) *Opening Doors: The Life and Work of Joseph Schumpeter, Vol. 1: Europe*. New Brunswick, NJ: Transaction Publishers.

Anderson, C. (2006) *The Long Tail: Why the Future of Business is Selling Less of More*. New York: Hyperion.

Anderson, C. (2012) *Makers: The New Industrial Revolution*. New York: Crown Business.

Andrejevic, M. (2007) *iSpy: Surveillance and Power in the Interactive Era*. Lawrence, KS: University of Kansas Press.

Arthur, W.B. (2009) *The Nature of Technology: What it is and How it Evolves*. New York: Free Press.

Banks, J. (2013) *Co-creating Videogames*. London: Bloomsbury.

Banks, J. and Deuze, M. (eds) (2009) *Co-creative Labour*, Special Issue of *International Journal of Cultural Studies*, 12(5).

Banks, J. and Potts, J. (2010) 'Consumer co-creation in online games', *New Media and Society*, 12(2): 253–70.

Barabási, A-L. (2003) *Linked: How Everything is Connected to Everything Else and What it Means*. New York: Plume.

Baulch, E. (2007) *Making Scenes: Reggae, Punk, and Death Metal in 1990s Bali*. Durham, NC: Duke University Press.

Bauman, Z. (2000) *Liquid Modernity*. Cambridge: Polity Press.

Baym, G. (2000) 'Constructing moral authority: "We" in the discourse of television news', *Western Journal of Communication*, 64: 92–111.

Baym, N. (2000) *Tune In, Log On: Soaps, Fandom, and Online Community*. Thousand Oaks, CA: Sage Publications.

Baym, N. (2010) *Personal Connections in the Digital Age*. Cambridge: Polity Press.

Beck, U. (1992) *Risk Society: Towards a New Modernity*. London: Sage.

Becker, H. (1982) *Art Worlds*. Berkeley, CA: University of California Press.

Beinhocker, E. (2006) *The Origin of Wealth. Evolution, Complexity, and the Radical Remaking of Economics*. Cambridge, MA: Harvard Business School Press.

Benkler, Y. (2006) *The Wealth of Networks: How Social Production Transforms Markets and Freedom*. New Haven, CT: Yale University Press.

Bennett, A. and Peterson, R. (2004) *Music Scenes: Local, Translocal, and Virtual*. Nashville, TN: Vanderbilt University Press.

Bennett, W.L. and Segerberg, A. (2012) 'The logic of connective action: Digital media and the personalization of contentious politics', *Information, Communication & Society*, 15(5): 739–68.

Bentley, R.A. (2009) 'Fashion versus reason in the creative industries', in M. O'Brien and S. Shennan (eds), *Innovation in Cultural Systems: Contributions from Evolutionary Anthropology.* Boston, MA: MIT Press. pp. 121–6.

Bentley, R.A. and Ormerod, P. (2010) 'Agents, intelligence, and social atoms', in M. Collard and E. Slingerland (eds), *Integrating Science and the Humanities.* Oxford: Oxford University Press.

Best, K. (2010) 'Living in the control society: Surveillance, users and digital screen technologies', *International Journal of Cultural Studies,* 13(1): 5–24.

Bickerton, D. (2009) *Adam's Tongue: How Humans Made Language, How Language Made Humans.* New York: Hill & Wang.

Boulding, K. (1977) 'Economic Development as an Evolutionary System', 5th World Congress of the International Economic Association. Tokyo: International Economic Association.

Boulding, K. (1981) *Evolutionary Economics.* Beverley Hills, CA: Sage Publications.

Boyd, B. (2009) *On the Origin of Stories.* Cambridge, MA: Harvard University Press.

Breen, M. (ed.) (1998) *Journalism: Theory and Practice.* Sydney: Macleay Press.

Bromley, M. (2014) 'Field maturation in journalism: The role of hackademics as a "motley crew"', *International Journal of Cultural Studies,* 17(1): 3–19.

Burgess, J. (2006) 'Hearing ordinary voices: Cultural studies, vernacular creativity, and digital storytelling', *Continuum,* 20(2): 201–14.

Burgess, J. and Green, J. (2009) *YouTube: Online Video and Participatory Culture.* Cambridge: Polity Press.

Butler, J. (1990) *Feminism and the Subversion of Identity.* London: Routledge.

Castells, M. (2001) *The Internet Galaxy: Reflections on the Internet, Business, and Society.* Oxford: Oxford University Press.

Chadwick, A. and Howard, P. (eds) (2008) *Routledge Handbook of Internet Politics.* London and New York: Routledge.

Choi, J. (2008) 'The New Korean Wave of U', in H. Anheier and Y. Raj Isar (eds), *The Cultural Economy.* Los Angeles, CA: Sage. pp. 148–154.

Cooke, P. and Lazzeretti, L. (eds) (2008) *Creative Cities, Cultural Clusters and Local Economic Development.* Cheltenham: Edward Elgar.

Council of Europe/ERICarts (2013) *Compendium of Cultural Policies and Trends in Europe,* 14th edn. Available from www.culturalpolicies.net.

Cowen, T. (2013) *Average is Over: Powering America Beyond the Age of the Great Stagnation.* New York: Dutton.

Crutzen, P. and Schwägerl, C. (2011) 'Living in the Anthropocene: Toward a new global ethos', *Yale Environment 360.* Available at: http://e360.yale.edu/feature/living_in_the_anthropocene_toward_a_new_global_ethos/2363/.

Crutzen, P. and Stoermer, E. (2000) 'The "Anthropocene"', *Global Change Newsletter,* 41: 17–18.

Cunningham, S. and Higgs, P. (2008) 'Creative industries mapping: Where have we come from and where are we going?', *Creative Industries Journal,* 1(1): 7–30.

Cunningham, S. and Higgs, P. (2009) 'Measuring creative employment: Implications for innovation policy', *Innovation: Management, Policy and Practice,* 11(2): 190–200.

Currid, E. (2007) *The Warhol Economy. How Fashion, Art, and Music Drive New York City* (new edn 2008). Princeton, NJ: Princeton University Press.

DCMS (1998, revised 2001) *Creative Industries Mapping Document.* London: Department for Culture, Media and Sport.
Deuze, M. (2008) 'The changing context of news work: Liquid journalism and monitorial citizenship', *International Journal of Communication*, 2: 848–65.
Diamond, J. (2012) *The World Until Yesterday: What Can We Learn From Traditional Societies?* New York: Viking.
Doctorow, C. (2009) *Makers.* New York: Harper/Voyager; and free download from http://craphound.com/makers/download/.
Dopfer, K., Foster, J. and Potts, J. (2004) 'Micro–meso–macro', *Journal of Evolutionary Economics*, 14: 263–79.
Douglas, M. (1966) *Purity and Danger: An Analysis of the Concepts of Pollution and Taboo.* London: Routledge.
Dutton, D. (2009) *The Art Instinct: Beauty, Pleasure and Human Evolution.* London: Bloomsbury.
Earls, M. (2007) *Herd: How to Change Mass Behaviour by Harnessing Our True Nature.* London: John Wiley.
Field, A. (2008) 'From D.Ds to Y.Y. to Park 97 to Muse: Dance club spaces and the construction of class in Shanghai, 1997–2007', *China: An International Journal*, 6(1): 18–43.
Fiske, J. and Hartley, J. (2003) *Reading Television*, 2nd edn. London and New York: Routledge (1st edn 1978).
Flew, T. (2012) *Creative Industries: Culture and Policy.* London: Sage.
Flew, T. (2013) *Global Creative Industries.* Cambridge: Polity Press.
Florida, R. (2002) *The Rise of the Creative Class. And How It's Transforming Work, Leisure and Everyday Life.* New York: Basic Books.
Florida, R. (2009) 'How the crash will reshape America', *The Atlantic*, March. Available at: www.theatlantic.com/magazine/archive/2009/03/how-the-crash-will-reshape-america/307293/.
Florida, R. (2010) 'Music scenes to music clusters: The economic geography of music in the US, 1970–2000', *Environment and Planning A*, 42: 785–804.
Gauntlett, D. (2011) *Making is Connecting: The Social Meaning of Creativity, from DIY and Knitting to YouTube and Web 2.0.* Cambridge: Polity Press.
Gauteng Department of Sport, Arts, Culture and Recreation (GDSACR) and British Council (2008) *Gauteng's Creative Industries: An Analysis.* Gauteng: GDSACR.
Giddens, A. (1998) *The Third Way: The Renewal of Social Democracy.* Cambridge: Polity Press.
Gilens, F. (2013) *Affluence and Influence: Economic Inequality and Political Power in America.* Princeton, NJ: Princeton University Press.
Gilens, F. and Page, B. (2014) 'Testing theories of American politics: Elites, interest groups, and average citizens', *Perspectives on Politics,* Fall.
Gillies, M. (2013) 'Capital gains and pains', *Times Higher Education*, 18 July. Available at: www.timeshighereducation.co.uk/comment/columnists/capital-gains-and-pains/2005766.article.
Goffman, E. (1971) *The Presentation of Self in Everyday Life.* Harmondsworth: Penguin.
Goldman, A. (1993) *Sound Bites.* London: Abacus.

Goldsmith, B., Lee, K. and Yecies, B. (2011) 'In search of the Korean digital wave', *Media International Australia*, 141: 70–77.

Graaf, J. de, Wann, D. and Naylor, T. (2001) *Affluenza: The All-Consuming Epidemic.* San Francisco, CA: Berrett-Koehler Publishers.

Granovetter, M.S. (1973) 'The strength of weak ties', *American Journal of Sociology*, 78 (6): 1360–80.

Grazian, D. (2004) 'The symbolic economy of authenticity in the Chicago blues scene', in A. Bennett and R.A. Peterson (eds), *Music Scenes: Local, Translocal, and Virtual*. Nashville, TN: Vanderbilt University Press. pp. 31–47.

Hall, S., Critcher, C., Jefferson, T., Clarke, J. and Roberts, B. (1978) *Policing the Crisis: Mugging, the State and Law and Order*. London: Macmillan.

Harari, Y.N. (2014) *Sapiens: A Brief History of Humankind*. London: Harvill Secker.

Hargreaves, I. (2011) *Digital Opportunity: A Review of Intellectual Property and Growth*. London: Intellectual Property Office. Available at: www.ipo.gov.uk/ipreview-finalreport.pdf.

Hargreaves, I., Bakhshi, H. and Mateos-Garcia, J. (2013) *A Manifesto for the Creative Economy*. London: Nesta. Available at: www.nesta.org.uk/sites/default/files/a-manifesto-for-the-creative-economy-april13.pdf.

Hartley, J. (1982) *Understanding News*. London: Routledge.

Hartley, J. (1996) *Popular Reality: Journalism, Modernity, Popular Culture*. London: Arnold [now Bloomsbury].

Hartley, J. (2005) 'Creative industries', in J. Hartley (ed.), *Creative Industries*. Malden, MA and Oxford: Wiley-Blackwell. pp. 1–40.

Hartley, J. (2008) *Television Truths: Forms of Knowledge in Popular Culture*. Malden, MA and Oxford: Wiley-Blackwell.

Hartley, J. (2009) *The Uses of Digital Literacy*. St. Lucia: UQP; New Brunswick, NJ: Transaction Press (2010).

Hartley, J. (2010) 'Creativity as emergence: Policy issues for creative cities', *5th Creative China Harmonious World International Forum on Cultural Industries*, 11 October, Beijing, China. Available at: http://eprints.qut.edu.au/39545/.

Hartley, J. (2012) *Digital Futures for Cultural and Media Studies*. Malden, MA and Oxford: Wiley-Blackwell.

Hartley, J. (2013) 'Authorship and the narrative of the self', in J. Gray and D. Johnson (eds), *A Companion to Media Authorship*. Malden, MA and Oxford: Wiley-Blackwell. pp. 23–47.

Hartley, J. and McWilliam, K. (2009) *Story Circle: Digital Storytelling Around the World*. Malden, MA and Oxford: Wiley-Blackwell.

Hartley, J. and Montgomery, L. (2009) 'Fashion as consumer entrepreneurship: Emergent risk culture, social network markets, and the launch of *Vogue* in China', *Chinese Journal of Communication*, 2(1): 61–76.

Hartley, J. and Potts, J. (2014) *Cultural Science: A Natural History of Stories, Demes, Knowledge and Innovation*. London: Bloomsbury Academic.

Hartley, J., Potts, J. and MacDonald, T. with Erkunt, C. and Kufleitner, C. (2012) *Creative City Index*, *Cultural Science*, 5(1) whole issue.

Hartley, J., Potts, J., Cunningham, S., Flew, T., Keane, M. and Banks, J. (2013) *Key Concepts in Creative Industries*. London: Sage Publications.

Hebdige, D. (1979) *Subculture: The Meaning of Style*. London: Routledge.
Hélie, M. (2012) *The Meaning of Emergent Urbanism, After A New Kind of Science*. Available at: http://emergenturbanism.com.
Herrmann-Pillath, C. (2010) *The Economics of Identity and Creativity: A Cultural Science Approach*. St. Lucia: UQP; New Brunswick, NJ: Transaction Press.
Herrmann-Pillath, C. (2013) *Foundations of Economic Evolution: A Treatise on the Natural Philosophy of Economics*. Cheltenham: Edward Elgar.
Higgs, P., Cunningham, S. and Bakhshi, H. (2008) *Beyond the Creative Industries: Mapping the Creative Economy in the United Kingdom*. London: Nesta. Available at: www.nesta.org.uk/library/documents/beyond-creative-industries-report.pdf.
Hobbes, T. (1651, this edn 1968) *Leviathan* (C.B. Macpherson, ed.). Harmondsworth: Penguin Books.
Hodgkinson, J. (2004) 'The fanzine discourse over post rock', in A. Bennett and R. Peterson (eds), *Music Scenes: Local, Translocal and Virtual*. Nashville, TN: Vanderbilt University Press. pp. 221–37.
Howard, S., Kjeldskov, J., Skov, M.B., Garnœs, K. and Grünberger, O. (2006) 'Negotiating presence-in-absence: Contact, content and context', *CHI 2006*, Montréal, Canada: ACM.
Howkins, J. (2001) *The Creative Economy: How People Make Money from Ideas*. London: Penguin.
Howkins, J. (2009) *Creative Ecologies: Where Thinking is a Proper Job*. St. Lucia: UQP; New Brunswick, NJ: Transaction Publishers (2010).
Hugo, V. (1831) *Notre Dame de Paris*. (1917 Harvard Classic Translation). Available at: http://www.bartleby.com/312/.
Hui, D. (2007) 'The creative industries and entrepreneurship in East and Southeast Asia', in C. Henry (ed.), *Entrepreneurship in the Creative Industries: An International Perspective*. Cheltenham: Edward Elgar. pp. 9–29.
Hurford, J. (2007) *The Origins of Meaning*. Oxford: Oxford University Press.
Hutter, M., Antal, A., Farías, I., Marz, L., Merkel, J., Mützel, S., Oppen, M., Schulte-Römer, N. and Straßheim, H. (2010) *Research Program of the Research Unit 'Cultural Sources of Newness'*. Berlin: Wissenschaftszentrum Berlin für Sozialforschung (WZB). Available at: http://bibliothek.wzb.eu/pdf/2010/iii10-405.pdf.
Iqani, M. (2012) *Consumer Culture and the Media: Magazines in the Public Eye*. Basingstoke: Palgrave Macmillan.
Jacobs, J. (1985) *Cities and the Wealth of Nations: Principles of Economic Life*. New York: Vintage.
Jeffries, A. (2013) 'At Maker Faire New York, the DIY movement pushes into the mainstream'. Available at: www.theverge.com/2013/9/23/4760212/maker-faire-new-york-diy-movement-pushes-into-the-mainstream.
Jenkins, H. (2006) *Convergence Culture*. New York: NYU Press.
Jenkins, H., Ford, S. and Green, J. (2013) *Spreadable Media: Creating Value and Meaning in a Networked Culture*. New York: NYU Press.
Jin, D.Y. (2012) 'Hallyu 2.0: The new Korean wave in the creative industry', *International Institute Journal*, 2 (1): 3–7. Available at: http://quod.lib.umich.edu/cgi/p/pod/dod-idx/hallyu-20-the-new-korean-wave-in-the-creative-industry.pdf?c=iij;idno=11645653.0002.102.

Jones, S. (ed.) (1998) *Doing Internet Research: Critical Issues and Methods for Examining the Net*. Thousand Oaks, CA: Sage Publications.

Kauffman, S. (1991) 'Antichaos and adaptation: Biological evolution may have been shaped by more than just natural selection. Computer models suggest that certain complex systems tend toward self-organization', *Scientific American,* August: 78–84. Available at: www.santafe.edu/media/workingpapers/91-09-037.pdf.

Kavanaugh, A., Reese, D.D., Carroll, J.M. and Rosson, M.B. (2005) 'Weak ties in networked communities', *The Information Society: An International Journal,* 21(2): 119–131.

Keane, M. (2007) *Created in China: The Great New Leap Forward*. London: Routledge.

Keane, M. (2011) *China's New Creative Clusters: Governance, Human Capital and Investment*. London: Routledge.

Keane, M. and Hartley, J. (eds) (2006) *International Journal of Cultural Studies*, 9(3) (September), special issue on *Creative Industries and Innovation in China*.

Kelly, S. (2013) 'Overview: Despite pushback, internet freedom deteriorates', in S. Kelly, M. Truong, M. Earp, L. Reed, A. Shahbaz and A. Greco-Stoner (eds), *Freedom on the Net 2013: A Global Assessment of Internet and Digital Media*. New York: Freedom House. pp. 1–13.

Kelly, S., Truong, M., Earp, M., Reed, L., Shahbaz, A. and Greco-Stoner, A. (eds) (2013) *Freedom on the Net 2013: A Global Assessment of Internet and Digital Media*. New York: Freedom House. Available at: http://freedomhouse.org/sites/default/files/resources/FOTN%202013_Full%20Report_0.pdf.

Kenway, J., Bullen, E., Fahey, J. with Robb, S. (2006) *Haunting the Knowledge Economy*. London: Routledge.

Kotov, K. and Kull, K. (2011) 'Semiosphere is the relational biosphere', in C. Emmeche and K. Kull (eds), *Towards a Semiotic Biology: Life is the Action of Signs*. London: Imperial College Press. pp. 179–194.

Kwanashie, M., Aremu, A., Okoi, K. and Oladukun, K. (2009) *The Impact of Culture and Creative Industries on Nigeria's Economy*. Available at: http://www.uis.unesco.org/culture/Documents/nigeria-pilot-research-impact-study-culture-industries.2009.pdf.

LaChapelle, D. (2006) *LaChapelle: Artists and Prostitutes*. Berlin: Taschen.

Lange, B. and Bürkner, H. (2012) 'Value creation in scene-based music production: The case of electronic club music in Germany', *Economic Geography*, 89(2): 149–69.

Lanham, R. (2006) *The Economy of Attention*. Chicago, IL: Chicago University Press.

Lapo, A. (2001) 'Vladimir I. Vernadsky (1863–1945), founder of the biosphere concept', *Int. Microbiol.*, 4(1): 47–9.

Lawler, S. (2008) *Identity: Sociological Perspectives*. Cambridge: Polity.

Lazzeretti, L., Capone, F. and Seçilmiş, E. (2014) 'Cultural and creative industries in Turkey: A benchmarking with Italy and Spain', paper presented to *Regional Studies Association European Conference*, Izmir, Turkey. Available at: www.regionalstudies.org/uploads/Luciana_Lazzeretti%C2%B0__Francesco_Capone%C2%B0__%C4%B0._Erdem_Se%C3%A7ilmi%C5%9F_PDF.pdf.

Leadbeater, C. (1999) *Living on Thin Air: The New Economy*. London: Viking.

Leadbeater, C. (2006) *We Think: Why Mass Creativity is the Next Big Thing*. London: Profile Books.

Leadbeater, C. (2010) *Cloud Culture: The Future of Global Cultural Relations*. London: Counterpoint.
Leadbeater, C. (2014) *The Frugal Innovator: Creating Change on a Shoestring Budget*. London: Palgrave Macmillan.
Leadbeater, C. and Wong, A. (2010) *Learning from the Extremes*. Available at: http://www.cisco.com/web/about/citizenship/socio-economic/docs/LearningfromExtremes_WhitePaper.pdf.
Leaver, T. (2012) *Artificial Culture: Identity, Technology, and Bodies*. London and New York: Routledge.
Lee, R.E. (2010) *Knowledge Matters: The Structures of Knowledge and the Crisis of the Modern World-System*. St. Lucia: University of Queensland Press; New Brunswick, NJ: Transaction Books (2011).
Lennon, S. and Abdullah, S. (2013) 'Creative industries as a new growth cluster for Brunei', *CSPS Strategy and Policy Journal*, 4.
Lessig, L. (2008) *Remix: Making Art and Commerce Thrive in the Hybrid Economy*. London: Bloomsbury. Available at: www.bloomsburyacademic.com/remix.htm.
Levit, G. (2000) 'The biosphere and the noosphere theories of V.I. Vernadsky and P. Teilhard de Chardin: A methodological essay', *Archives Internationales D'Histoire des Sciences*, 144 (50): 160–76.
Levit, G. (2011) 'Looking at Russian ecology through the biosphere theory', in A. Schwarz and K. Jax (eds), *Ecology Revisited: Reflecting on Concepts, Advancing Science*. Dordrecht: Springer.
Levy, P. (1997) *Collective Intelligence: Mankind's Emerging World in Cyberspace*. New York and London: Plenum Trade.
Li, C. and Bernoff, J. (2008) *Groundswell: Winning in a World Transformed by Social Technologies*. Cambridge, MA: Harvard Business School Press.
Li, S. (2010) 'The online public space and popular ethos in China', *Media Culture and Society*, 32(1): 63–83.
Li, W. (2011) *How Creativity is Changing China*. London: Bloomsbury.
Licoppe, C. (2004) '"Connected" presence: The emergence of a new repertoire for managing social relationships in a changing communication technoscape', *Environment and Planning D: Society and Space,* 22(1): 135–56.
Lipari, L. (2010) 'Listening, thinking, being', *Communication Theory*, 20(3): 348–62.
Loasby, B. (1999) *Knowledge, Institutions and Evolution in Economics*. London: Routledge.
Lobato, R. (2010) 'Creative industries and informal economies: Lessons from Nollywood', *International Journal of Cultural Studies*, 13: 337–54.
Lobato, R. and Thomas, J. (2012) 'The business of anti-piracy: New zones of enterprise in the copyright wars', *International Journal of Communication*, 6: 606–25.
Lotman, Y. (1990) *Universe of the Mind: A Semiotic Theory of Culture*. Bloomington, IN: Indiana University Press.
Lotman, Y. (2009) *Culture and Explosion*. Berlin: Mouton de Gruyter.
Luhmann, N. (1991) 'What is communication?', *Communication Theory*, X: 251–9.
Luhmann, N. (2012) *Theory of Society, Vol. 1*. Stanford, CA: Stanford University Press.
MacNeilage, P. (2008) *The Origin of Speech*. Oxford: Oxford University Press.

Macpherson, C.B. (1962) *The Political Theory of Possessive Individualism: Hobbes to Locke.* Oxford: Oxford University Press.

Malbon, B. (1999) *Clubbing: Dancing, Ecstasy and Vitality.* London: Routledge.

Mandelker, A. (1995) 'Logosphere and semiosphere: Bakhtin, Russian organicism, and the semiotics of culture', in A. Mandelker (ed.), *Bakhtin in Contexts: Across the Disciplines.* Evanston, IL: Northwestern University Press. pp. 177–90.

Martinez, S. (n.d.) *Gaming, Film and Digital Animation: Mexico's Creative Industry's Climb to Recognition.* Available at: www.nearshoreamericas.com/wp-content/uploads/whitepappers/developing-nations-contributed-43x100-of-total-world-trade-creative-industries-2008.pdf.

Marwick, A. and boyd, d. (2011) 'I tweet honestly, I tweet passionately: Twitter users, context collapse, and the imagined audience', *New Media and Society*, 13(1): 114–33.

Maxwell, R. and Miller, T. (2011) 'Eco-ethical electronic consumption in the smart-design economy', in T. Lewis and E. Potter (eds), *Ethical Consumption: A Critical Introduction.* London: Routledge. pp. 141–55.

Maxwell, R. and Miller, T. (2012) *Greening the Media.* New York and Oxford: Oxford University Press.

Mayer, V. (2014) 'Creative work is still work', *Creative Industries Journal*, 7 (1): 59–61.

Mazzucato, M. (2013) *The Entrepreneurial State: Debunking Public vs. Private Sector Myths.* London and New York: Anthem Press.

McCloskey, D. (2010) *Bourgeois Dignity: Why Economics Can't Explain the Modern World.* Chicago, IL: University of Chicago Press.

McGuigan, J. (2010) *Cultural Analysis.* London: Sage.

McKay, G. (ed.) (1998) *DiY Culture: Party and Protest in Nineties Britain.* London: Verso.

Mesoudi, A. (2007) 'A Darwinian theory of cultural evolution can promote an evolutionary synthesis for the social sciences', *Biological Theory*, 2(3): 263–75.

Metcalfe, J.S. (2008) *Restless Capitalism – The Evolutionary Nature of Competition.* Princeton, NJ: Princeton University Press.

Metcalfe, J.S. (n.d.) *Restless Capitalism: Increasing Growth and Returns in Enterprise Economies.* Manchester: CRIC. Available at: www.cric.ac.uk/cric/staff/J_Stan_Metcalfe/pdfs/restcapit.pdf.

Metcalfe, J.S. and Ramlogan, R. (2005) 'Limits to the economy of knowledge and knowledge of the economy', *Futures*, 37(7): 655–74.

Miller, T. (2004) 'A view from a fossil: The new economy, creativity and consumption – two or three things I don't believe in', *International Journal of Cultural Studies*, 7(1): 55–65.

Minter, A. (2013) *Junkyard Planet: Travels in the Billion-Dollar Trash Trade.* London: Bloomsbury.

Mokyr, J. (2009) *The Enlightened Economy. An Economic History of Britain 1700–1850.* New Haven, CT: Yale University Press.

Montgomery, L. (2010) *China's Creative Industries: Copyright, Social Network Markets and the Business of Culture in a Digital Age.* Cheltenham: Edward Elgar.

Morozov, E. (2011) *The Net Delusion: How Not to Liberate The World.* New York: Public Affairs (Perseus); London: Allen Lane.

Morozov, E. (2013) *To Save Everything, Click Here: The Folly of Technological Solutionism*. New York: PublicAffairs/Perseus Books.

Neuwirth, R. (2011) *Stealth of Nations: The Global Rise of the Informal Economy*. New York: Pantheon.

O'Connor, J. (2005) 'Cities, culture and "transitional economies": Developing cultural industries in St. Petersburg', in J. Hartley (ed.), *Creative Industries*. Malden, MA and Oxford: Wiley-Blackwell. pp. 244–58.

O'Connor J. (2010) *The Cultural and Creative Industries: A Literature Review* (2nd edn). Newcastle-upon-Tyne: Creativity, Culture and Education (CCE) Series.

Ong, W. (2012) *Orality and Literacy. 30th Anniversary Edition with New Chapters by John Hartley*. London: Routledge.

Ormerod, P. (2007) *Why Most Things Fail: Evolution, Extinction and Economics*. London: Wiley.

Packard, V. (1960) *The Waste Makers*. New York: David McKay Co.

Pagel, M. (2012a) *Wired for Culture: The Natural History of Human Cooperation*. London: Allen Lane.

Pagel, M. (2012b) 'The culture bandwagon', *New Humanist*. Archived at: www.eurozine.com/articles/2012-02-21-pagel-en.html.

Papacharissi, Z. (ed.) (2010) *A Networked Self: Identity, Community, and Culture on Social Network Sites*. New York: Routledge.

Piketty, T. (2014) *Capital in the Twenty-First Century*. Cambridge, MA: Belknap/Harvard University Press.

Popper, K. (2002) *The Logic of Scientific Discovery*. London: Routledge.

Postman, N. (1985) *Amusing Ourselves to Death: Public Discourse in the Age of Show Business*. New York: Penguin.

Potts, J. (n.d.) 'Art and innovation: An evolutionary economic view of the creative industries', *UNESCO Observatory* (University of Melbourne Faculty of Architecture refereed e-journal). Available at: http://education.unimelb.edu.au/__data/assets/pdf_file/0017/1105721/art-innovation.pdf.

Potts, J. (2008) 'Creative industries & cultural science: A definitional odyssey', *Cultural Science Journal* 1(1). Available at: http://cultural-science.org/journal/index.php/culturalscience/article/view/6/15.

Potts, J. (2009) 'Do developing economies require creative industries? Some old theory about new China', *Chinese Journal of Communication*, 2(1): 92–108.

Potts, J. (2010) 'Can behavioural biases in choice under novelty explain innovation failures?', *Prometheus*, 28 (2): 133–48.

Potts, J. (2011) *Creative Industries and Economic Evolution*. Cheltenham: Edward Elgar.

Potts, J. and Cunningham, S. (2008) 'Four models of the creative industries', *Cultural Science Publications*. Available at: http://cultural-science.org/FeastPapers2008/StuartCunninghamBp.pdf.

Potts, J., Cunningham, S., Hartley, J. and Ormerod, P. (2008) 'Social network markets: A new definition of the creative industries', *Journal of Cultural Economics*, 32(3): 167–85.

Potts, J. and Montgomery, L. (2009) 'Does weaker copyright mean stronger creative industries? Some lessons from China', *Creative Industries Journal*, 1(3): 245–61.

Prince, R. (2010) 'Globalising the creative industries concept: Travelling policy and transnational policy communities', *Journal of Arts Management, Law and Society*, 40: 119–39.
Puckett, J. et al. (2002) *Exporting Harm: The High-Tech Trashing of Asia*. Basel: The Basel Action Network (BAN); Seattle, WA: Silicon Valley Toxics Coalition (SVTC).
Radjou, N., Prabhu, J. and Ahuja, S. (2012) *Jugaad Innovation: Think Frugal, Be Flexible, Generate Breakthrough Growth*. San Francisco, CA: Jossey-Bass.
Redmond, S. (2010) 'Avatar Obama in the age of liquid celebrity', *Celebrity Studies*, 1(1): 81–95.
Richerson, P. and Boyd, R. (2005) *Not By Genes Alone: How Culture Transformed Human Evolution*. Chicago, IL: Chicago UP.
Roodhouse, S. (2010) *Cultural Quarters: Principles and Practice*. Bristol: Intellect Publishers.
Ross, A. (2007) 'Nice work if you can get it: The mercurial career of creative industries policy', in G. Lovink (ed.), *My Creativity Reader: A Critique of Creative Industries*. Amsterdam: Institute of Network Cultures. pp. 17–40.
Runciman, W.G. (2009) *The Theory of Cultural and Social Selection*. Cambridge: Cambridge University Press.
Ruutu, K., Panfilo, A. and Karhunen, P. (2009) *Cultural Industries in Russia: Northern Dimension Partnership for Culture*. Copenhagen: Nordic Council of Ministers, TemaNord Publications, 590.
Saefullah, H. (2011) *The Silenced Protest: Punk and Democratisation in Indonesia*, unpublished working paper.
Sahlins, M. (1974) *Stone Age Economics*. New York: Aldine de Gruyter. (Reissued 2011 by Routledge.)
Sahlins, M. (1976) *Culture and Practical Reason*. Chicago: University of Chicago Press.
Samson, R. and Pitt, D. (1998) *The Biosphere and Noosphere Reader: Global Environment, Society and Change, with a Foreword by Mikhail Gorbachev*. London: Routledge.
Sawyer, K. (2005) *Social Emergence: Societies as Complex Systems*. Cambridge: Cambridge University Press.
Schlesinger, P. (2009) 'Creativity and the experts: New labour, think tanks, and the policy process', *International Journal of Press-Politics* 14(1): 3–20.
Schumpeter, J. (1942) *Capitalism, Socialism, and Democracy*. New York: Harper & Brothers.
Senft, T. (2008) *Camgirls: Celebrity and Community in the Age of Social Networks*. New York: Lang.
Sennett, R. (2012) *Together: The Rituals, Pleasures, and Politics of Cooperation*. New Haven, CT: Yale University Press.
Shirky, C. (2008) *Here Comes Everybody*. London: Allen Lane.
Silver, D., Clark, T. and Rothfield, L. (2005) *A Theory of Scenes*, unpublished manuscript, University of Chicago. Available at: http://cas.uchicago.edu/workshops/money/PDF/ Clark Silver Rothfield2005 A Theory of Scenes.
Simatupang, T., Rustiadi, S. and Situmorang, D. (2012) 'Enhancing the competitiveness of the creative services sectors in Indonesia', in T. Tullao and H. Lim (eds), *Developing ASEAN Economic Community (AEC) into A Global Services Hub*. ERIA Research Project Report 2011-1, Jakarta: ERIA. pp. 173–270.

Spigel, L. (1992) *Make Room for TV: Television and the Family Ideal in Postwar America*. Chicago, IL: University of Chicago Press.

State Council, PRC (2006) *National 11th Five Year Plan for Cultural Development*. Beijing: State Council, PRC.

State Council, PRC (2014) *Suggestions on Promoting the Development of International Cultural Commerce*. Beijing: State Council, PRC.

Stockwell, F. (2000) *A History of Information Storage and Retrieval*. Jefferson, NC: McFarland & Co.

Straw, W. (1991) 'Systems of articulation, logics of change: Communities and scenes in popular music', *Cultural Studies*, 5(3): 368–88.

Straw, W. (2001) 'Scenes and sensibilities', *Public,* 22/23: 245–57.

Sullins, L.L. (2006) '"Phishing" for a solution: Domestic and international approaches to decreasing online identity theft', *Emory International Law Review,* 20(2): 397–434. Available at: http://bit.ly/hrHTfK.

Taylor, T.D. (2005) 'Book review of A. Bennett and R.A. Peterson (Eds.), *Music Scenes: Local, Translocal, and Virtual*', *Notes,* 61(4): 1026–28.

Throsby, D. (2010) *The Economics of Cultural Policy*. Cambridge: Cambridge University Press.

Tomaselli, K. and N. Mboti (2013) 'Film Cities, Film Futures: Political Economy of Production, Distribution, Exhibition', paper presented at *Archaeology of the Future* conference, Bayreuth University, Germany, January. Available at: http://ccms.ukzn.ac.za/files/articles/African_cinema/film%20cities%2018%20jan%2013.pdf.

Towse, R. (2014) *Advanced Introduction to Cultural Economics*. Cheltenham: Edward Elgar.

Turkle, S. (1997) *Life on the Screen: Identity in the Age of the Internet*. New York: Touchstone.

UKTI (2011) *UK Creative Industries in India: A Guide to Architecture, Design and Digital Content*. UK: Trade and Industry Department. Available at: http://bis.ecgroup.net/Publications/UKTradeInvestment/SectorReports/111107.aspx.

UNCTAD (2008) *Creative Economy Report 2008: The Challenge of Assessing the Creative Economy Towards Informed Policy-making*. Available at: www.unctad.org/creative-economy.

UNCTAD/UNDP (2010) *Creative Economy Report 2010*. Available at: http://unctad.org/en/pages/PublicationArchive.aspx?publicationid=946.

UN/UNDP/UNESCO (2013) *Creative Economy Report 2013 Special Edition: Widening Local Development Pathways*. Available at: www.unesco.org/new/en/culture/themes/creativity/creative-economy-report-2013-special-edition/.

Vaidhyanathan, S. (2005) *The Anarchist in the Library: How the Clash Between Freedom and Control is Hacking the Real World and Crashing the System*. New York: Basic Books.

Veblen, T. (1898) 'Why is economics not an evolutionary science?', *Quarterly Journal of Economics*, 12. Available at: http://socserv.mcmaster.ca/econ/ugcm/3ll3/veblen/econevol.txt.

Veblen, T. (1899) *The Theory of the Leisure Class: An Economic Study of Institutions*. Available at: www.gutenberg.org/files/833/833-h/833-h.htm.

Vernadsky, V. (1938) 'Scientific thought as a planetary phenomenon' [extracts], trans. and introduced by W. Jones, *21st Century,* Spring–Summer 2012. Available at:

www.21stcenturysciencetech.com/Articles_2012/Spring-Summer_2012/04_Biospere_Noosphere.pdf.

Vernadsky, V.I. (1943) 'Some words about the noösphere', *21st Century*, Spring 2005: 16-21. Available at: https://www.21stcenturysciencetech.com/translations/The_Noosphere.pdf.

Wang, F., Kuehr, R., Ahlquist, D. and Li, J. (2013) *E-Waste in China: A Country Report*, United Nations University Institute for Sustainability and Peace. Available at: http://collections.unu.edu/eserv/UNU:1624/ewaste-in-china.pdf.

Wang, W.J., Yuan, Y. and Archer, N. (2006) 'A contextual framework for combating identity theft', *Security & Privacy, IEEE* 4(2): 30–8.

Wang, Y.Z. (2007) 'Cultural industries' and 'Creative industries', in X.M.H. Zhang et al. (eds), *Development of Cultural Industries in China 2007*. Beijing: Social Science Academic Press. pp. 40–5.

Warner, M. (2002) 'Publics and counterpublics', *Quarterly Journal of Speech*, 88(4): 413–25. Available at: http://knowledgepublic.pbworks.com/f/warnerPubCounterP.pdf.

Whitson, J.R. and Haggerty, K.D. (2008) 'Identity theft and the care of the virtual self', *Economy and Society*, 37(4): 572–94.

Williams, J.P. (2006) 'Authentic identities: Straightedge subculture, music, and the internet', *Journal of Contemporary Ethnography*, 35(2): 173–200.

Wilson, E.O. (1998) *Consilience: The Unity of Knowledge*. New York: Vintage Books.

Winnicott, D.W. (1971) *Playing and Reality*. London: Tavistock Publications.

Yoshimoto, M (2003) 'The status of creative industries in Japan and policy recommendations for their promotion', *NLI Research*. Available at: www.nli-research.co.jp/english/socioeconomics/2003/li031202.pdf.

Yousafzai, M. with Lamb, C. (2013) *I Am Malala. The Girl Who Stood Up for Education and was Shot by the Taliban*. London: Weidenfeld & Nicolson.

Zappavigna, M. (2011) 'Ambient affiliation: A linguistic perspective on Twitter', *New Media and Society*, 13: 788–806.

Zittrain, J. (2008) *The Future of the Internet: And How to Stop It*. New Haven, CT: Yale University Press; London: Penguin. Available at: http://futureoftheinternet.org/.

INDEX

3D printing 75, 111

aggressive parochialism 172, 174
Akyol, R.A. 156
Alibaba Group 141
Anderson, C. 107, 108, 109, 115, 116
Andrejevic, M. 186, 214
Anthropocene 22
Arthur, W.B. 4, 23, 68
Assange, J. 186
Australian Research Council 44, 55

Baidu 92
Bailey, J. 67
Bakhshi, H. 65–6
Banks, J. 56, 106
Barabási, A-L. 53
Baran, P. 182
Baulch, E. 123, 151
Bauman, Z. 89
Baym, G. 172
Baym, N. 92, 219
Beck, U. 191
Becker, H. 121
Bell, G. 11, 13, 14
Benkler, Y. 96, 183, 190
Bennett, A. and Peterson, R. 120
Bennett, W. and Segerberg, A. 186
Bentley, R.A. 51
Best, K. 186
Beyoncé theory 228–9
Blair, T. 64
  Blairite 65
Bollywood 137, 153
Boulding, K. 23, 25
boyd, d. 95
Breen, M. 173

Bromley, M. 30
Brown, G. 46, 64
Burgess, J. 37, 56, 104
'but surely?' questions 170–5, 180, 184, 195
Butler, J. 89, 123

Capital of Culture, European 154, 162
Castells, M. 56
CCI (Centre of Excellence for Creative Industries & Innovation) 32, 38, 47, 55
celebrity 50, 53, 87, 187, 200, 224
  cyber- 97
  micro- 91, 95
  wiki- 95
Cerf, V. 183
Chadwick, A. and Howard, P. 190
Choi, J. 159
clash of systems 23, 47, 73, 76, 77
complex systems 8, 18, 37, 53, 55, 58, 59, 60, 73, 176–9, 212, 213
conceptual community 4, 25, 67, 174, 201
Cooke, P. and Lazzeretti, L. 6, 76–7, 173
copyright 32, 43, 61, 71, 73, 75–6, 88, 108, 115–6, 137, 187–90, 217
  industries 3, 45, 189
  see also: intellectual property
Corndog 84–8, 94–6
Cowen, T. 176
creative city/cities 48, 58, 69, 70, 72, 75, 77, 78, 126, 133, 151, 155
  Guadalajara 149
  –network 161–2
  Tokyo 158
Creative City Index 221

creative citizen/citizenship 58, 70, 72, 74, 77, 79
creative class 48, 110, 143, 152, 200
creative cluster 48, 56, 58, 66, 70, 71, 77, 109–10, 124, 136–7, 163
Creative Commons 115
creative culture 76, 78, 79
creative destruction 10, 36, 44, 52, 60, 74, 75
creative economy 3–4, 6–8, 17, 44, 57, 58–9, 65, 66, 77, 79, 103–4, 129–30, 174–5, 190, 201, 220,
  Brazil 131–3
creative industries 3–7, 15, 25, 26–7, 28–9, 30–3, 35–6, 60–1, 62–5, 173
  Brazil 131–3
  China 139–40, 157
  European Union 162
  as fiction 223
  as future-sphere 35
  history of 57–8
  India 137
  Indonesia 150–1
  innovation and 77, 104
  Japan 158–9
  Korea 159–60
  mediated 126
  Mexico 148–9
  Nigeria 153
  phases of 69–75
  policy 8, 25–8, 33, 45, 49, 59, 64, 130–1, 178, 212
  practice 221–3, 224–6
  Russia 134–6
  as social technology of distributed innovation 59–60, 77, 175
  South Africa 142–3
  systems approach to 67, 213–4
  Turkey 154–5
  United Nations 161
  users and 76
  see also: social network markets
Crook, C. 200
cultural industries 3, 57, 124, 134, 137, 223–4, 228
  Africa 163

cultural industries *cont.*
  China 139–40
  Mexico 148
  South Africa 142
  Turkey 155
cultural science 8, 17, 18, 19, 23, 60, 61–3, 220, 221, 228
culture 5–6, 7, 11, 18, 23, 26, 45, 57, 59, 78, 96, 210–11, 227
  arts and 32, 65, 135, 158
  Chinese 47
  consumption, domain of 12
  convergence- 140
  'cute' 157, 158
  digital 133
  DIY 37, 50, 66, 105, 218–9
  evolutionary approaches to 60, 62, 213
  and knowledge 18–20, 211, 213–4
  literary 21
  maker 106, 113, 114
  pop, popular 35, 67, 85, 134, 141, 148, 157, 158, 229
  print 169
  public 7, 47
  resistant 157
  shanzhai 114–5
  as source of newness and innovation 8–9, 103, 105
  as system 18, 67
  and technology 12–13, 14, 72, 141
  see also: deme; semiosphere
culture industries 57
Cunningham, S. 59, 106
Currid, E. 59, 72, 121–2, 123

Davies, D. 181
DCMS (Dept. Culture Media and Sport, UK) 8, 28, 31, 32–3, 35, 41, 45–7, 49, 66, 71, 142, 154, 200
deme(s), demic 5, 9, 26, 27, 36, 38, 75, 86, 88, 103, 110, 172–4, 181, 199, 209–10, 211, 212, 213, 215
Deng Xiaoping 198
Deuze, M. 89, 106
Diamond, J. 5, 88

discourse public 4, 26, 174
DIWO [do-it-with-others] 108
DIY [do-it-yourself] 52, 75, 95, 106,
    108–11, 112, 219, 220, 222, 226, 228
  aesthetic 225
  citizenship 202
  disciplines 220
  ethos 107
  team 226
Doctorow, C. 107
Dopfer, K., Foster, J., Potts, J. 36, 212
Douglas, M. 193
Dr Strangelove 181
Dumb Ways to Die 49, 53

Earls, M. 52
Eco, U. 169, 170
Eschenburg, J. 144
Etsy 103

Facebook 26, 35, 50, 52, 75, 133, 150 184
Field, A. 124
Flew, T. 29, 220
Fitzgerald, B. 38, 56
Flickr 50
Florida, R. 48, 125, 138, 163, 200
'forever' 229
Freedom House Index 185

Gates, B. 83, 198
Gauntlett, D. 106, 219
Gevinson, T. 226–9
Giddens, A. 64
Gil, G. 130–1
Gilens, F. 186, 190
Goffman, E. 90, 91, 123
Goldman, A. 123
Goldman Sachs 61, 130, 147
Google, Inc. 29, 50, 70, 203
Graaf, J. de 191
Granovetter, M. 122
Grass-Mud-Horse 94
Grazian, D. 120
Green, J. 37, 56
Greenpeace 192, 194
Gillies, M. 76

Guiyu (China) 49, 192, 195, 204
Guo, Shengkun 184–5

hack/hacker 107, 163, 217
  hackathons 119
  hackerspaces 109, 112
Hall, S. 41
Hallyu (Korean wave) 158, 159, 160
Harari, N. 6
Hargreaves, I. 33, 66, 73, 79, 187
HAXLR8R 113
Hebdige, D. 123
Hélie, M. 78, 125
Herrmann-Pillath, C. 18, 51, 56,
    105, 220
Higgs, P. 71, 104
Hodgkinson, J. 120
Hollywood 32, 47, 61, 122, 153
Howard, S. 93
Howkins. J. 71, 76, 123
Huawei 114, 141
Hugo, V. 169–70
Hui, D. 159
Hutter, M. 5, 9, 36, 105

i-D Magazine 224–6, 227–8
India Design Mark 137–8
industrial revolution 9, 34, 68, 108,
    113, 115, 217
innovation 5, 8–9, 10, 12, 14, 27, 33,
    35–7, 59, 70, 78, 95, 104,
    105–6, 108, 126, 138, 174, 210,
    212, 215
  creative 44, 48, 49–50, 73, 74, 76, 144,
    175
  cultural 139–40
  -culture 77
  enabled 77
  frugal 125, 164
  Jugaad 116
  knowledge 43
  -network 58, 70, 72
  shanzhai 114–5
  social 77
  sustained 220, 228
  user-led 46, 56

Intel Corporation 10–11, 14, 15
intellectual property (IP) 3, 31, 34, 36, 43, 45–6, 56, 66, 70–1, 73, 77–8, 103, 187, 189, 213, 222
   China 114–5, 139, 141, 142
   rights (IPR) 31, 73, 78, 115, 142, 156, 160, 187, 189
   WIPO 76, 161
   see also: copyright
Internet Society, The 183
Iqani, M. 8

Jacobs, J. 22
Jeffries, A. 113
Jenkins, H. 48, 190
Jiaoshou ('Shouting Beast') 84–6, 89–96
Jiaoshou Weekly 94
Jin, D.Y. 160
Jobs, S. 67
Jones, S. 190
Jugaad (India) 116

K-pop 160
Kahn, B. 183
Kauffman, S. 176, 178, 179, 216
Kavanaugh, A. 88
Keane, M. 47, 56, 139, 141
Kelly, S. 185
Kenway, J. 173
Kickstarter 75, 112
Krugman, P. 198
Kwanashie, M. 152
Kyary Pamyu Pamyu 51

LaChapelle, D. 122
Lamartine, A. de 154
Lange, B. and Bürkner, H. 120
Lanham, R. 51, 106
Lapo, A. 20, 24
Lawler, S. 91
Lazzeretti, L. 154
   see also: Cooke and Lazzeretti
Leadbeater, C. 36, 45, 83, 97, 116, 197, 220, 228

Leaver, T. 8
Lee, R.E. 8, 216
Lennon, S. and Abdullah, S. 130
Lessig, L. 52
Levi, P. 88, 97
Li, C. and Bernoff, J. 52
Li, Shubo 93
Li, Wuwei 33, 140
Licoppe, C. 93
Lipari, L. 93
Loasby, B. 49
Lobato, R. 116, 153
Lotman, Y. 3, 6, 16–24, 37, 42, 68
Luhmann, N. 22, 172, 177

Macpherson, C.B. 96
maker 106–117
   culture 37, 106, 114, 115
   movement 37, 106, 107, 108–12, 114, 115, 116, 117, 125, 126, 163, 202, 219
makerspaces 109–114, 115, 119
Malbon, B. 123
Manifesto for the Creative Economy 66
Martinez, S. 148, 149
Marwick, A. 95
Marx, K. 180
Maxwell, R. and Miller, T. 23, 194–5
Mayer, V. 223
Mazzucato, M. 216
McCloskey, D. 217
McDowell, A. 122
McGray, D. 158
McGuigan, J. 6, 173
McKay, G. 123
McLuhan, M. 169–70
Metcalfe, J.S. 49, 201
microproductivity 4, 37, 70, 73, 79, 95–6, 103, 106, 107, 126, 202, 218
milieu 122
   see also: scenes
millennials 10, 11, 14, 15
Miller, M. 64, 205
Miller, T. 6, 173
   see also: Maxwell and Miller

Index

Minter, A. 195
micro-meso-macro (MMM) 35–6, 36–7, 212–3, 229
Mokyr, J. 9. 34, 108
Montgomery, L. 51, 56, 61, 78, 142, 189
Moore's law 10, 11, 15, 49, 75
Morozov, E. 84, 186
Moss, K. 41, 49, 53

Nelson, T. 83
NESTA 33, 65, 163
Neuwirth, R. 116
newness 5, 9, 11, 14, 23, 35–8, 72, 74, 103–4, 105, 106, 117, 125–6, 174, 175, 187, 190, 194, 201, 202, 212, 220, 224–5
night-time economy 120
Nokia 29, 115
Nollywood, 116, 153
noösphere 16, 17, 18, 21, 23, 24, 35, 96
Notre Dame de Paris 169
Novikov, T. 135

Obama phones 115
O'Connor, J. 6, 134, 156, 173
Occupy (movement) 197, 199, 202, 218
O'Neill, J. 61, 129, 130, 145, 147–8, 164
Ong, W.J. 170
open access 183, 184, 189, 216

Packard, V. 191
Pagel, M. 5, 26, 172, 179, 211
Pangestu, M. 150, 151
Papacharissi, Z. 72, 219
Park, Geun-Hye 160
Piketty, T. 186, 198–201, 205
poised system 176, 178–9, 183, 185, 190, 216
Popper, K. 28
  Popperian 173
Postman, N. 191
Potts, J. 5, 9, 28, 36, 50, 51, 56, 59, 61, 68, 69, 75, 78, 97, 105, 126, 220
  Hartley, J. and Potts, J. 5, 8, 9, 17, 21, 26, 172, 195

Pozible 75, 112
precariat 217, 223
Preston, P. 200
Prince, R. 25, 26–7, 29, 33, 55, 67, 174, 201
Psy 160
Puckett, J. 192
Pussy Riot 134, 136

ReaGilè Project (South Africa) 144, 157
Redmond, S. 89
Roberts, L. 182
Rookie Mag 227–9
Rosen, J. 218, 219
Ross, A. 6, 173
Rowling, J.K. 46, 106
Runciman, W.G. 22, 68
Ruutu, K. 134

Sachs, J. 190
Saefullah, H. 123–4
Sahlins, M. 106, 196
Samson, R. and Pitt, D. 20
Sawyer, K. 22, 68
scenes 78, 119–26, 144, 164, 219
  art 135
  design 136
  music 131
Schumpeter, J. 9, 36, 209
  Schumpeterian 52, 75, 210
Seeed Studio 112, 115
Sefton-Green, J. 64, 68
self-organising (systems) 18, 26, 36, 65, 76, 86, 122, 126, 183, 185, 212, 216
  theory of 177, 178
semiosphere 16–18, 20–4, 35, 36, 37, 72, 174, 211, 213, 214
Senft, T. 89, 91, 95
Sennett, R. 106
shanzhai culture 110, 114–5
Shirky, C. 72
Silver, D. 123
Simatupang, T. 150
Smith, C. 45, 46, 58
Snowden, E. 185, 186, 199

social learning 75–6, 78, 122, 126, 210
social network markets 28, 50–2, 59, 60, 75, 78, 97, 108, 126, 150
social technology 59–60, 74, 175
Spigel, L. 12
Stiglitz, J. 198
Straw, W. 120, 121
subculture 86, 123
Sullins, L. 88
'swimming lesson' 222, 224

Taylor, T. 120
team/teamwork 8, 43, 62, 87, 112, 224–8
Tencent 86, 141
Thomas, J. 116
Three Bigs 3, 16, 27, 34–5, 37, 38, 175, 193, 202, 213, 214, 221
Three Buts 30, 171, 175, 180–203, 214, 215, 221
Throsby, D. 220
Tobreluts, O. 135
Tolokonnikova, N. 136
Tomaselli, K. and N. Mboti 144
Towse, R. 220
Turing, A. 181
translation 23, 36, 174
Tudou 85, 92, 96
Tudou Video Festival 85, 91
Turkle, S. 89
Twitter 35, 75, 184

UNCTAD 60, 131, 148, 153, 155, 161
UNESCO 133, 161, 162
United Nations 161

universal-adversarialism 172–4
urban semiosis 5, 70, 72, 73, 75, 77, 78, 125, 126

Vaidhyanathan, S. 190
Veblen, T. 23, 53, 191, 196, 211
Vernadsky, V.I. 16–24, 37

Wales, J. 83–4
Wang, F. 192, 193
Wang, W.J. 88
Wang Y.Z. 139
Warner, M. 26, 174, 201
Weinstock, T. 225–6
Wessler, R. 114
Whitson, J. and Haggerty, K. 88
WikiLeaks 186, 199, 202
Wikipedia 50, 75, 83–4,
Williams, J.P. 119
Wilson, E.O. 5, 174
Winnicott, D. 90
Wozniak, S. 106–7

Yi, Zhenxing 89
  see also: Jiaoshou
Yousafzai, M. 202–3
YouTube 35, 37, 44, 49, 50, 51, 70, 75, 77, 84, 85, 96, 160
Yudhoyono, S.B. 130, 150
Yue Minjun 141

Zappavigna, M. 91
Zhang Yin (Cheung Yan) 198
Zhukova, D. 136
Zittrain, J. 175, 183, 190, 217